RENEWALS: 691-4574
DATE DUE

WITHDRAWN
UTSA LIBRARIES

Conserving America's Neighborhoods

ENVIRONMENT, DEVELOPMENT, AND PUBLIC POLICY
A series of volumes under the general editorship of
Lawrence Susskind, *Massachusetts Institute of Technology,
Cambridge, Massachusetts*

CITIES AND DEVELOPMENT
Series Editor: Lloyd Rodwin, *Massachusetts Institute of Technology,
Cambridge, Massachusetts*

CITIES AND CITY PLANNING
Lloyd Rodwin

THINKING ABOUT DEVELOPMENT
Lisa Peattie

CONSERVING AMERICA'S NEIGHBORHOODS
Robert K. Yin

Other subseries:

ENVIRONMENTAL POLICY AND PLANNING
Series Editor: Lawrence Susskind, *Massachusetts Institute of Technology,
Cambridge, Massachusetts*

PUBLIC POLICY AND SOCIAL SERVICES
Series Editor: Gary Marx, *Massachusetts Institute of Technology,
Cambridge, Massachusetts*

Conserving America's Neighborhoods

Robert K. Yin

The Case Study Institute
Washington, D.C.
and
Massachusetts Institute of Technology
Cambridge, Massachusetts

PLENUM PRESS • NEW YORK AND LONDON

Library of Congress Cataloging in Publication Data

Yin, Robert K.
  Conserving America's neighborhoods.

  (Environment, development, and public policy. Cities and development)
  Bibliography: p.
  Includes index.
  1. Neighborhood – United States – Conservation and restoration. I. Title. II. Series.
HT123.Y56   307.7'6   81-23359
ISBN 0-306-40795-7   AACR2

© 1982 Plenum Press, New York
A Division of Plenum Publishing Corporation
233 Spring Street, New York, N.Y. 10013

All rights reserved

No part of this book may be reproduced, stored in a retrieval system, or transmitted,
in any form or by any means, electronic, mechanical, photocopying, microfilming,
recording, or otherwise, without written permission from the Publisher

Printed in the United States of America

Preface

Over the years I have conducted numerous neighborhood studies, alternately focusing on specific geographic areas, public programs, and types of citizen actions. Because most of these efforts were done on a project-by-project basis, it did not readily occur to me that these separate investigations also represented an aggregate statement about American neighborhoods: the continuing and complex relationship between public policy and neighborhood life.

A suggestion by Lloyd Rodwin, the senior editor for this series, provided the opportunity to reexamine the various manuscripts, and to select (and in some cases, considerably edit) those bearing most on this overall theme. Thus each of the chapters in this book is a commentary on the potential uses of public policy for preserving the most cherished aspect of contemporary neighborhoods—the social life within them. In some cases the policy actions may have only an indirect effect on neighborhoods. For instance, a whole portion of the book is devoted to the role of research in understanding neighborhood conditions; public policy is relevant because research, these days, has itself become a public policy enterprise. In other cases the policy effects are direct and pervasive—the support of citizen organizations, the delivery of neighborhood services, and the provision of timely and relevant information to residents.

I do not know whether the relationship between public policy and neighborhoods is the same or as intimate outside the United States. The reference to "America's" neighborhoods in the title of this book is intended, therefore, as a forewarning about the potential limitations of my analysis. Eventually, I would in fact like to do comparative studies of neighborhood issues in other countries, but for the time being I have been more than preoccupied learning about the American scene, which I still find a challenging task.

The separate origins of each of the chapters in this book have been acknowledged in the source footnote to each chapter. The chapters have been heavily edited to improve their stylistic and substantive consistency, although the original purpose and setting of each work has been preserved. Most of the materials are not more than a few years old, yet in some places the nature of the evidence already appears dated. This phenomenon I again take as a sign of the complexity of the policy–neighborhood relationship; both public policies and neighborhoods are rapidly changing, and the resulting relationship is extraordinarily dynamic. Thus there is a certain risk in having produced this book. Some may view it simply as a documentation of a peculiar past. My own hope is that it can serve as an agenda for the future, by presenting a coherent portrait of the relevant neighborhood issues and offering some modest suggestions (especially in Chapters 4 and 12) about new initiatives.

The research in this book has benefited from the advice and assistance of many individuals. In this sense, the book is a creature of diverse contributions, although I alone am responsible for the final product.

Chronologically, The New York City-Rand Institute provided an initial array of research problems (1970–1972), most of them developed in conjunction with the "fire project." Colleagues at NYC-Rand who were especially supportive were Edward Blum, Rae Archibald and Jan Chaiken (now working in Rand's Santa Monica office), and Peter Szanton (an unusual leader, who is now with the firm of Hamilton, Rabinovitz, and Szanton, in Washington, D.C.). NYC-Rand no longer exists, but those of us who worked there all consider it to have been a unique and rewarding research venture.

Second, the teaching of courses on urban neighborhoods, at MIT's Department of Urban Studies and Planning (1972 to the present) created another setting for integrating lessons about neighborhoods. Again, an extremely talented set of colleagues helped to contribute to the evolution of my ideas: Tunney Lee, Lloyd Rodwin, Rob Hollister (now at Tufts University), Larry Susskind, Phillip Clay, David Birch, Lisa Peattie, Rolf Goetze, and Deborah Auger. Among other activities, some of us shared the teaching of summer courses on neighborhood planning (1977 and 1979), and most of the group participated in a year-long series of seminars on the neighborhood.

Another set of earlier experiences was related to The Rand Corporation and its Washington, D.C. office, where I worked from 1973 to 1978. My research became more intensively focused on the federal context for neighborhood development. During this time, too, I had the opportunity to work with Peter Ujvagi (now a local official in Toledo, Ohio) and to assist the National Commission on Neighborhoods in designing its research activities. This experience yielded new insights into the dynamics of neighborhood politics at the national level.

PREFACE

Finally, a slightly different experience resulted from service on the peer review committee (1975–1979) of the Center for Studies of Metropolitan Problems (National Institute of Mental Health). The Center was led by Elliot Liebow, himself one of the most sensitive neighborhood observers I have met. The committee included several prominent experts on neighborhood research, including one who eventually reviewed an earlier draft of the present manuscript, Marc Fried (of Boston College). I am especially thankful to Marc for his comments. Over the years, the Metro Center's deliberations were remarkable in at least one respect: Because no single academic discipline has a monopoly over neighborhood research, the committee constantly argued about the basic evidence and analytic strategies involved in such research. These discussions, in retrospect, served as excellent seminars.

My own neighborhood research continues to this day. At The Case Study Institute, one current project has to do with the role of neighborhoods in the Community Development Block Grant program, and a second project focuses on neighborhood grass-roots organizations that have succeeded without government sponsorship. Steven Gale and Phyllis Kaniss at the University of Pennsylvania have been the major sponsors/colleagues on the first project, and Cicero Wilson and Robert Woodson of The American Enterprise Institute have served in a similar capacity on the second.

Thus, this book may be seen as but a midpoint in a continuing stream of neighborhood research. In addition, the strength of my interests in neighborhoods derives from some personal roots. The West Side of Manhattan was a very real neighborhood home for seventeen years, and forays into other parts of New York provided daily exposure to neighborhood differences and change—phenomena that New Yorkers take for granted (in New York, the object is to survive, not to study). To those responsible for this neighborhood upbringing—father and family and the memory of my mother—I dedicate this book.

ROBERT K. YIN

Contents

Introduction xi

PART I CITIZEN INITIATIVES 1

Chapter 1 Correlates of Power in Citizen Organizations 3

Chapter 2 How Citizens Influence Their Municipal Services 17

Chapter 3 Patrolling the Neighborhood Beat 26

Chapter 4 Revenue Sharing with the Community Sector? 51

PART II GOVERNMENT INITIATIVES 63

Chapter 5 Neighborhood Service Delivery: Historical Development and the Crisis of the 1960s 65

Chapter 6 The (In)equity of Information Systems in Education 80

Chapter 7 Can Public Housing Help? 92

Chapter 8 The Neighborhood Library as an Information and Referral Center 102

PART III RESEARCH INITIATIVES   117

Chapter 9   Neighborhood Fact-Gathering: How Can We Study Neighborhoods Better?   119

Chapter 10   Using Participant-Observation to Study Urban Neighborhoods   132

Chapter 11   Fire Alarms as Urban Social Indicators   158

Chapter 12   Improving the Evaluation of Neighborhood Intervention Programs   169

Index   191

Introduction

THE NEIGHBORHOOD BEAT

Most people have fond memories of the neighborhood in which they were raised. The everyday activities of neighborhood life, including encounters with friendly neighbors, shopkeepers, clergy, and service personnel all provided a supportive environment for growing up.

Residential neighborhoods, whether urban or suburban, have continued to serve this social function. Moreover, neighborhood life has been a source of support for adults as well as children. The variety of social interactions, the use of public and private spaces for leisurely activities, and the provision of commercial and public services to satisfy daily needs all help an individual to live securely and feel self-fulfilled. In short, neighborhood life has been a key aspect of American life, to be likened to employment, familial, and educational experiences.

No doubt, just as with these other experiences, neighborhood life can also become dysfunctional. Indeed, the problems of crime in the streets, inadequate housing, burglaries, and the underprovision of services are neighborhood problems that have drawn widespread public attention over the last two decades. If one's own neighborhood has these problems, daily life can be threatening and unpleasant instead of supportive, to the point of instilling a pervasive fear of the neighborhood environment (Jacobs, 1961, pp. 31–32; Suttles, 1972, p. 234). Short of relocating to another neighborhood, it may be extremely difficult to find ways to deal with these conditions.

But whether supportive or threatening, the neighborhood beat has been a fact of American life. Cooley (1909/1956) regarded neighboring relationships as a basic form of human interaction, and in this sense the neighborhood constitutes a social unit, essential to our cultural fabric. Thus participation in neighborhood life is as fundamental as participation in American society as a whole; or to put it another way:

> The importance of the neighborhood begins with the importance of citizenship. To be a citizen is to participate in civic affairs. "Participate" is the key concept. To simply live in a place, and not participate in its civic affairs, is to be merely a resident, not a citizen. (Morris and Hess, 1975, p. 7)

Conversely, when neighborhood life goes awry, we may rightfully be regarded as "a nation of strangers" (Packard, 1972).

CONSERVING NEIGHBORHOOD LIFE

The purpose of this book is to describe different approaches for preserving the neighborhood as a social unit. The book is organized into three parts, emphasizing citizen actions, governmental actions, and research actions.

Citizen actions, whether organized or individually based, must be considered the most important of these three. Citizens must participate and use their own resources for maintaining and strengthening their neighborhoods, as only residents themselves can determine the type of neighborhood life they are to have. Fortunately, a fundamentally voluntary spirit, entailing formal and informal associations (Tocqueville, 1840/1961), has been ingrained in the American culture. Showing how citizen actions can be effective in contemporary settings is the aim of the first part of this book.

In contrast, governmental actions have commonly been associated with formalized programs, usually initiated by the federal government. This impression has been created by the large-scale efforts undertaken by the federal government over the past fifteen years in the fields of housing, education, crime prevention, and neighborhood economic development (Yin, 1980). Nevertheless, to maintain and strengthen neighborhoods the most relevant unit of government continues to be at the local level. Counties and municipalities are the ones that define land use and that provide such neighborhood services as water supply and sewers, schools, police and fire protection, and the upkeep of public places such as streets and parks. In fact, the federal government may be regarded as providing only one direct neighborhood service—the postal service. Thus the chapters in Part II serve mainly as a reminder of the local role, covering initiatives made by local governments even when, as with public housing, federal funds may be the ultimate source of financial support.

Research actions are also relevant for maintaining and strengthening neighborhoods. Existing investigations have added substantially to our knowledge about neighborhood life, and future research is needed so that the full dynamics of such life can be understood. The researcher may assist by mon-

INTRODUCTION

itoring neighborhood conditions, to guide citizens in taking whatever actions are desirable. But the researcher can also inform citizens about processes such as residential mobility (e.g., Rossi, 1980) and about the results of specific actions—that is, what occurred and why. Thus Part III contains chapters on various research initiatives aimed at illuminating neighborhood life.

Not included in this book are several topics that though related to neighborhoods, are so intertwined with nonneighborhood processes that inclusion would have meant a drastically expanded volume. Such topics include housing construction and rehabilitation, real estate and capital investment markets, and the locational patterns of employment centers. The reader is referred to other sources to cover these topics. For instance, Rolf Goetze has written an excellent series of books on the role of housing programs in developing neighborhood confidence (1976, 1979; Goetze, Colton and O'Donnell, 1977). Similarly, other investigations have examined the role of financial institutions in fostering or retarding neighborhood change (e.g. Lachman and Downs, 1978; Public Affairs Counseling, 1976). Although these private sector activities may be important to neighborhood life, a thorough rendition of such topics would have to go beyond neighborhood issues and would ultimately require an exploration of housing, finance, or microeconomics.

In sum, the theme on which this book has been based is that of the American neighborhood as a *social* unit. The actions that can be taken to improve the quality of everyday life, and thereby to conserve the socially significant role of neighborhoods in this country, are covered in the course of the book.

CAN NEIGHBORHOODS SURVIVE?

The prospects for American neighborhoods have been enhanced by recent trends, especially in urban neighborhoods. In numerous places across the country, physical signs of improvement are evident where deterioration was once prevalent. Many of the improvements, reflected by the upgrading of housing structures and the in-migration of young professionals (e.g., Auger, 1979; Clay, 1979; Laska and Spain, 1980; Rosenthal, 1980) are occurring in those very transitional neighborhoods whose destinies were uncertain just fifteen or twenty years ago. "Neighborhood revitalization" and the gentrification of neighborhood populations have therefore become prominent phenomena during the last few years (Rosenthal, 1980).

Of course, few would claim that the neighborhoods with the greatest problems—the ghettos—have necessarily improved. Similarly, physical deterioration may have accelerated in a new ring of neighborhoods, those located in the innermost suburban areas (Sternlieb and Lake, 1975). Nevertheless, the future of neighborhoods seems to be on an upswing that contrasts sharply with the era of the 1960s, marked by urban riots and massive population flights from neighborhoods. Although numerologists will still debate whether migratory patterns have significantly changed—for example, whether there is a population shift back to the city (e.g., Abravanel and Mancini, 1980; Lipton, 1977)—a psychological optimism about the future of neighborhoods has become prevalent. Part of the optimism also involves the realization that large-scale community development efforts, such as urban renewal, may actually have positive effects if judgment is withheld for a suitable period of time (Sanders, 1980), because most development efforts require ten to twenty years to allow for the land acquisition, land clearance, and reconstruction processes to be completed.

Whether these emerging physical signs will be accompanied by a true revival of neighborhood life is still unclear. Physically attractive neighborhoods are only one part of the story. If such neighborhoods are limited to only a small segment of the population—the very rich, for example—or if neighborhood organizations and interactions fail to reemerge even in these physically attractive neighborhoods, the social functions of neighborhoods will still have been lost. To this extent the civilizing force of neighborhood life may also remain uncaptured. Thus an alternative scenario would be the evolution of a faceless and alienated society, some of whose members happened to live in physically attractive neighborhoods.

One hopes that the likelihood of this scenario varies from slim to zero. If neighborhoods as social units cannot survive, few mechanisms will remain to counter the trends toward self-indulgence, self-centered attitudes, and ultimately a socially corrupt society. Alternative mechanisms such as the family and the church have also been declining, so that the loss of a sense of neighborhood could have truly devastating effects (Bronfenbrenner, 1974).

The more desirable outcome is the conserving and rebuilding of the neighborhood as a social unit. This does not imply an artifactually serene or segregated life in which cultural diversity, age mixture, and life-style differences are suppressed. (Such a homogenizing effect was, in fact, associated with the "neighborhood unit" movement, in which physical planners implicitly followed a unicultural approach to neighborhood life—see Perry [1939] and Isaacs [1949].) The vigor of neighborhood life, and the role of the neighborhood as a genuine social unit require the accommodation of different life-styles within the same geographic area. Participation in neighborhood organizations, social interactions in carrying out the functions of daily life, and neighboring relationships are all ways in which a diversity of tastes can be acknowledged and yet life can be continued in a civilized manner.

However, this more desirable outcome has, until now, been more a depiction of America's past than her future. The challenge before us is to conserve this precious resource—the neighborhood as a social unit—and to

INTRODUCTION

combine it with the new technologies evolving in other facets of American life. Only such a combination of old and new is likely to prepare us to face the future.

THE FEDERAL ROLE IN CONSERVING NEIGHBORHOODS

A few words must also be said about the role of the federal government in conserving neighborhoods as social units. Too often in the past federal programs have been designed with the neighborhood as a target of "intervention" (Glickman, 1980). In only a few cases, as with the Neighborhood Reinvestment Corporation (e.g., Ahlbrandt and Brophy, 1975) and the work of the National Commission on Neighborhoods (1979), has sufficient attention been given to indigenous efforts, whether undertaken by private enterprises at the local level or by citizen groups. More commonly, federal programs have imposed unachievable priorities on specific neighborhoods or citizen organizations, have set unrealistic time schedules, and have frequently fostered the long-term destruction of self-help efforts.

Federal support is needed, but it will succeed only under certain conditions. New programs must be judged first by their ability to regenerate rather than to cripple local efforts. Second, programs need to be in place over a long period of time, and not be redesigned every few years to reflect whimsically shifting priorities at the national level. Third, the programs must be based on a supportive rather than an interventionist posture. Overseas, for instance, the federal government's AID programs are, at least in theory, intended to provide long-term support for the development of foreign capabilities rather than to impose specific interventions; a counterpart program aimed at American neighborhoods does not exist. In short, the objectives of any new federal programs should be to conserve and reinforce social relationships within neighborhoods and to assure the development of self-sustaining local efforts. The ultimate criterion for a successful program must be the satisfaction of the residents or participants in the program, and not the short-term accomplishment of impossible tasks beyond neighborhood capabilities—such as the reduction of crime or the construction of a specific number of housing units.

The policy challenge at the federal level will not be met by the re-creation of task-specific programs. *Nor will the challenge be met by a massive withdrawal of federal support.* The challenge will be met only when a way has been found to make federal programs into neighborhood programs, some ideas for which are in this book. Only then can citizens share in the resources that ultimately govern their destinies. Under the aegis of a federal administration led by Ronald Reagan, one would like to think that this more enlightened policy posture is still possible.

REFERENCES

Abravanel, Martin D., and Mancini, Paul K. "Attitudinal and Demographic Constraints." In *Urban Revitalization*, edited by Donald B. Rosenthal, Beverly Hills, Calif.: Sage Publications, 1980, pp. 27–47.

Ahlbrandt, Roger S., and Brophy, Paul C. *Neighborhood Revitalization:Theory and Practice*. Lexington, Mass.: Lexington Books, 1975.

Auger, Deborah. "The Politics of Revitalization in Gentrifying Neighorhoods: The Case of Boston's South End." *Journal of the American Planning Association* 1979, 45, 515–522.

Bronfenbrenner, Urie. "The Origins of Alienation". *Scientific American* 1974, 231, 53–61.

Clay, Phillip L. *Neighborhood Renewal: Middle-Class Resettlement and Incumbent Upgrading in American Neighborhoods*. Lexington, Mass.: Lexington Books, 1979.

Cooley, Charles Horton. *Social Organizations: A Study of the Larger Mind*. 1909. Reprint., Glencoe Ill.: Free Press, 1956.

Glickman, Norman J., ed. *The Urban Impacts of Federal Policies*. Baltimore: Johns Hopkins University Press, 1980.

Goetze, Rolf. *Building Neighborhood Confidence*. Cambridge, Mass.: Ballinger, 1976.

Goetze, Rolf. *Understanding Neighborhood Change*. Cambridge, Mass.: Ballinger, 1979.

Goetze, Rolf; Colton, K. W., and O'Donnell, V. F. *Stabilizing Neighborhoods: A Fresh Approach to Housing Dynamics and Perceptions*. Cambridge, Mass.: Public Systems Evaluation, 1977.

Isaacs, Reginald R. "Attack on the Neighborhood Unit Formula." *Land Economics* 1949, 25, 73–78.

Jacobs, Jane. *The Death and Life of Great American Cities*. New York: Vintage Books, 1961.

Lachman, M. Leanne, and Downs, Anthony. "The Role of Neighborhoods in the Mature Metropolis." In *The Mature Metropolis*, edited by Charles L. Leven. Lexington, Mass.: Lexington Books, 1978, pp. 207–224.

Laska, Shirley Bradway, and Spain, Daphne, eds. *Back to the City: Issues in Neighborhood Renovation*. New York: Pergamon Press, 1980.

Lipton, Gregory S. "Evidence of Central City Revival." *Journal of the American Planning Association* 1977, 45, 136–147.

Morris, David, and Hess, Karl. *Neighborhood Power: The New Localism*. Boston: Beacon Press, 1975.

National Commission on Neighborhoods. *People, Building Neighborhoods*. Washington, D.C.: U.S. Government Printing Office, 1979.

Packard, Vance. *A Nation of Strangers*. New York: McKay, 1972.

Perry, Clarence A. "The Neighborhood Unit Formula." *In Housing for the Machine Age*. New York: Russell Sage Foundation, 1939, pp. 49–76.

Public Affairs Counseling. *The Dynamics of Neighborhood Change*. Report prepared for the U.S. Department of Housing and Urban Development, Washington, D.C., 1976.

Rosenthal, Donald B., ed. *Urban Revitalization*. Beverly Hills, Calif: Sage Publications, 1980.

Rossi, Peter H. *Why Families Move*. 2d ed. Beverly Hills, Calif.: Sage Publications, 1980.

Sanders, Heywood T. "Urban Renewal and the Revitalized City: A Reconsideration of Recent History." In *Urban Revitalization*, edited by Donald B. Rosenthal. Beverly Hills, Calif.: Sage Publications, 1980.

Sternlieb, George, and Lake, Robert W. "Aging Suburbs and Black Homeownership." *Annals*, 1975, 422, 105–117.

Suttles, Gerald D. *The Social Construction of Communities*. Chicago: University of Chicago Press, 1972.

INTRODUCTION

Tocqueville, Alexis de. *Democracy in America*. 2 vols. New York: Shocken Books, 1961. (Originally published, 1840.)

Yin, Robert K. "Creeping Federalism: The Federal Impact on the Structure and Function of Local Government," In *The Urban Impacts of Federal Policies*, edited by Norman J. Glickman. Baltimore: Johns Hopkins University Press, 1980, pp. 595–618.

I
Citizen Initiatives

Neighborhood life revolves around the activities of its residents. In every neighborhood, the daily activities and neighboring relationships are essential to the development of a sense of community. Among these activities a special subset has drawn public attention over the years. These are the concerted actions citizens take in relation to some neighborhood program or problem, and they are the topic of Part I of this book.

Typically, the concerted action leads to the formation of some organized citizens' group. As formal entities these groups may exist for only a short period of time, as many will be directed at a single issue and will disappear when the issue is resolved. Some of the groups, however, may serve multiple purposes and may eventually develop a sustained source of support. Whatever the longevity and whatever the issue, there appear to be some general principles regarding the operations of these groups. Thus, the following four chapters cover the ways these groups can be organized, their usefulness in collaborating with municipal officials in improving neighborhood services, and their role in fostering a sense of voluntarism.

Chapter 1 provides some empirical evidence regarding the important characteristics of citizen organizations. These characteristics are mainly judged in relation to impact; whether they were associated with a greater degree of citizen influence over programmatic issues. Chapter 2 places the role of citizen organizations in a broader municipal context, showing how the collective activities are but one source of feedback that can be made available to municipal officials. Other information about residents' needs and priorities can be derived by monitoring urban indicators, by holding neighborhood meetings, by establishing grievance procedures, or by locating government facilities close to the neighborhoods being served. All these alternatives are commonly found within municipalities across the country, and are therefore worth reviewing.

Chapter 3 analyzes one type of direct activity that has been sponsored by citizen organizations—crime prevention patrols. The chapter explores patrol experiences in depth, developing further insight into the difficulties and benefits of operating citizen organizations, as well as into the contemporary crime problem that plagues many neighborhoods. In reviewing these patrol activities, the reader should recall Jane Jacobs's observations about neighborhood life:

> The first thing to understand is that the public peace—the sidewalk and the street peace—of cities is not kept primarily by the police, necessary as police are. It is kept primarily by an intricate, almost unconscious network of voluntary controls and standards among the people themselves, and enforced by the people themselves. . . . No amount of police can enforce *civilization* where the normal, casual enforcement of it has broken down. (1961, pp. 31–32, emphasis added)

Thus the patrol activities, rather than being viewed as a competitor to the police, may be considered a contemporary attempt to revive the basic responsibilities of citizens.

Chapter 4 starts from a totally different perspective: that the desirable citizen initiatives are usually the ones taken on a voluntary basis. The chapter goes on to discuss the serious policy dilemma posed by this observation—how to foster government sponsorship and support of voluntary activities, itself a potentially contradictory situation. The chapter, based on work that the author did on behalf of the U.S. National Commission on Neighborhoods, raises the speculative possibility that government support can be provided without undermining the essential, voluntary nature of citizen organizations.

In sum, the first part of this book calls attention to the most important ingredient of contemporary American neighborhoods: the concerted actions of residents. Such actions are the primary resource that must be conserved and sustained in the future; they are the essence of neighborhood.

REFERENCES

Jacobs, Jane. *The Death and Life of Great American Cities*. New York: Vintage Books, 1961.

1
Correlates of Power in Citizen Organizations

THE VITALITY OF CITIZEN ORGANIZATIONS

Organized citizen action has been a hallmark of American democracy (Tocqueville, 1840/1961). At the neighborhood level, residents have frequently formed organizations to deal with common needs. In turn, these groups have often become an integral part of a neighborhood's social fabric. Citizen organizations have therefore been among the most important ways through which citizens have helped to improve neighborhoods.

The development and support of these types of groups became a controversial issue in the 1960s. Federal initiatives emphasized the devolution of power to citizen-dominated organizations that would oversee the delivery of services (Sundquist, 1969). Locally elected officials noted that they, as representatives of the citizenry, had a prior claim to this role, and conflicts ensued. Yet whichever side of the controversy one favored, certain knowledge about citizen organizations was still lacking. Among the key questions were:

- *In what kinds of neighborhoods is a citizen organization most likely to be successful?* The presence of a strong community identity, the

---

This chapter is based on excerpts from Robert K. Yin, William A. Lucas, Peter L. Szanton, and J. Andrew Spindler, *Citizen Organizations: Increasing Client Control over Services* (Santa Monica, Calif.: Rand Corporation 1973), pp. 47–67. The original research was supported by the U.S. Department of Health, Education and Welfare, although none of the stated views or conclusions reflects the official position of that department.

homogeneity of the community, the proportion who are poor, and the nature of the region or city are said to be related to success.
- *For what kinds of services is an organization most likely to be successful?* Attention must be given to how services are funded, the inherent nature of the services, and the organization of the agency delivering the services.
- *What organizational features, authority, and functions does a citizen organization need in order to be successful?* The success of a citizen organization can be related to the type of organizational form chosen, the existence of a committee structure, the procedures used in selecting the participants, the specific duties they are given, and the skills and experience of the participants.

To answer these questions, the experiences reported in fifty-one previously published case studies of citizen organizations were examined.[1] These case studies covered a variety of situations in health, education, social services, and planning in which a citizen organization had exerted influence over service programs. The case studies were first examined for some evidence regarding outcomes. By "successful citizen influence" was meant any of three outcomes—that citizens had

1. Implemented their views (*program impact*)
2. Brought more effective cooperation among the groups in the community being served (*community impact*)
3. Developed new organization and management skills for the participants (*skill development*)

The case studies were then examined for salient neighborhood, service, and organizational characteristics, and these were correlated with these three outcomes.

In general, neither the neighborhood nor service characteristics were major correlates of successful citizen organizations. Among the neighborhood characteristics, a moderate-size target population (5,000 to 20,000 residents) and the prior existence of a shared community identity were partial correlates of success. However, among the service characteristics, none was found to be related to the three outcomes of program impact, community impact, or skill development. Because of these results it was possible to examine more closely the organizational characteristics related to successful organizations,

---

[1]The full methodology and listing of the case studies may be found in Yin, Lucas, Szanton, and Spindler (1973). Descriptions of the general methodology may be found in Yin and Heald (1975) and Yin, Bingham, and Heald (1976).

regardless of their community or program characteristics.[2] The overall goal, summarized at the end of this chapter, was the identification of an organizational model for successful citizen action—a model that can be implemented (or thwarted) where desired.

ORGANIZATIONAL CHARACTERISTICS

Organizational Authority and the Proportion of Citizen Participants

The first relevant characteristic has to do with a citizen organization's charter. The case studies showed that governing boards are generally more successful than advisory committees in having *program impact*. A serious problem of interpretation remains, however, because the greater the legal authority of the organization, the fewer are the number of actual consumers of services found on the committee or board. For example, surveys of welfare boards have revealed few welfare recipients or even low-income people as board members. In fact, whereas one-third of the committees had two or more welfare recipients, none of the boards had even two recipients. Three-fourths of the boards had no low-income participants of any kind (O'Donnell and Reid, 1971). Is the greater program impact of governing boards attributable to their greater power, or to the *absence* of consumer members?

At stake is one of the critical questions about citizen organizations: the proportion of board members that should come from the community being served. Citizens from the target group have rarely been allowed to dominate service-linked citizen organizations that have considerable authority. One possible inference is that negative consequences are associated with having a strong, citizen-dominated board. The data from the fifty-one case studies suggest that this assumption is incorrect.

These findings are supported by a separate study of health centers, which also found that the proportion of participants from the consumer population was not related to program effectiveness (Langston et al., 1972). The study, whose purpose was to evaluate neighborhood health centers, surveyed approximately 9,500 families, including users of health centers, nonusers in the health center areas, and comparable respondents in a matched area for each of twenty-one centers. Objective information was gathered about the services the center provided, the management structure, the integration of funding,

---

[2]That is not necessarily to say that there were no interaction effects, with some organizational features having differential consequences under different programs or in different communities. Unfortunately, the number of cases did not permit systematic analysis of this question, and the only evidence of interaction was idiosyncratic and not susceptible to generalization.

outreach activities, and many other features of the center. *Program effectiveness* was measured by twenty-eight subjective factors from interviews and fifteen objective characteristics of the centers, including:

- Thirteen measures of appropriate utilization of the center, for example, are fewer appointments broken; is there home care; are there fewer untreated needs?
- Five convenience measures, for example, how long is the waiting time; how crowded is the center?
- Three satisfaction measures, for example, do users like the doctors; is the doctors' treatment respectful and dignified?
- Fifteen comprehensiveness measures, for example, how many tests are administered; is there pre- and postnatal care?

These were all aggregated into one performance score. The score thus reflects objective and specific definitions of program effectiveness for comparable services, in addition to the report of on-site evaluations made subjectively by local administrators. Citizen participation was measured by the proportion of service beneficiaries on the boards of these neighborhood centers, which varied from under 25 percent to 100 percent. In all cases the proportion of beneficiaries was substantial. When the degree of participation was correlated with the program effectiveness measure, it was found that there was no relationship between the two.

The conclusion appears to be that, after a certain proportion of beneficiary representation is achieved, other factors determine the success or failure of the citizen organizations. All-citizen boards may represent a neighborhood point of view better than boards with only one-third or one-half of their members drawn from the target community population (Mogulof, 1970), but there is nevertheless a case to be made for having substantial numbers of service managers and providers present to supply another perspective and to explain some of the complexities of service delivery. For these reasons, an optimal strategy would be a "citizen-dominated" board (50 to 60 percent citizen representation), but with the condition that both providers and citizens each comprise at least one-third of the board.

Budgetary Control

Beyond the distinction between governing boards and advisory committees, certain functional responsibilities are also critical. The reason is that there may be weak boards as well as committees with some significant powers.

Analysis of the fifty-one case studies showed that budget control was a key to organizational success. Such control is, of course, an ultimate power in any organization, for it is the concrete instrument through which policy changes are most often put into effect. The success of the citizen organizations in having program impact was determined by the following question: *Does the organization have substantial influence over the service budget* (see Table 1)? About 80 percent of the organizations with budgetary influence also had program impact. Moreover, control over the budget also provided opportunities for managerial responsibility, and 83 percent of the organizations with substantial budgetary influence also indicated development of new leadership skills among the citizen participants.

"Substantial influence" over the budget means much more than merely reviewing or approving the local application for funds. Although mere approval of a project application, including its budget, at first glance seems to be a powerful authority, participants are frequently confronted with a prepared application and given a simple choice: They can approve an unfamiliar or disagreeable application package and obtain the money for the locality, or they can fail to approve it, miss the deadline, and not have a project at all. Assurances that the citizen organization will be able to exercise future influence are frequently made, but that opportunity rarely occurs. The "sign-off" function itself may therefore not be critical and, as predicted, the case studies showed that program impact was *not* related to simple sign-off authority: *Is the sign-off of the citizen organization required on funding requests by the service organization* (see Table 2)? In other words, mere sign-off requirements, in contrast to deeper citizen involvement in formulating and debating the budget and approving changes, do not by themselves contribute to significant *program impact*.

Grievance Investigation

Circumstances may not always permit the granting of sweeping authority to a citizen organization. Thus among other functions that citizen organizations

Table 1

	Budget influence[a]	
Program impact	Yes (N = 19)	No (N = 24)
No or trivial implementation of citizen views	21%	62%
Significant or high implementation of citizen views	79	38
Total	100	100

[a]Throughout the tables, the data do not include case studies that lacked the information needed to answer the question.

Table 2

	Sign-off authority	
Program impact	Yes (N = 16)	No (N = 26)
No or trivial implementation of citizen views	44%	54%
Significant or high implementation of citizen views	56	46
Total	100	100

have fulfilled has been the investigation of individual complaints about the staff and administration of the services. Citizens can usually deal with the concrete issues involved in grievances. The specific information regarding a complaint can often be grasped quickly, and a complaint may lead to focused decisions that are made in a relatively short time, permitting even new participants to take part in discussions in a meaningful way. Such discussions also increase participant contact with both staff and users, and may have a variety of positive consequences for the citizen organization that go well beyond the narrow grievance-investigation function itself.

In the cases where a citizen organization had substantial influence in the investigation of complaints, the case studies showed that the participants were successful in other respects. Participants were able to implement their views in 74 percent of those cases where they had influence in grievance investigation, whereas they were successful in only 23 percent of the cases in which grievance investigation was absent: *Does the citizen organization have substantial influence in the investigation of complaints that individual citizens have about staff and program* (see Table 3)? A closer examination of the thirteen cases in which an organization had no influence in the complaint process also showed that in only one case was there an increase in *skill development*; in only one case was there a significant *community impact*.

Staff and Participant Expertise

Another important organizational characteristic for a citizen organization is whether it should have staff under its own control. As Table 4 indicates, the presence of staff was associated with a 75 percent success rate in having program impact: *Does the citizen organization have its own staff?* This feature appears to be of central importance to success in affecting services, and the reasons are not difficult to infer. The availability of staff makes continuity and

Table 3

Program impact	Grievance investigation	
	Yes (N = 30)	No (N = 13)
No or trivial implementation of citizen views	26%	77%
Significant or high implementation of citizen views	74	23
Total	100	100

expertise available to the citizen organization that cannot otherwise be attained. Participants who only put in several hours a week cannot keep up with the details of service programs in sufficient depth to exercise meaningful influence unless they start with considerable expertise in the area. The participants in what became an embittering experience with the Philadelphia Model Cities stated that one lesson they learned was: "Community organizations must have the dollars to hire their own staff technicians, and must be able to direct that staff and hold it accountable" (Arnstein, 1972). When the citizens in an organization are economically disadvantaged, typically without the time, education, and other resources available to the middle class, the absence of staff may be a crippling weakness. Moreover, the fact that staff can serve as a vehicle for providing training and experience to members of the target population may also account for the strong correlation between the organization's having staff resources and *skill development*: In cases where an organization had its own staff, 76 percent were judged to have developed significant new organizational skills among members of the target community.

Table 4

Program impact	Own staff	
	Yes (N = 20)	No (N = 26)
No or trivial implementation of citizen views	25%	58%
Significant or high implementation of citizen views	75	42
Total	100	100

Indigenous Service Staff

There may also be additional support for effective participation if the service staff (as opposed to the staff of the citizen organization) is drawn from the target population. Whether or not they are hired by the citizen organization, service staff from the local community often provide useful information and support. In addition, the employment of indigenous staff in the delivery of service appears to improve program effectiveness. The previously cited study of neighborhood health clinics collected data on the proportion of the staff indigenous to the clinic service areas as well as on the extensive measures of program effectiveness. The relationship between the aggregate performance measures and the proportion of indigenous staff is weak but positive (Langston *et al.*, 1972). The study also suggested a possible explanation for this outcome: A low frequency of professional staff–citizen problems was strongly related to a high proportion of indigenous service staff.

Another study has also noted that strong forms of citizen participation are more likely to be associated with a more frequent employment of indigenous paraprofessionals (Community Change and Public Sector, 1972). It thus seems that when strong organizations are established and indigenous paraprofessionals are employed on the service staff, the result is both a higher likelihood of having a *program impact* and, as a matter of course, a higher probability of improved staff–client relations.

Training, Reimbursement, and Prior Expertise

As an alternative to staff, one might consider increasing the expertise of the participants. That could be done by training, by attracting more knowledgeable individuals with pay or at least reimbursement for expenses, and/or by recruiting participants with prior experience in citizen organizations. Training was provided in only ten of the fifty-one case studies, and pay and reimbursement in eight. The small number of cases limits the reliability of the results, but in two-thirds of the cases where training was provided, the participants developed new skills and were successful in getting their views translated into policy. Reimbursement and pay were unrelated to success, but that may be the result of how the money was allocated. Frequently, individuals have been reimbursed only after a delay of many months, and observers have complained that such a reimbursement schedule is not a meaningful incentive.

Indications that the presence of knowledgeable participants does make a difference were brought out by a different question: whether at least a substantial minority of participants from the target population had prior experience in citizen participation or community organization. The case studies showed a consistently higher rate of success for *program impact* among those organizations with experienced participants. Of twenty-two cases with experienced participants, 68 percent implemented their views compared to a 42 percent success rate among the cases without such participants.

Tenure and Specialization

Whether or not prior experience is available, another way of strengthening citizen participation may be to assure that participants remain active and thus develop expertise. The effects of longevity of participation could not be closely examined, however, because in 86 percent of the case studies where a judgment was possible, one-half or more of the participants had only been involved for two years, or for the life of the organization if it was less than two years old.

As for functionally specialized committees, their effect may be to permit the participants to choose those topics where their interests and knowledge are greatest, and to keep track of a narrower range of problems and activities. Consistently with that view, 67 percent of those cases where functional committees operated were associated with successful *program impact,* compared to 47 percent success among cases without such committees.

In summary, of all of these personnel characteristics, the most important way of giving citizen organizations the capacity to exercise power is to provide them staff over which they have control. The use of indigenous paraprofessionals on the service staff is also important. Training, remuneration, and the use of specialized committees for the citizen organization are additional factors that will further support the citizen participants and increase their expertise.

Organizational Structure, Level, and Membership Selection

With remarkable consistency, the case studies showed that none of the previously considered characteristics was related to the other outcome in question: *community impact.* For the most part it appears that the effects of a citizen organization on the community it represents are more a function of the structure of the organization, and not of its power and duties. Considered here are the basic structure of the organization, the level at which it is organized, and the means used in selecting citizens from the target community.

Constituent Organizations

The growing number and diversity of organizations in many communities, all purporting to represent or serve similar target populations, make it important to consider what organizational form citizen participation should take.

Some organizations are simple in structure; others are complex in that they are "umbrellas" bringing together a variety of other active organizations. These umbrella organizations occasionally have their own constituent organizations organized at a lower level of aggregation (such as neighborhood councils as part of a citywide organization); or the constituents can be well-established, independent organizations that participate in the organization (e.g., the selection of delegates by and from welfare rights organizations, churches, and other organizations on a community action agency board). In either event there are costs and benefits. Simple organizations are easy to join, as a new board member only has to learn the politics of one unitary organization; delegates to umbrella organizations must deal with the politics of constituent organizations that may influence the behavior of their colleagues. But the umbrella organization can often tap the significant resources of its constituent organizations, whereas a unitary organization often stands alone in trying to influence a service agency.

A more complex structure does make it less likely that the participants will hold common views and more difficult for them to hold common positions. In 60 percent of the case studies where citizen participants represented constituent organizations in umbrella organizations, the citizen organization was *not* able to implement participant views beyond a trivial degree. On the other hand, organizations with such a structure provided a forum for different points of view within the target community, and appeared to lead to greater interorganizational coordination. Thus umbrella organizations are much more likely (77 percent) to have a community impact—that is, a unifying effect on their communities—than are unitary organizations (see Table 5). These results indicate a potential conflict between two desirable consequences: The structure associated with success in bringing the community together is also associated with decreased participant influence over the services.

A potential resolution to this problem may be found by considering the effects of organizational structure and the key factor of staff as they operate

Table 5

Community impact	Type of organizational structure	
	Umbrella ($N = 13$)	Unitary ($N = 32$)
Unifying effect on community	77%	34%
No effect or fragmenting effect on community	23	66
Total	100	100

Table 6

	Organizational structure and staff resources (Number of cases)			
	With staff		Without staff	
Program impact	Umbrella	Unitary	Umbrella	Unitary
No or trivial implementation of citizen views	1	2	5	12
Significant or high implementation of citizen views	7	2	2	10

together. Although the number of cases is limited, the pattern is suggestive. Umbrella organizations with staff have a successful *program impact,* as do unitary organizations with staff. Unitary forms without staff do not do well, but umbrella organizations without staff do worst of all. It appears that staff, perhaps by providing continuity and cohesion, are equally effective in umbrella organizations in enabling the citizen organization to implement citizen views. The results suggest that citizen organizations impact if they have their own staff. Without staff, umbrella organizations appear to be self-defeating as a means of increasing citizen influence (see Table 6).

Level of Organization

The earlier discussion of community characteristics showed that the size of the target population made some difference, but that the nature of the community was not a large factor. A separate but consistent finding is that it makes little or no difference whether the city organization is operated at the county, metropolitan, city, or neighorhood level.

The only evidence that suggested the desirability of one level over another was that city and county organizations seemed to have a greater likelihood (59 percent) of community impact than did the organizations based on smaller areas. Those in smaller, more homogeneous neighborhoods, villages, and suburbs probably have less diversity in the first place, so the fact that they have less frequent (37 percent) community impact may not be that important.

Membership Selection Procedures

Boards and executive committees of citizen organizations can be selected in three ways. They can be *appointed,* whether by state or local officials, by the administrator of the services performer, or by some professional or community group. They can be *elected,* either by the community or by some organization or group within the community. They can be *self-selected,* in that those who come to open meetings are presumed to be those both interested and able to speak for others, or in the sense of a self-constituted group setting up a nonprofit organization.

The case study data suggested that appointment is the weakest method. The reasons are probably varied. Because those appointing tend to choose citizens already known as prominent figures, this process seems less likely to help develop skills for participants not previously involved in community activities. The dangers of cooptation are quite great, as individuals friendly to the wishes of management of the services are frequently chosen (Austin, 1972). In either event, less than one-half of the case studies that had appointment procedures were successful in influencing the program, compared to 60 percent of those relying on election and self-selection.

Both self-selection and appointment have limited impact on the broader community, probably because the process of selection occurs with little fanfare. Whereas only 30 percent of the cases relying on appointment or self-selection had a community impact, 81 percent of those using elections had this effect. Self-selection is somewhat better than appointment, however, in that individuals with widely differing views can express them and take active roles in the organization's activities. But just as the appointment procedure may lead to citizens who are too passive, self-selection opens the door to ephemeral and/or rancorous participation. Even when it is structured so that the citizens are informed and cooperative in attitude, the potential abuses are evident to the professionals and managers of the services, making implementation difficult.

The data therefore suggest that election mechanisms are the most desirable. One reason may be that elections are the only way to establish the fact that a few citizens represent and speak for a larger number of citizens. General elections are not always successful, however, because the turnout is frequently quite small, raising questions about the legitimacy of the elected representatives. A comparison by Peterson (1970) of efforts at participation in Chicago, Philadelphia, and New York reinforces the conclusion that elections are the better form, but suggests that elections within constituent organizations, or among delegates or organizations, may well be the best form among the many election procedures available.

THE SUCCESSFUL ORGANIZATIONAL MODEL

In sum, the experience from fifty-one case studies of citizen participation showed that certain organizational features do appear to be correlated with a substantial devolution of power to citizen organizations. Three of these features are of prime importance:

- Meaningful influence over the budget
- Investigation of complaints
- Staff responsible to the citizen participant organization

The ancillary benefit of positive community impact is maximized if the structure of the organization is umbrella-like, and if elections for a citizen organization's officers are held by constituent organizations. At the same time, the case studies suggested that some organizational features are *not* related to the likelihood of success. These are: sign-off authority, the geographic level of the organization, and whether the service program is funded directly by the federal government or through state and local agencies.

The overall pattern of findings suggests the development of a general model for citizen organizations. Where citizens are interested in maximizing three types of outcomes—impact over services, community impact, and skill development—the previously identified features may be considered the structural and functional characteristics to be implemented. The model will still have to be tailored to specific local situations and types of services, but the findings showed no systematic relationships with these conditions, and the model may therefore provide a general set of guidelines. Whether these guidelines are to be used by citizens themselves in designing their own organizations (e.g., Alinsky, 1971) or whether government mandates should identify these features can only be determined by the politics of each neighborhood scene.

REFERENCES

Alinsky, Saul D. *Rules for Radicals: A Practical Primer for Realistic Radicals.* New York: Random House, 1971.

Arnstein, Sherry R. "Maximum Feasible Manipulation." *Public Administration Review* 1972, *32*, 388.

Austin, David M. "Resident Participation: Political Mobilization or Organizational Co-optation?" *Public Administration Review* 1972, *32*, 409–420.

Community Change, Inc., and Public Sector, Inc. "A Study of Consumer Participation in the Administrative Process in Various Levels of HSMHA's Service Projects." Mimeographed. Sausalito, Calif., 1972.

Langston, Joann H. et al.*Study to Evaluate the OEO Neighborhood Health Center Program at Selected Centers.* Rockville, Md.: Geomet Report No. HF-71, 1972.

Mogulof, Mervin. *Citizen Participation: A Review and Commentary on Federal Policies and Practices.* Washington, DC: Urban Institute, 1970, p. 20.

O'Donnell, Edward J., and Reid, Otto M. "Citizen Participation on Public Welfare Boards and Committees." *Welfare in Review* 1971, *9*, 1–9.

Peterson, Paul E. "Forms of Representation: Participation of the Poor in the Community Action Program." *American Political Science Review* 1970, *64*, 491–507.

Sundquist, James S. *Making Federalism Work: A Study of Program Coordination at the Community Level.* Washington, DC: Brookings Institution, 1969.

Tocqueville, Alexis de. *Democracy in America.* 2 vols. New York: Shocken Books, 1961. (Originally published, 1840.)

Yin, Robert K., and Heald, Karen. "Using the Case Survey Method to Analyze Policy Studies." *Administrative Science Quarterly* 1975, *20*, 371–381.

Yin, Robert K., Bingham, E., and Heald, K. "The Difference that Quality Makes: The Case of Literature Reviews." *Sociological Methods and Research,* 1976, *5*, 139–156.

2
How Citizens Influence Their Municipal Services

CITIZEN PARTICIPATION

Citizen participation in community affairs can be approached from many angles. The most common one has been the increased role of citizens in the use of federal funds, stemming from urban development programs such as the urban renewal, Community Action, and Model Cities programs, but now also including citizen advisory boards in special services such as education and transportation.[1] However, an alternative approach to citizen participation emphasizes the influence of citizens over the actions of municipal officials. Because of the frequent turnover in federal programs, this alternative approach may be more significant to the urban scene; the full array of municipal services can be affected, and these are the services that will endure regardless of any changes in the mixture of federal programs. From this point of view, the goal is to have municipal officials—that is, the people who work in city hall or in the line agencies actually delivering services to neighborhoods—listen more closely to what residents say.

To improve officials' capacity for listening, there is an array of citizen feedback mechanisms. Some of these mechanisms represent weak forms of

---

This chapter is based on a previously unpublished paper, first presented at the Neighborhood Concepts of Local Government Seminar, Fort Wayne, Indiana, September 1975, sponsored by the City of Fort Wayne, and later issued as "Citizen Feedback Mechanisms in Municipal Services" (Santa Monica, Calif.: Rand Corporation, 1976).
[1] For more on this aspect of citizen participation, see Chapter 1.

feedback in the sense that all they involve is getting information from citizens; others are strong forms in that they call for neighborhood control and power over services (Yin and Yates, 1975). The purpose of this chapter is to call attention to the full array of mechanisms, and thereby to indicate the basic framework of *bureaucratic* governance that exists in most cities. Such governance is to be distinguished from the *political* governance structures that have more commonly drawn attention: voter behavior, machine politics, and job patronage. Although these political activities often set the tone for the broader direction of municipal services, the bureaucratic governance structures are more important on a day-to-day basis.

In reviewing the alternative feedback mechanisms one should keep three lessons in mind. First, no single mechanism is best. Different agencies and different cities have different needs, and the appropriate mechanism depends on the particular situation. Second, initiative from the local level is needed to make a citizen feedback mechanism work best. There is very little, for instance, that can be done by federal officials other than to cite the experience of other cities, because only local officials will understand how best to make the necessary adaptations in their own city. Third, the feedback mechanisms do not usually result in a clear and unambiguous signal from the citizenry. In fact, the opposite is more likely to be the case—and municipal officials will still have to decide how to deal with the varying and often competing needs of their constituents.

TYPES OF CITIZEN FEEDBACK MECHANISMS

Citizen feedback mechanisms may be divided into those that fall outside the executive branch of local governments and those that fall within its purview. Only the latter category is the topic of this chapter. However, it is useful to remember that those mechanisms falling outside the executive branch—for example, contacting one's legislative representative or pursuing cases in the courts—can also influence municipal service activities. In the last few years, for instance, the courts have dealt with the important question of equity and the distribution of municipal services, in which residents of one neighborhood may receive poorer services than residents in another neighborhood, even though both groups may pay similar taxes and should receive the same amounts of services. Other types of mechanisms outside the executive branch are civic organizations and the mass media. Every city has its range of civic organizations that express the views of special interest groups, and the mass media often help provide such forms of citizen feedback as newspaper hotlines and investigative reporting by the local television station.

HOW CITIZENS INFLUENCE THEIR MUNICIPAL SERVICES

Some of the problems with these mechanisms outside the jurisdiction of the executive branch are that they tend to work slowly, and that many citizens cannot use them without special resources. For instance, both time and money are needed to pursue cases in court. Moreover, these mechanisms are also somewhat ineffective because they lack direct links to the municipal services about which citizens complain. In fact, it is these shortcomings that have led to the development of new forms of citizen feedback within the executive branch. This chapter therefore discusses five such mechanisms, treating them in the order of ascending financial and political costs.

Urban Indicators

Urban indicators, based on the records *already* maintained by every municipal agency, are one of the cheapest ways of getting citizen feedback. An examination of fire alarm data in New York City, for instance, reveals that false alarms have a rhythmic pattern, with a peak that tends to occur around July 4.[2] Although the pattern seems to be an obvious reflection of youths being on the street in the hot summer, that may not be the case. An examination of the false alarms in Detroit reveals that Detroit's pattern is exactly the reverse. Thus a different explanation of urban activity in Detroit would have to be developed in comparison to that for New York. The point, however, is that different cities have different service needs, and the existing municipal records can often serve as indicators of these needs. Many indicators do have regular patterns, and officials can easily and cheaply monitor them for deviations. The deviations may indicate that important citywide or neighborhood conditions have changed, and the information may suggest further inquiry by citizens and officials.

Another kind of indicator is the relocation patterns of families. Every city has some agency, such as the American Red Cross or the welfare department, that keeps records of the times when, because of an emergency, families have had to relocate. Mapping such patterns sometimes gives clues about the neighborhoods that are likely to need help in the future. Families on welfare in particular may move because of an emergency, and they may relocate to a neighborhood that is experiencing the early stages of decline. To the extent that officials monitor the relocation patterns, two municipal actions could result: improved services intended to help the relocated family adjust to its new neighborhood, and further inquiry concerning the general conditions of the neighborhood. In sum, urban indicators are derived from records that are already on hand; all that is necessary is to monitor them with an analytic eye.

[2] See Chapter 11.

Neighborhood Meetings

A second kind of feedback mechanism is the neighborhood meeting. Data on the frequency of such meetings are occasionally reported in the *Municipal Yearbook* (e.g., Stenberg, 1972), and show that meetings are a common mechanism, whether convened by chief executives, legislative bodies, or city boards and commissions. Interestingly, the meetings appear to be found more frequently in large cities (those over 100,000) than in small cities (those between 25,000 and 100,000).

Meetings are certainly an easy and low-cost way of increasing feedback, discussion, and personal contact between officials and citizens. Meetings are most frequently used to ascertain citizens' responses to plans for building new facilities. However, as a feedback mechanism, meetings usually do not give residents much power. Often residents do not have sufficient time to prepare for a meeting, and they may not have the resources to present their case effectively. Nevertheless, even though there is little real control over services on the part of residents, meetings are an important mechanism because they do allow for an exchange of views, and changes in proposed plans can occur.

Grievance Procedures

A third type of feedback mechanism, grievance procedures, is slightly more expensive but provides more feedback and control. Grievance procedures are probably the most prevalent mode of citizen feedback (see Table 7). Citywide grievance mechanisms usually involve a single telephone number a resident can call or a single place a resident can visit if he or she has a problem.

Table 7
Citywide Complaint Mechanisms

Mechanisms	Large cities[a] (N = 90)		Small cities[b] (N = 380)	
	Number	Percent	Number	Percent
Special telephone number	43	48	93	24
Special complaint bureau	52	58	109	29
Ombudsman or community service officer	41	46	76	20

Source: Stenberg, 1972.
[a]More than 100,000 population.
[b]25,000 to 100,000 population.

The typical citywide grievance procedure is not intended to displace the numerous complaint mechanisms operated by individual municipal agencies (not shown in Table 7). On the contrary, citywide grievance procedures are specifically intended to deal with those situations where a resident does not know to which agency to turn. Suppose there is the body of a dead dog on the roof of a building, and a resident wants to get the carcass removed. Now, whom should the resident call? It might be the sanitation department, the housing department, or the health department. There are numerous other occasions when a citizen does not know just whom to call or is unaware of the detailed organization of government agencies. Because citywide grievance procedures can be given better publicity than the complaint procedures of single agencies, more people are likely to be aware of them. And, a citywide grievance mechanism may be able to deal effectively with a problem because it has arisen before in some other neighborhood.

In one especially interesting type of grievance procedure, a single person—an ombudsman (or ombudsperson)—serves in a citywide capacity. Several cities have tried this approach. The office of ombudsman originated in Europe, where an ombudsman was appointed by the legislative branch and citizens would then bring their problems to this individual, who could in turn recommend new legislation. In American cities the ombudsman has most frequently been attached to the mayor (or executive branch). Figure 1 is a map showing some of the states and cities that at one time or another have had some kind of ombudsman. In Dayton, Ohio, which has about 250,000 people in the central city and is the city that has had an ombudsman for the longest perion of time, the operation required about $100,000 annually. There were about twelve staff people working full-time, and they dealt with about 5,000 complaints a year (Yin, 1972). What makes an ombudsman work better or worse is the individual's personality, the backing received from the mayor, and the extent to which the mayor only uses the ombudsman as a public relations official.

Neighborhood Facilities

In many cities, city governments have located multipurpose facilities that are within walking distance (about half a mile at the most) of the residents in the neighborhoods. Besides being local centers for receiving citizens' complaints, these facilities sometimes serve as places where residents can pay their local taxes or water bills. In other words, functions normally carried out in a downtown city hall can be decentralized in this way to a neighborhood facility.

One of the most well-known examples of neighborhood facilities has been the "little city halls" in Boston. Boston has had fourteen little city halls

CHAPTER 2

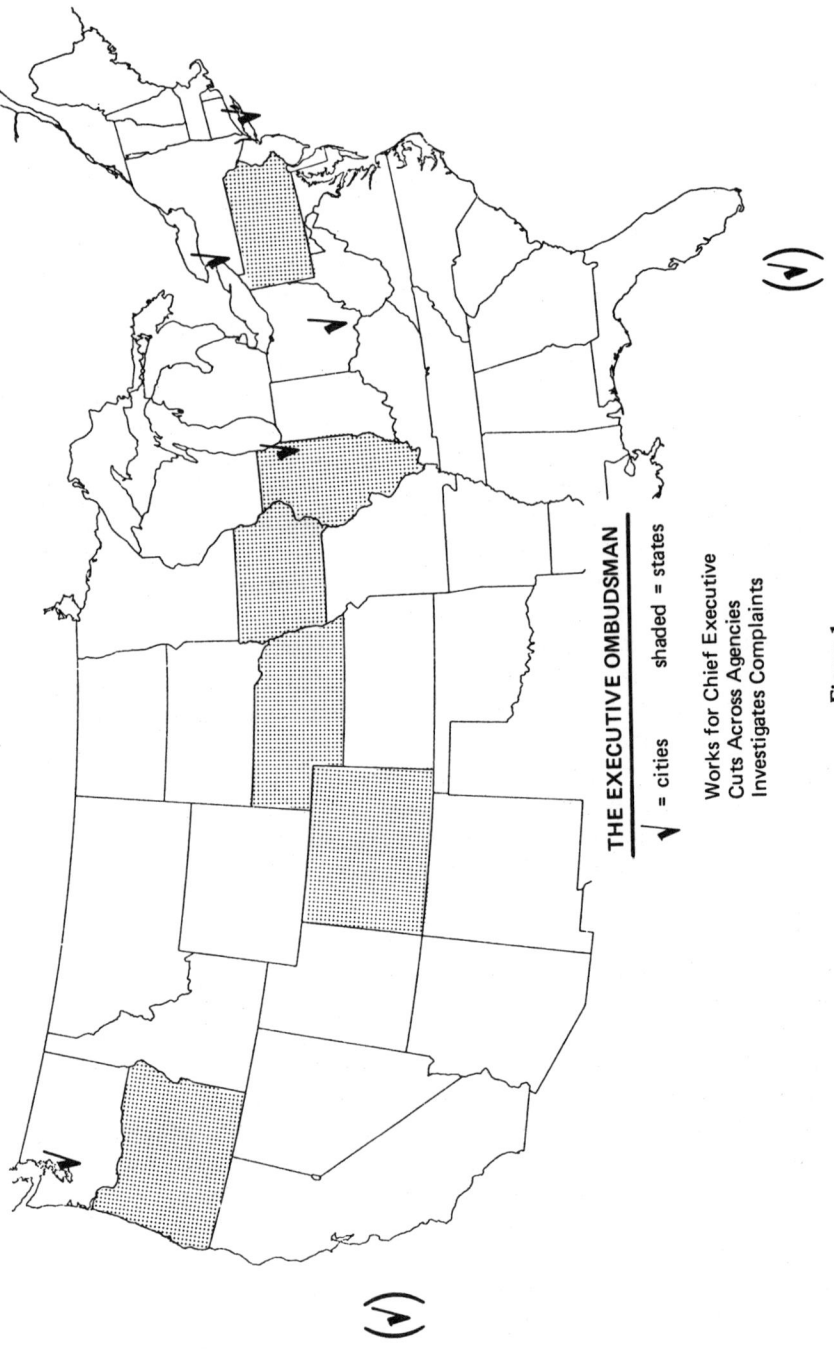

Figure 1

HOW CITIZENS INFLUENCE THEIR MUNICIPAL SERVICES

covering its neighborhoods, and the entire operation required about $1.5 million a year in the early 1970s. There were about 100 staff people who handled from 70,000 to 80,000 complaints a year, which is no small undertaking. The city halls are not necessarily located in new buildings; they can be trailers or storefronts.

Moreover, a city does not necessarily have to start from scratch. Too often it is forgotten that there already are neighborhood facilities. In Somerville, Massachusetts, a suburb of Boston that just touches on Cambridge and Boston and has about 100,000 people, there are five branch libraries.[3] Most residents are within walking distance (half a mile) of at least one of these libraries, and those who are not may be near firehouses or other municipal buildings that could serve as community centers. To operate an information and referral service or a grievance procedure, the existing library staff could be trained, under certain conditions, to perform those activities, so that a city would not even have to start with a totally new staff.

Neighborhood Organizations

The fifth and last kind of feedback mechanism covers programs with which most officials are well acquainted. These programs have frequently, but not always, stemmed from the federal Community Action and Model Cities efforts and involve a neighborhood organization formed either through elections or municipal appointments. The organization may have considerable resources at its disposal and may attempt to improve the services in the neighborhood or to deal with residents' problems.

An earlier study of federally supported organizations identified those factors in neighborhood organizations that made them powerful in the sense that neighborhood residents could influence service agencies.[4] Of the possible organizational features and functions, three were most frequently correlated with the occurrence of citizens' power: paid staff, a grievance procedure, and review over budget formulation. Of these three, the availability of paid staff turned out to be of greatest importance. Not surprisingly, some of the most serious political battles concerning local organizations are often over the question of paid staff: Those who do not want a powerful organization do not want to give it enough resources to hire its own staff. If one considers neighborhood organizations in their most powerful form, one is starting to consider neighborhood government; however, there are two important qualifications: A genuine neighborhood government must be constitutionally based—that is, there must be some provision for it in the city charter or the state consti-

---

[3]For more on the possible role of branch libraries, see Chapter 8.
[4]See Chapter 1.

tution—and the neighborhood government must have some kind of taxing authority.

CONCLUSIONS

These various approaches suggest at least three important lessons about the ways citizens can influence municipal services. First, effective feedback and participation require that citizens have the same level of decentralized or centralized organization as the relevant municipal service. Neighborhood-based indicators, meetings, and organizations can create all sorts of pressure on city hall or on local agencies, but if the local agencies are centralized and do not operate on a district basis, it may be difficult for them to respond directly to a neighborhood's problem. To take but a simple example, suppose that a neighborhood has two or three playgrounds in need of repair and that residents set priorities by deciding which playground is to be repaired first. If the public works or recreation department is not controlled at the district level, the district official must send a requisition to a central office that does not necessarily discriminate according to neighborhoods (e.g., see Yin, Hearn, and Shapiro, 1974). The requisition ends up on a pile of other requisitions that is dealt with according to a sequence imposed by administrative accident rather than by local priorities, and the citizen feedback mechanism has only a frustrating effect.

Second, if a feedback mechanism does not lead to a perceptible response, the mechanism may fall into disuse. In a grievance procedure that fails to produce some result, even the official who is supposed to deal with the complaints—the ombudsman or the neighborhood complaint officer—will be frustrated. In some cases, for example, the neighborhood complaint officer may have difficulty reaching the relevant city department or agency to file a complaint on behalf of a resident. If this situation occurs frequently enough, the complaint system may adapt by closing shop in a unique way: The neighborhood complaint officer might tie up the telephone line by continually talking to friends; the complaint office might move out of its storefront location to a less accessible place; or the office might fail to publicize its presence. In short, the citizen feedback mechansim would still exist but would not be easy for residents to use.

Third, as stated at the outset, no single mechanism works best. Different mechanisms become differentially advantageous depending on the nature of the problem, a city's prior history of citizen participation, and the specific line agency involved. The best results may indeed stem from multiple efforts in which a variety of feedback mechanisms, including surveys and polls, are used over a variety of situations.

REFERENCES

Stenberg, Carl W. "Decentralization and the City." *Municipal Yearbook,* 1972, Washington, D.C.: International City Management Association, 1972.

Yin, Robert K. "Cable-TV and Public Interest Programs in Dayton." In *Cable Communications in the Dayton Miami Valley,* In L. L. Johnson *et al.,* Santa Monica, Calif.: Rand Corporation, 1972.

Yin, Robert K, and Yates, Douglas. *Street-Level Governments: Assessing Decentralization and Urban Services.* Lexington, Mass: Lexington Books, 1975.

Yin, Robert K., Hearn, R.W., and Shapiro, P. "Administrative Decentralization of Municipal Services." *Policy Sciences* 1974, 5, 57–70.

3
Patrolling the Neighborhood Beat

RESIDENT PATROLS AND GUARDS

Citizen Crime Prevention

In the face of rising crime rates and a declining sense of security, urban residents have initiated a variety of crime prevention efforts. Although improved architectural design (Newman, 1972) and increased protection by the local police department have been common demands, many residents have also felt that their own vigilance and active concern over neighborhood conditions can play an important role in assuring an adequate level of residential safety. Typical crime prevention activities have taken a wide variety of forms, including property identification campaigns, programs to make residents more aware of good crime prevention practices, increased use of security devices, and programs to encourage citizens to report suspicious incidents (see National Advisory Commission, 1974; U.S. Chamber of Commerce, 1970).

The purpose of this chapter is to examine one category of crime prevention activities—resident patrols and guards—and to review in an exploratory manner the available evidence about them. The formation of resident

---

This chapter is based on excerpts from Robert K. Yin, Mary E. Vogel, Jan M. Chaiken, and Deborah R. Both, *Patrolling the Neighborhood Beat: Residents and Residential Security* (Santa Monica, Calif.: Rand Corporation, 1976). The research was supported by a grant from the U.S. Department of Justice, although none of the stated views should be construed as representing the official policies of that department.

patrols and guards represents an important form of citizen participation in neighborhood affairs. Unlike other crime prevention activities, most of which require residents only to be more alert and sensitive to crime prevention in their daily routines, a patrol or guard activity demands active organizational support and personal commitment.

Previous investigations of resident patrols have laid some useful but limited groundwork. Some studies have intensively examined one type of patrol activity. Knopf (1969) and Anderson et al. (1974), for instance, studied youth patrols that emerged during outbreaks of civil disorder. Although such studies have been illuminating in regard to single types of patrols, they did not develop a comparative framework for assessing different types of patrols and guards. Other studies have examined a wide variety of citizen crime prevention activities (e.g., Washnis, 1977), including patrols and guards, but used only limited sources of information and an informal set of research methods. In some cases these studies have openly restricted themselves to descriptive and nonevaluative observations. Marx and Archer (1971, 1972), for instance, examined twenty-eight self-defense groups but made no attempt to evaluate the patrols or to discuss outcomes; Brown (1969) merely listed the prominent patrol and guard projects that appeared in several cities during the 1960s. In contrast, this chapter

- Identifies the variety of resident patrol and guard activities
- Reports on preliminary evidence with regard to the outcomes of these criteria

Definition of Resident Patrol and Guard Activities

A resident patrol or guard may be defined as a citizen crime prevention activity with four characteristics. First, there must be a *specific patrol or surveillance routine*. Patrol personnel, whether resident volunteers or guards paid by residents' groups, maintain a regular, fixed schedule of crime prevention duties. The duties exist on a routine basis and are not merely triggered by specific crime incidents. This criterion excludes those activities (e.g., taxi patrols) in which a person reports emergencies observed in the course of other occupational responsibilities. However, it does include those situations in which a person serves on a part-time basis—but for a specific shift—in a patrol function.

Second, the routine of the patrol must be aimed at *preventing criminal acts*. On this basis, local chapters of the Ku Klux Klan or vigilantes in Queens, New York organized only to harass congregating homosexuals (Bird, 1969) would be excluded because of the personal and political interests represented by those persecuting groups. By emphasizing the prevention of criminal acts, the definition also excludes groups that perform only such tasks as identifying or remedying hazardous environmental conditions, including unlit areas, broken locks, weak railings, and malfunctioning traffic signals.

Third, the patrol or guard activity must be *administered by a citizen or residents'* (e.g., homeowners' or tenants') *organization or public housing authority*. The formal organization may be weak and may include substantial participation by the local police department. It must, however, have some formal role structure—for example, a hierarchy of roles, with patrol members having different types of assignments—and be a resident organization, or a nonpolice organization acting under the direction of residents. For instance, guards hired by realty companies or landlords would be excluded because such guards are paid from some portion of the rent, and tenants usually have no influence or control over the provision of the service. However, guards hired by condominium owners through their homeowners' association would be included. These nuances aside, the third criterion mainly excludes spontaneous resident patrol activities that might arise in an emergency, unless the activities were subsequently formalized and organized, and it also excludes volunteer patrol or guard functions organized and administered solely by the local police department.

Fourth, the activity is directed primarily at *residential rather than commercial areas*. The patrols or guards are concerned with the security of neighborhood activities that take place in public as well as private areas. This criterion excludes situations in which private police are hired to protect retail stores, transportation depots, warehouses, and other commercial and industrial facilities.

TYPES OF PATROLS

Many different activities can satisfy these four criteria for defining a resident patrol. For example, the following would all fall within the definition:

- An armed community protection group
- A volunteer automobile radio patrol
- A volunteer foot patrol
- An escort service staffed by youths
- A uniformed private police force
- Hired guards patrolling in marked automobiles
- A public housing vertical patrol
- A public housing stationary patrol
- Elderly watchmen and gatekeepers at a retirement village

To evaluate these patrol efforts it is necessary to partition the patrols into a few analytically useful groups. Such a typology helps to develop generalizations about the various patrol efforts and facilitates the application of the appropriate evaluative criteria to each patrol. For instance, a patrol that prohibits its members from intervening in a crime in progress should not be assessed by the number of arrests that its members make, whereas a private police force with special arrest powers may be appropriately assessed by such a standard.

Possible Criteria for a Typology

The ideal typology would be one that classified all patrols on the basis of some simple characteristic and that led to the clustering of patrols that had the same experience. The particular characteristic could come from one of several aspects of patrol operation. For example, at the crudest level, any patrol involves: a crime problem, an organization to lead and carry out crime prevention activities, a set of goals, a patrol routine or activity, an implicit (if not explicit) relationship to the police, and some outcome. Patrols may vary in any of these components, and each can potentially be used as the basis for a typology. However, some components hold more promise than others.

A typology based on either the *problem* or the *outcome* does not permit the analyst to group patrols for purposes of evaluation or policy intervention. For instance, any classification by outcome is unmanageable because the outcome represents that which one wants to learn about a posteriori—that is, a dependent variable. The requirement for a patrol typology, in contrast, is a need for some a priori means of grouping patrols. Classification by the problem is similarly unhelpful because crime problems are not necessarily stable. Thus, for purposes of policy intervention, it would be unwise to develop a set of procedures for some crime problem only to have the nature of the problem change as implementation takes place.

Grouping patrols by *organizational structure* is a feasible approach, but raises another issue. The organizational structure may vary in ways that are unrelated to the main efforts of a patrol. A complex, bureaucratic structure, for instance, may be found among either stationary or mobile patrols, but an evaluation of patrols would be more relevant if it accounted for this difference in function rather than the degree of bureaucratization.

The *goals* of a patrol effort constitute an attractive but deceptive basis for classification. The patrol ideology may be poorly stated or even misleadingly represented, as the stated goals of an organization may bear little or no relation to its actual activities (Wilson, 1973). For example, in the case of patrols in which the monitoring of another group of residents is a covert objective, formal statements of goals are apt to be misleading.

The patrol's *relation to the police* presents analogous difficulties for classification, although the nature of such relations has been used in the past to classify patrols (e.g., Marx and Archer, 1972). First, definitional problems are likely to arise over whether a patrol enjoys an adversary, supportive, or neutral relationship with the police. The empirical assessment of such relationships is difficult, especially in light of the occurrence of cooptation tactics in conflict-ridden communities. Second, the choice of the appropriate respondent to classify the patrol as an adversary or supporter also poses a problem, as the opinions of the police and patrol members may differ.

Patrol activities, in contrast to all of the preceding, are a more attractive basis for creating a useful typology. First, the activities are observable and hence potentially measurable. Second, patrol activities are susceptible to policy intervention (e.g., federal support can be provided or withheld from patrols that do not follow a prescribed set of activities). For these reasons, distinctions among patrol activities appear to be a useful foundation on which to develop a patrol typology.

Criteria Used: Patrol Activities

The main set of decisions related to patrol activities has to do with: (a) whether the police are also the object of patrol monitoring, (b) the type of area being patrolled, and (c) whether the patrol also engages in other than crime prevention activities (see Figure 2). Regardless of their other activities, patrols that monitor the police—which may be called *community protection patrols*—are considered a distinct type of patrol. The usual reason for such monitoring is that residents (or the patrol members) perceive themselves to be victims of poor police service, or even of unreasonable harassment and persecution. This type of patrol is distinguished because of its differential impact on patrol outcomes, over and above such questions as the type of area the patrol covers.

A second important aspect of deployment is the type of area covered. Among the patrols that perform crime prevention activities only, *building patrols*[1] are organized mainly to protect residents of a specific building or group of buildings and usually operate as stationary guards or foot patrols. The universe of residents being protected by building patrols is easily identified, and the residents often form a tenants' or homeowners' association (the public housing authority can serve in this capacity as well) that directly represents the residents and supervises the patrol. *Neighborhood patrols* cover

---

[1]This term will be used throughout to refer to patrols that cover a single building, a housing project, or a well-defined residential compound.

PATROLLING THE NEIGHBORHOOD BEAT

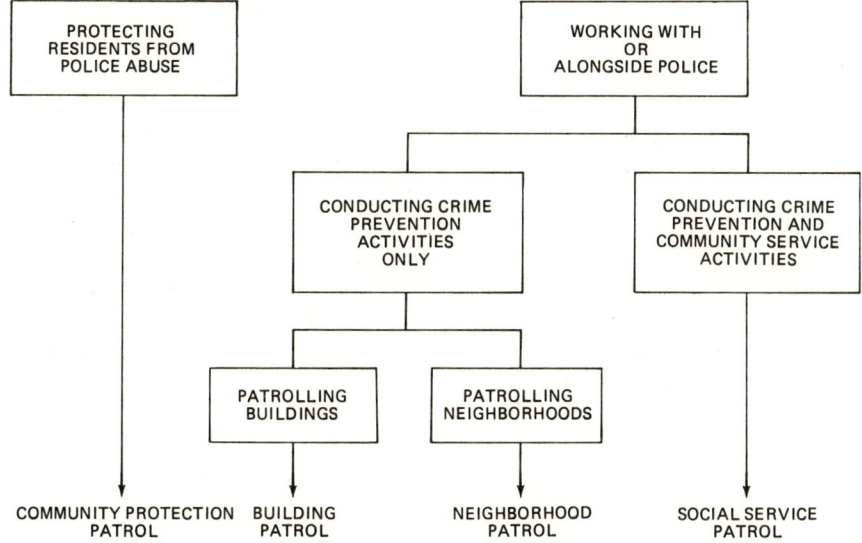

Figure 2. Types of patrols, based on patrolling activity.

a less well-defined group of residents and a much larger geographic area, and usually operate on foot or in automobiles. Furthermore, whereas building patrols have little obvious need for coordination with the police (the local police are seldom concerned with the protection of specific buildings or private residential compounds), that is not the case with neighborhood patrols, where the activities of the patrol overlap, at least in theory, with those of the local police.

Finally, one variant of both building and neighborhood patrols is important enough also to be treated separately. This variant is a *social service patrol*, which may cover either a building or a neighborhood, but engages in community service functions other than crime prevention, for example, civil defense or sanitation, or the employment of youths as part of a job opportunity program. Although the social service patrols are a variant of both building and neighborhood patrols, they will be treated separately because a different set of outcomes may be associated with them.

PATROL OUTCOMES

The outcomes of patrol efforts were examined by relying on information from two sources:

- Thirty-two patrols were the subject of intensive study, with interviews and observations conducted in the field.[2]
- Eleven patrols were studied by others and described in previous evaluation reports.

The discussion is organized according to the patrol typology: *building patrols, neighborhood patrols, social service patrols,* and *community protection groups*. These four types of patrols appear to produce different types of outcomes.

Table 8 lists the patrols that were studied by type, project name[3] and location, and source of information. Throughout the discussion of each patrol type, these patrol projects will be referred to (in parentheses) as *illustrative examples* of points being made in the text. For each type, the outcomes to be reviewed are: (1) crime reduction, (2) changes in the residents' sense of security, (3) police–community relations, (4) police coverage, (5) vigilantelike (i.e., dysfunctional) outcomes, and (6) effects on citizen participation.

Building Patrols

The main objective of building patrols is the protection of specific buildings and their adjacent grounds or of private residential compounds. The buildings or compounds protected may vary from high-income, high-rise dwellings (Harbor View, Santa Rosa) to low-income housing for the elderly (Broadmoor Towers, Fenwick Lane) to detached houses whose only access is from a private road (Burbank Mews). The patrol may operate on foot, only within and immediately around a building (Broadmoor Towers, Santa Rosa), or may use a car to cover an entire residential complex (St. Louis Housing Authority).

Whatever the physical setting, building patrols are a distinctive type of resident patrol for several reasons. First, the patrols operate in an area in which local police activity is minimal. This fact means that a building patrol may be expected to have little field contact, if any, with the police. Second, the building patrol is generally supervised by an official organization that in some way represents the tenants or owners of the buildings being protected. Such organizations include public housing authorities, tenants' associations, homeowners' associations, and management services that maintain the build-

---

[2]For each of these patrols a brief case study narrative was written: See Volume 2 of the study from which this chapter is an excerpt. The 32 were selected from a larger number of 226 patrols that had actually been identified.
[3]Fictitious names have been substituted for the actual patrol names because of the desires of the respondents that were interviewed.

Table 8
Patrols Described in Interviews and Evaluations by Type, Name, and Location

Type of patrol	Field interviews	Evaluations[a]
Building patrols	Belle Isle (New Orleans) Brigadoon Manors (D.C.) Broadmoor (Baltimore) Burbank Mews (New Orleans) Casa Vargas (Boston) Fenwick Lane (Baltimore) Harbor View (Boston) Mayberry Glen (D.C.) St. Louis Housing Authority Santa Rosa (San Diego)	Cuyahoga (Cleveland) Low-Income Towers (New York City)
Neighborhood patrols	Avalon (Chicago) Azalea Hills (Norfolk) Belmont (Baltimore) Bloomfield (New Orleans) Boonton (St. Louis) Burwick (D.C.) Civilian Observation (Chicago) Forest Hills (Houston) Lincoln Park (Detroit) Millbank (Brooklyn) Rangefield (Boston) Stapleton Place (Boston) Thornton Heights (Baltimore) Voorsted Park (Brooklyn) 54th Ward (Brooklyn)	Beachview (N.Y.C.) Childguard (N.Y.C.) Loch Raven (Baltimore) Safeblock (N.Y.C.)
Social service patrols	Bay Youth (D.C.) Caldwell Township (Detroit) California Neighborhood Safety Team (Los Angeles) CORPS (Detroit) Livingston (Detroit) Triquonic (Newark)	Bromley-Heath (Boston) Community Patrol (N.Y.C.) Hartford Security (Hartford) WEFF (Grand Rapids) Youth Courtesy (D.C.)
Community protection groups	Alliance for Safety (New Orleans)	

[a]Patrols that were studied in previously published reports.

ing on behalf of a tenants' association. In one case, a housing authority had organized over 800 volunteers to serve in twenty high-rise projects (Cuyahoga).

Third, the main duties of the patrol are related to the goal of preventing crime and keeping unwanted strangers out of buildings or the immediate area. Surveillance is often made easier by the existence of fences, walls, natural barriers, or isolation from the surrounding community (Brigadoon Manors). The patrol typically involves a guard stationed at a building entrance or gate who admits (signs in and checks credentials of) visitors and watches for suspicious activities, often with the aid of television monitors and other electronic aids. Fourth, except for public housing projects, patrol members are usually paid guards. Paid guards may be selected from among residents (Brigadoon Manors, St. Louis Housing Authority), or they may be furnished on a contractual basis by a private security firm (Casa Vargas, Harbor View).

These four distinctive features of building patrols appear to make a difference in the types of outcomes that can be expected from the patrols, as well as to provide some explanation for the outcomes reported in the project narratives.

Crime Reduction

Because the patrols operate around specific buildings, and because the universe of residents being protected is well defined, the crime reduction impact of a building patrol is, in principle, not difficult to measure. At the same time, most of the building patrols in our study were not formed in response to a crime problem in the building. Only a few of the buildings (Casa Vargas, St. Louis Housing Authority) had any serious residential crimes before their patrols were formed. In the other cases, the patrols emerged as a *preventive* measure and were able to maintain a fairly crime-free environment. Prevention appeared especially important when the building was located in a neighborhood that was perceived to be unsafe. The lack of a prior history of crime problems within a building thus makes it difficult to assess most of these building patrols on the basis of reductions in crime incidents, or even on the basis of the seriousness of any single crime incident. Most building patrols had encountered no crime-related incidents (Brigadoon Manors, Broadmoor, Burbank Mews, Cuyahoga, Fenwick Lane, Santa Rosa). Others reported such minor incidents as calling the police to remove a drunk (Casa Vargas, Harbor View). Only two patrols reported dealing with domestic quarrels and other confrontations of a more serious nature (Mayberry Glen, St. Louis Housing Authority).

As a result there was little effort in the available evaluations of building patrols to assess the actual levels of crime or victimization among residents.

Generally, crime reduction was simply not a relevant outcome. Even in those few cases where the patrols had been initiated because of crimes or vandalism in the building, there was still no systematic attempt to assess the effect of the patrol, although the patrol coordinators and local police usually felt that crime had declined (St. Louis Housing Authority).

Sense of Security

The well-defined universe of residents being protected again makes it possible, in principle, to measure improvements in residents' sense of security.[4] However, any comprehensive survey of residents' attitudes was beyond the scope of inquiry. Nevertheless, patrol personnel and police indicated that the visibility of the building patrols, both in their predictable deployment at some desk or station and in their uniformed presence, appeared to be a positive factor in increasing the residents' sense of security. The only complaints mentioned by respondents were related to patrol behavior that only marginally affected residents' sense of security. Sleeping or drinking on the job, discourtesy, and incompetence were among the most frequent complaints (Burbank Mews, Casa Vargas, Harbor View). These complaints, it should be pointed out, probably resulted from the fact that many of the patrols were paid guards from whom better service had been expected.

Police–Community Relations and Police Coverage

These outcomes are discussed together because, with one major exception, neither appears to be important in assessing building patrols. Inasmuch as the local police do not, as a rule, protect specific buildings, they are not usually consulted when the building patrols are established. Moreover, once the patrol has begun operations there is minimal contact in the field between the patrol members and the regular police. This general lack of contact at either the planning or operational level is one reason that changes in coverage are also likely to be minimal.

The one major exception has to do with large public housing projects that have had some history of apparently inadequate coverage by the local police (Casa Vargas, Mayberry Glen, St. Louis Housing Authority). In these situations the patrols had been formed in part because of inadequate police coverage and because police–community relations had not been satisfactory. Racial or linguistic differences between the residents and the police might

---

[4]In some cases the residents of a building may include the perpetrators of crime in that area. Of course, it is not the sense of security of the perpetrators but that of the victims of crimes and of other residents that patrols seek to improve.

have contributed to this poor relationship. Under these circumstances, according to a few reports, the formation of a building patrol had helped to improve police–community relations. In one case the police undertook responsibility for training the patrol members at the police academy (St. Louis Housing Authority); in return, the police felt that they could call on the building patrol to assist them when they responded to a call in the project.

Vigilante Behavior

The building patrols had few reports of vigilantism (e.g., reports of citizen harassment or overzealous activity by the patrol). Most of the complaints about these patrols, as previously noted, had to do with unsatisfactory performance of duties by patrol members; in at least one case the result was that the private security company hired for the service was replaced (Casa Vargas). In one case (Belle Isle) there was a complaint that a guard was too aggressive, but the complaint referred only to his attempts to reduce radio and television noise in the building.

The lack of vigilantism may be attributable in part to the fact that building patrols are usually sponsored by an organization officially representing the residents or tenants. This auspice provides the patrol with a degree of legitimacy that reduces the likelihood of the patrol's being unwelcome; the continued supervision of the patrol by the organization means that the residents have some control, although sometimes only indirectly, over the patrol members' behavior and tenure. These conditions appear to reduce the likelihood of dysfunctions and to result in few complaints of patrol abuse or vigilantism.

Citizen Participation

Possibly because building patrols tended to be organized by an existing citizen organization or public housing authority, the formation of the patrol appeared to have little, if any, effect on citizen participation. There were no instances among our cases where the formation of a building patrol eventually led to other organized activities or projects on the part of the residents.

Conclusions

Building patrols attempt to regulate access to specific buildings chiefly by stationing a guard at the entrance; only occasionally do they include foot or automobile patrols among their duties. The most significant though tentative findings are the following: First, building patrols may keep crime at low levels and increase residents' sense of security. The fact that areas protected by building patrols are small and enclosed may facilitate the effective screening and identification of intruders or potential troublemakers. Furthermore, anecdotal evidence strongly suggests that residents feel safer in the presence of visible building patrols.

Second, building patrols are the subject of few complaints or reports of vigilantism. The fact that building patrols are frequently sponsored by organizations representing the residents being protected appears to legitimate these patrols in carrying out their work. The findings of previous research and the field work for this study were in agreement that virtually all complaints regarding these patrols were minor and that paid guards who performed poorly were replaced.

Third, changes in police coverage and police–community relations did not generally ensue from building patrol activity. Because these patrols operate in areas in which the police tend not to patrol, there is little reason for the patrol to maintain contact with the police and little, if any, prior police coverage is likely to be affected.

Fourth, public housing patrols raise a few exceptions both in terms of the crime problem they face and the relation between residents and the local police. The crime problem in public housing, unlike that in wealthier areas, may be largely an internal one (Fairley and Liechenstein, 1971). Although some crime is perpetrated by intruders and can be prevented by monitoring the access to a building, additional measures may be required to abate crime perpetrated by residents themselves. Furthermore, public housing patrols sometimes do affect police–community relations and police coverage. In several projects, patrols were called to assist local police when a crime was reported. By mediating encounters between police and residents, patrols appear to have helped ease relations, with the result that police encounter less hostility from residents and respond more readily to calls from the project.

Neighborhood Patrols

Neighborhood patrols, in contrast to building patrols, usually have a poorly defined area of surveillance. The area may cover many blocks, may not have strict boundaries, and may not be patrolled as intensively as are buildings. Few neighborhood patrols, for instance, are on duty twenty-four hours a day. Moreover, because neighborhood patrols cover mainly the streets and other public areas rather than buildings, the patrols frequently coordinate their activities with those of the local police, and there is likely to be more field contact between the patrol and police. Finally, because of the neighborhood patrol's difficulty in distinguishing residents who belong to the area from those who are strangers, it also must operate somewhat differently from the building patrol. Whereas the building patrol may concentrate on screening strangers and keeping them off the premises, the neighborhood patrol can focus only on observed behaviors that appear undesirable or suspicious, a task that requires more judgment; the task may also easily lead to the reporting of embarrassing false alarms to the police or to the perception by other residents that the patrol has been unnecessarily provocative.

Beyond these general characteristics, neighborhood patrols can take a wide variety of forms. They are found in neighborhoods of different income levels and ethnic composition. They may be on foot or in cars. The patrol may cover certain areas in relation to such activities as children walking to and from school (Childguard), or may watch the streets from a strategic vantage point inside an apartment (Safeblock). In most cases, however, neighborhood patrols cover their beat in an automobile. The car may be marked or unmarked, manned by a volunteer or a private security guard, and follow a regular or irregular routine. In most cases, when the patrol observes a suspicious incident, it reports the observation by radio to a base station or to the police (Boonton, Civilian Observation Patrol, 54th Ward, Millbank, Stapleton Place, Thornton Heights). In some cases an armed patrol will itself intervene (Bloomfield, Burwick, Forest Hills, Lincoln Park). In one case (Rangefield) the patrol covered a small area; on observing a suspicious incident, the patrol would blow a whistle to call the police.

These characteristics of neighborhood patrols both distinguish them from building patrols and establish constraints on any evaluation of them. More of the six outcomes are relevant than was the situation with the building patrols.

Crime Reduction

The majority of the neighborhood patrols emerged in relation to a chronic or severe crime problem in the neighborhood (e.g., burglaries, purse snatchings, and undesirable juvenile activities). One high-income neighborhood had been the scene of robberies, rapes, and even murder (Bloomfield). The patrol was formed as part of a neighborhood association, and extra fees were collected to hire guards through a private security company. In another case an increase in crime or perceived danger in the neighborhood led citizen-band radio buffs to organize a mobile patrol that took advantage of their radio expertise (Civilian Observation Patrol). There were a few cases, however, where neighborhood patrols had begun even though there was no crime problem (Azalea Hills, Boonton, Burwick, Lincoln Park).

The nature of the area covered by the neighborhood patrols makes it difficult to assess changes in crime incidence. First, the area patrolled is usually smaller than and not coterminous with areas for which police statistics are kept. Second, even if the boundary problem could be overcome, any changes in crimes reported to the police would be difficult to interpret because successful patrol efforts could result in an increase or a decrease in the proportion of crimes reported. Third, in most cases the patrols have operated for too short a period or too intermittently to expect that their effects would be measurable by any aggregate statistics. Fourth, the universe of residents being protected is not well defined as it was in the case of the building patrols, and any victimization survey might not cover the right respondents. For all these reasons, it is not surprising that only a few of the existing patrol evaluations made any attempt to analyze the patrol's effect on crime reduction. One evaluation found no effect on the crime rate in the area, but the evaluation was faulty to the extent that the crime rates in the other areas of the city were not presented, so that the analysis did not establish any baseline expectation for the crime trends in the neighborhood (Loch Raven).

An alternative way of examining the neighborhood patrol's effect on crime is to determine the types of incidents that the patrol has encountered. Patrols intervene in numerous incidents, often quite serious in nature. Of the patrols studied, many had intervened in burglaries in progress (Belmont, Bloomfield, Forest Hills, Lincoln Park, Millbank, Safeblock). Two (Bloomfield, Civilian Observation Patrol) claimed frequent calls to the police (one or two per night), as well as responses to police calls for assistance for an officer in distress. Other patrol activities included dealing with vandalism and theft, dispersing teen gangs, and settling family disputes. Because the patrols usually receive no feedback from the police regarding the disposition of an incident reported to the police, whether the patrol calls the police directly or via a base station (Boonton), the actual frequency and severity of incidents validly reported cannot be satisfactorily documented. In one case (Civilian Observation Patrol) a patrol member reported seeing a suspected rapist on the street (the police had previously circulated a picture of the suspect); the next morning he read in the newspaper that the rapist had been apprehended, but never found out whether his tip had been the correct one. The provision of such feedback would certainly raise the incentives for patrol members, as well as provide guidance about the quality of the patrol's work. In sum, however, there was little evidence on which to base the patrol's overall effect on crime reduction.

In spite of this inability to formally assess the overall effect, one can point to a few features of patrol operations that may influence a patrol's success in preventing crime. Close supervision of the patrol and direct accountability to a residents' organization or association seem to enhance a patrol's crime reduction capability (Burwick, Forest Hills, Lincoln Park). Systematic training of patrol members in the procedures for observing and reporting incidents (as opposed to those situations where the members are trained merely by riding around with a more experienced member) may also improve the crime reduction capability. Similarly, the use of an unmarked car by a mobile patrol may increase the likelihood of the patrol's having the opportunity to intervene in a crime such as a burglary. However, the use of weapons does not appear to be a consistent correlate of the patrol's ability to deal with most types of residential crime, as both armed (Bloomfield) and unarmed (54th Ward, Stapleton Place) patrols reported having dealt with serious incidents.

Sense of Security

A neighborhood patrol may have either of two contrasting effects on residents' sense of security. On the one hand, the patrol may increase the sense of security of its members. This effect appears to occur especially in those cases where the patrol was initiated by a small group of residents who themselves had been the victims of crime, or felt they were directly threatened by increases in crime (Safeblock, Thornton Heights). The patrol activity in such cases appeared to lead to a heightened sense of security because the patrol provided a systematic way of calling for help. On the other hand, the same patrol may have a neutral or even negative effect on the sense of security of the other residents of the community (Safeblock, Thornton Heights, Belmont). This kind of effect may be reflected in complaints by the residents that the patrol unnecessarily stirs fears, harasses residents, or otherwise acts in a suspicious, vigilantelike manner (Azalea Hills, Voorsted Park).

There was, however, no systematic evidence regarding changes in the sense of security of either the patrol members or the residents. Many patrols had received complaints about their activities from residents: In one case residents disapproved of the overzealous behavior of one patrol member (who was subsequently suspended); in another case teenagers objected to the patrol's breaking up teenage street gatherings. Although such complaints were in the minority, informal comments regarding the increased sense of security attributable to the neighborhood patrols were not as uniformly positive as they had been in the case of the building patrols.

Police–Community Relations

The patrols usually have a direct effect on patrol–police relations, and to the extent that the patrol represents the community, this relationship may then affect police–community relations. There are several aspects of patrol–police relations. First, if there is little coordination between the patrol and the police, the police may simply be indifferent to or ignore the patrol (Boonton, Millbank); on the other hand, a neighborhood patrol that makes no attempt to coordinate its activities with the police may be perceived by the police to be a potential vigilante group (Safeblock). Second, in some cases where there had been good coordination with the police in the planning and operation of the patrol, the result may be perceived by the residents as employing unnecessarily harassing tactics (Thornton Heights). Third, if the patrol is active and assertive, the police may consider it a competitor and may react either by treating the patrol members condescendingly (Lincoln Park) or by trying to recruit patrol members into an auxiliary police unit (54th Ward). Fourth, if the patrol is subservient or plays the role of companion to the police, the police may perceive the patrol as a buff group rather than as a serious patrol (Azalea Hills).

These subtleties suggest the complex nature of police–patrol relations. Perhaps the most important aspect of such relations, however, is that the police—by giving or withholding endorsement—can either provide the patrol with a degree of legitimacy or raise questions about its activities.

Police Coverage

Once again, the fact that neighborhood patrols operate in the same territory covered by the local police means that these patrols, unlike building patrols, may have some effect on police coverage. As was to be expected, virtually no evidence was available concerning police deployment patterns, either before or after the patrol was formed. In one case, however, it was claimed that patrol activities had helped to educate residents to complain effectively to the police and that as a result an extra policeman had been assigned to the neighborhood on Friday nights (Rangefield). In another case the police admitted that their coverage of the neighborhood had been curtailed as a result of the effectiveness of the patrol (Stapleton Place). In a third case where a patrol had apparently been effective, the police claimed that there had nevertheless been no decrease in their coverage of the neighborhood (Bloomfield).

Vigilante Behavior

Although for the most part neighborhood patrol activities were accepted by the residents, several patrols were the subject of complaints alleging physical violence or the violation of individual rights. One patrol, seriously criticized by residents for harassing teenagers, was opposed by the local press as being a vigilante group (Azalea Hills). Another patrol (Lincoln Park) learned that it had recruited the leader of a radical rightist group only when the police refused him a concealed-weapons permit. Other groups were perceived as having overzealous members who would unnecessarily harass pedestrians (Voorsted Park), antagonize other community groups (Thornton Heights), or irresponsibly use dangerous weapons (Safeblock).

One factor possibly related to these complaints of vigilantism was that the patrol members had generally been recruited on the basis of cliques or friendship groups. In contrast, the more a patrol had been organized under a broad organizational auspice, the fewer the complaints about vigilantelike behavior. Quite possibly, patrols based on cliques tend to produce this type of behavior because the members use the patrol to pursue narrow self-interests that may conflict with the self-interests of others in the neighborhood, whereas organization-recruited patrols must pursue policies that represent the common interest.

Citizen Participation

Neighborhood patrols appeared to have little effect on citizen participation in other neighborhood activities. A few patrols, however, had some contrary experiences. In one case participation ultimately increased as the patrol activity was completely preempted by the formation of a neighborhood association, and the patrol voted itself out of existence (Safeblock). In another case the patrol was one of several functions of an existing neighborhood organization; the patrol maintained signs announcing its presence throughout the neighborhood, helped educate residents about crime prevention practices, and was able to raise a substantial amount of money to purchase a patrol car and to support the office costs of operating the patrol (Millbank).

Conclusions

Neighborhood patrols operate in broader, less clearly defined areas than building patrols. Although some neighborhood patrols are limited to stationary watch or foot–patrol duties, most include automobile patrolling. The evidence about neighborhood patrols from previous research is as sparse as that on building patrols. The patrols constitute a marginal increment to police protection and are thinly distributed over large areas. It is not always clear what resident population should be specified for a patrol evaluation, whether the patrols have a measurable impact, and whether any impact measured could be attributed to the patrol rather than to other influences. On the basis of informal evidence, however, the following tentative statements may be made about the outcomes of neighborhood patrols.

First, it is unclear to what extent neighborhood patrols reduce crime or increase residents' sense of security. Anecdotal evidence suggested that patrols do report to the police numerous crime incidents ranging from assaults and robberies to juvenile pranks. The patrols, however, rarely receive feedback from the police about the disposition of the incident. Second, regarding residents' sense of security, neighborhood patrols occasionally generated more unease than did building patrols, primarily because the nature of the patrols' duties was unclear to the residents.

Third, information regarding changes in both police coverage and police–community relations was largely inaccessible. No previous systematic research on these topics was identified. On the basis of the field work it appears that neighborhood patrols may have no direct effect on police–community relations. Although there is an intermediate outcome in terms of police–patrol relations, the relationship appears to be a complex one requiring further study.

Fourth, in relation to vigilante behavior, more serious complaints were raised regarding neighborhood than regarding building patrols. Among the factors frequently associated with such behavior were: recruitment on the basis of friendship, and operation of voluntary patrols in low crime areas. In the latter case, members tended to grow bored and to seek out more interesting although sometimes illicit activities.

Social Service Patrols

Social service patrols are building or neighborhood patrols that also perform social service functions. The main reason for attempting to distinguish this variant type of patrol is that social service patrols tend to have other crime prevention functions that go beyond the immediate objectives of building or neighborhood patrols.

These functions fall into two main categories. First, the social service patrol may be organized around a variety of community responsibilities, among which patrolling may be only one. The patrol may, for instance, operate an ambulance service (Triquonic), perform civil defense functions, such as giving assistance during a tornado (Caldwell Township, Livingston, WEFF), or be formally involved in other community projects, such as beautification and cleanup, youth placement, family counseling, food co-ops, and collective gardens (Bromley-Heath). Second, the social service patrol may be organized as much to provide employment opportunities for youths as to perform crime prevention functions (Bay Youth, Community Patrol, Hartford Security). There may be a purposeful attempt to recruit as patrol members youths who are suspected of causing some of the neighborhood's crime problems. In the words of one coordinator, "We try to take the baddest kids on the block and turn them around." Again, although a building or neighborhood patrol's main function may be to reduce crime, its potential employment and cooptation objectives in dealing with youths are sufficiently different to warrant placing it in a different category.

Another reason for distinguishing these social service patrols is that police and community residents may actually perceive them in a different manner from building or neighborhood patrols. One social service patrol, for instance, had been so active in its civil defense activities that the police claimed not to perceive the patrol's purpose primarily as crime prevention (Livingston). Another patrol, organized as part of a Model Cities program (Hartford Security), might again have been viewed as part of a community development rather than strictly crime prevention effort.

Because many of the anticipated outcomes of social service patrols are similar to those of building or neighborhood patrols, the following discussion focuses more on the effects that appeared relevant only for social service patrols.

Crime Reduction

The patrol's effect on crime reduction is first related, of course, to whether it operates as a building patrol (Bromley-Heath, Hartford Security), or as a neighborhood patrol (Bay Youth, California Neighborhood Safety Team, Community Patrol, CORPS, Livingston, WEFF, Youth Courtesy). The same problems of measurement and anticipated effects that were previously discussed in relation to building or neighborhood patrols are relevant, and in this respect the social service patrols did not appear to have had experiences that were significantly different from those of building or neighborhood patrols.

A second major effect on crime reduction was, however, specifically related to social service patrols. Since social service patrols had in a few cases deliberately recruited youthful troublemakers as patrol members, it might be argued that these patrols would have a potentially greater effect on crime reduction than would building and neighborhood patrols. There was little evidence, however, with regard to this potential effect on crime reduction. For example, there was no instance in which youths recruited for the patrol and those eligible but not ultimately recruited were compared for their subsequent criminal activities. Such an analysis could have shed some light on the patrol's presumed effect on crime reduction.

Sense of Security

Two existing evaluations of social service patrols had informally sampled residents' attitudes—one by means of retrospective survey questions and the other through comparative analysis of two paired neighborhoods, only one of which was patrolled (WEFF, Youth Courtesy). This information suggested that the visible presence of the social service patrols and their escort services had enhanced residents' feelings of safety, especially among the female respondents. In another case (Triquonic) the existence of a white ethnic patrol may have enhanced feelings of security among the residents of the same ethnic group.

In most cases the social service patrols might be expected to have had a positive effect on residents' sense of security, because the patrols' duties include emergency assistance and other community services in addition to the patrol function. In these other duties the patrol members were likely to become acquainted with a larger group of residents, and the residents perceived the patrol in much the same way they perceived Red Cross volunteers or other community service groups. To this extent feelings of security, not only in relation to crime but also in relation to other community hazards, may have increased (Caldwell Township, Livingston).

Police—Community Relations

As with neighborhood patrols, the important effect of social service patrols is not on police–community relations directly, but on patrol–police relations, which in turn may have an effect on police–community relations.

The patrol–police relationship can take both positive and negative forms. Where the social service patrol helped the local police to enter a hostile housing project or neighborhood, the patrol appeared to have had a positive effect on police–community relations because the police felt safer and the residents felt that the police were more responsive (Bromley-Heath). In other cases (Community Patrol, Bay Youth), such police–community hostilities were not overcome, and because the patrol members were accused of being snitchers or stoolies, the existence of the social service patrol may only have aggravated relations. In one such case (Community Patrol) field contact between the patrol members and the police was discouraged because of fears that the patrol would become too closely identified with the police.

There was another nuance in the relationship of one social service patrol and the police, where it was felt that the policemen on the beat enjoyed good relations with the patrol (indeed, some of the policemen were members of the patrol in their off-hours) but the police headquarters disapproved of the patrol and suspected it of having vigilante tendencies. (Other patrols may have had the reverse situation: approved by headquarters police but not welcomed by the precinct police.) Finally, there was one case of potential competition between the patrol's activities and policemen's opportunities to work overtime (Livingston). These examples all suggest again the complexity of patrol–police relations and the difficulty of drawing any general conclusions about police–community relations on the basis of existing data.

Police Coverage

Social service patrols would be expected to have little effect on police coverage, and none of the police interviewed admitted to any changes in deployment patterns as a result of the patrol. Concrete evidence on changes in police deployment patterns, much less analysis of patterns before and after the emergence of a patrol, appeared not to have been included in any previous studies of social service patrols.

Vigilante Behavior

Some of the social service patrols appeared vulnerable to the same vigilantism as the neighborhood patrols. In particular, when a patrol had been organized informally by close friends or within one segment of a heterogeneous community, and when there was little formal coordination between the patrol and the police, the patrol was accused of excessively harassing other residents and hence acting somewhat as a vigilante group (Triquonic).

The social service patrols were also vulnerable to another type of problem that appeared related to the youth orientation of the patrol—that is, that the formation of the patrol could lead to antagonisms between the youths in a neighborhood who had been chosen to join the patrol and those who had not. Because of their knowledge of neighborhood problems and people, the youths who became patrol members could in one sense perform patrol duties more responsively than the local police; but in another sense the youths could take advantage of their patrol membership to harass other youths in the community. However, there was no direct evidence that such situations occurred, nor were there any complaints by residents about patrol members' behavior.

Citizen Participation

There appeared to be two outcomes concerning citizen participation. The first had to do with the employment function of the youth patrols and the fact that the paraprofessional employment is usually regarded as a form of citizen participation. To the extent that the patrols raised hopes among the youths for permanent employment or for opportunities for more advanced positions in doing police work, the social service patrols may have suffered from some of the same problems as other social welfare programs such as Model Cities and Manpower programs. In two cases (Community Patrol, Hartford Security), the patrol members expressed the opinion that the patrol duties should have been permanent or on a full-time basis.

Second, the very classification of a patrol in this group indicates that the patrol has become an organizational nucleus that supported one or more citizen efforts to provide services to their communities.

Conclusions

Social service patrols perform functions similar to those of building and neighborhood patrols; in addition, they undertake tasks not connected with crime prevention, such as community beautification, flood control, and youth employment. The following tentative conclusions can be drawn about this type of patrol.

First, the evidence about crime reduction or increases in residents' sense of security because of social service patrols is limited in essentially the same way as for the two other types of patrols. One important distinction is that social service patrols occasionally attempt to reduce crime by recruiting youthful offenders into their ranks and redirecting the energies of those youths toward crime prevention. Unfortunately, the anecdotal reports contained in the field work did not provide sufficient evidence to comment on the efficacy of this strategy. Previous research on social service patrols did include two informal evaluations that touched on residents' sense of security. These studies suggested fairly widespread awareness of the social service patrols on the part of residents and generally positive effects on residents' sense of security. However, in other cases where the patrols were involved mainly with activities other than crime prevention, residents as well as the police may have perceived the patrol as a social service and not as a genuine crime prevention effort.

Second, evidence concerning patrol effects on police coverage and police–community relations was again inaccessible. Although the field work revealed a complex dynamic of police–community relations, the main possibility appeared to be that, perhaps because of the greater visibility of the social service patrols, both positive and negative outcomes may have been more extreme than in the case of other patrols.

Third, the field work suggested some vigilantism potentially distinctive to social service patrols: Where such patrols had recruited from the youth factions in the neighborhood, the patrol experience had the potential to become one more occasion for strife among the factions.

Community Protection Patrols

Community protection groups are distinguished by the fact that, in addition to serving as either building or neighborhood patrols and in addition to other social service activities they may undertake, the groups also *monitor the police*. They do so because of their fear of harassment by the police, based on previous incidents or on a generally antagonistic relationship with the police.

The emergence of community protection groups has been associated mainly with the civil rights movement and urban riots during the 1960s. In particular, several black patrols were formed in southern cities, often in response to urban disorders, to protect themselves and other black residents from recriminations from the white community. The field work, however, did not uncover any existing community protection groups at the sites contacted, although such groups may well exist among blacks as well as other inner-city residents. For further research, special efforts would have to be made to locate such groups, as few would easily admit to such activities.

A leader of one defunct community protection group was located in the course of the field work, and a historical account was written about his patrol (Alliance for Safety). The patrol was mainly active in the mid-1960s during the civil rights movement; patrol members were armed to protect black leaders and residents against attacks by the Ku Klux Klan, other white residents, and the police. The patrol, operating as a mobile radio patrol, dealt with constant threats of assassination, as well as harassment. Although the patrol felt that the police were a source of harassment, the current police chief (who was a member of the force at the time) told us that the police provided adequate protection for black residents. Because it is difficult to generalize about community protection groups from this single case, no hypotheses were attempted about the outcomes resulting from these efforts.

SUMMARY

This study, though it only assessed the patrol experience in an exploratory fashion, has suggested the following previously unreported findings.

First, *there appear to be numerous patrols across the country, in neighborhoods of varied income and racial composition.* The full range of field work revealed 226 patrols at 16 sites, either central cities or major suburbs. The patrols varied widely in cost, but most were operated on a small budget and on a volunteer basis. The major expenditures are related not to arms, but to citizen-band radios and other communications equipment, uniforms, gasoline and maintenance for patrol cars, and the administrative costs of maintaining records and files. Most of the patrols, other than those organized by public housing authorities, receive no public financial support. The main implication is that if the patrols are at all effective they are likely to be a desirable citizen crime prevention alternative because of their low cost.

Second, patrols may usefully be divided into four types in order to consider their effectiveness: building, neighborhood, social service, and community protection patrols. The relatively small and contained areas covered by building patrols facilitate an evaluation of their effect on crime, and in most cases, though no formal evaluation was possible, *building patrols seemed to be effective in preventing crime.* Because building patrols are often formally sponsored by residents' or tenants' organizations, the patrol operations tend to be highly visible and legitimated, factors that may contribute to their efficacy. In contrast, although there is some evidence that neighborhood patrols perform valuable services, the broad and ambiguously defined areas they protect make any assessment of their impact difficult. Furthermore, the neighborhood patrols are the subject of more residents' complaints than are building patrols. As for social service or community protection patrols, a general lack of evidence about them precludes any major conclusion as to their crime prevention capability.

Third, *contemporary resident patrols are occasionally susceptible to vigilantism, with neighborhood patrols appearing to be more inclined to vigilantism than building patrols,* particularly when members are selectively recruited from within a friendship group (e.g., a citizen-band radio group) or on the basis of social compatibility with the patrol leader or members. In such cases the patrol, often representing a splinter group within the community, may be the subject of a greater number of residents' complaints and more serious ones than other patrols. Vigilantism may also emerge when patrol and surveillance become dull, a situation that may occur particularly when crime abates; in the absence of other rewarding organizational activity, neighborhood patrol members may tend to engage in novel but dysfunctional ventures (e.g., harassment of teen-agers and chasing speeders).

Finally, *several implementation factors influence a patrol's ability to operate and to achieve its goals: personnel, organizational affiliation, and bureaucratization.* Those patrols appear to operate best whose personnel are matched to the level of coverage the patrol seeks to provide—that is, members feel that they have neither too much nor too little to do. Recruiting and maintaining this supply of personnel is a major organizational task. Patrols that carefully screen and train their applicants appear to engender a commitment among their members that reduces attrition. The recruitment and screening procedures employed by a patrol also seem to influence members' general proclivities for vigilantism.

Patrols that maintain neighborhood organizational affiliations also tend to operate more effectively. A patrol of this kind is frequently more representative of the community it patrols, is viewed by residents as more legitimate, can be monitored by the residents, receives financial resources from the neighborhood organization, and may even be able to rely on the organization to perform maintenance activities during periods when the patrol operates at a reduced level. Bureaucratization, involving a paid administrator, maintenance of logs and other records, prearranged scheduling, and quality control of members' behavior in the field is a third implementation factor that seems to enhance a patrol's ability to operate effectively.

REFERENCES

Anderson, William A. et al. "Urban Counterrioters." *Society* 1974, *11*, 50–55.

Bird, David. "Trees in a Queens Park Cut Down as Vigilantes Harass Homos." *New York Times*, 2 July 1969, pp. 1, 29.

Brown, Richard M. "The American Vigilante Tradition." In *Violence in America*, vol. 1, edited by the National Commission on the Causes and Prevention of Violence. U.S. Government Printing Office, Washington, D.C.: 1969, pp. 121–180.

Fairley, William, and Liechenstein, Michael. *Improving Public Safety in Urban Apartment Dwellings: Security Concepts and Experimental Design for New York Housing Authority Buildings.* New York: New York City–Rand Institute, 1971.

Knopf, Terry Ann. *Youth Patrols: An Experiment in Community Participation.* Waltham, Mass.: Lemberg Center for the Study of Violence, Brandeis University, 1969.

Marx, Gary T., and Archer, Dane. "Citizen Involvement in the Law Enforcement Process: The Case of Community Police Patrols." *American Behavioral Scientist* 1971, *15*, 52–72.

Marx, Gary T., and Archer, Dane. *Community Police: An Exploratory Inquiry.* Cambridge, Mass: Harvard–MIT Joint Center for Urban Studies, 1972.

National Advisory Commission on Criminal Justice Standards and Goals. *Call for Citizen Action: Crime Prevention and the Citizen.* Washington, D.C.: Law Enforcement Assistance Administration, 1974.

Newman, Oscar. *Defensible Space.* New York: Macmillan, 1972.

U.S. Chamber of Commerce. *Marshaling Citizen Power against Crime.* Washington, D.C.: 1970.

Washnis, George J. *Citizen Involvement in Crime Prevention.* New York: Praeger, 1977.

Wilson, James Q. "If Every Criminal Knew He Would Be Punished if Caught . . ." *New York Times Magazine*, 28 January 1973.

4
Revenue Sharing with the Community Sector?

The case studies conducted by the National Commission on Neighborhoods[1] provide concrete illustrations of how residents can act together to improve their neighborhoods. A consistent theme throughout these cases was the importance of *voluntary activities,* which included:

- The numerous hours contributed by community leaders and residents
- Membership dues, donations, and other fundraising efforts
- Contributions of staff or facilities by local church groups or private welfare agencies

These voluntary activities are the essence of American citizen participation. The appropriate federal role should be to stimulate rather than thwart such activities.

IMPORTANCE OF THE COMMUNITY SECTOR

As a whole, these voluntary activities may be considered part of the *community sector* in American life, by which is meant the collection of citizens and institutions that make significant contributions to neighborhood life.

This chapter is based on a previously unpublished paper, submitted to the National Commission on Neighborhoods in 1979. See its report, *People, Building Neighborhoods* (Washington, D.C.: U.S. Government Printing Office, 1979). The author designed the case studies presented in that report.

[1]The commission, created by Congress in 1978, operated for eighteen months.

The importance of the community sector may be observed in many commonplace ways. For instance, municipal officials know that, when residents no longer sweep their stoops or take care of their immediately surrounding sidewalks, no amount of municipal sanitation service can compensate to make the neighborhood clean again. Similarly, residents must usually take the initiative to monitor the need for housing repair, to take care of family needs and childrearing, and to make their neighborhoods livable. All of these efforts, enhanced by voluntary helping institutions (including business contributions and social welfare agencies), constitute the community sector. The community sector has assumed significant economic proportions that in part can only be measured when municipal or federal services are needed to replace goods or services previously provided by the community sector. Such replacement may be more costly but less effective, and thus the long-term goal should be to promote a viable and healthy community sector rather than displacing it with government-directed efforts.

THE ROLE OF COMMUNITY ORGANIZATIONS

Community organizations are a major set of institutions in the community sector and are the main vehicle through which government can support the community sector. For this reason, the Commission on Neighborhoods conducted a series of forty case studies to determine how such organizations operate and how they might best be supported in the future.

As a group, the case studies illustrated the diversity of community organizing that exists across the country. In most instances, however, the case studies covered groups that

- Had been largely founded by residents or organized by the local ministry
- Were about five years old
- Had made significant contributions to neighborhood improvement, either working with or independently of city government
- Had continued to grow and to confront new neighborhood problems

The case studies were unable to document fully the membership and financial resources available to each of these organizations over time. However, it should be pointed out that in most instances the work of these community organizations has been known at a national level even though the organizations have not been dominated by support from the Ford Foundation or federal government funds. (A list of the organizations that were studied is given at the end of this chapter.)

The case studies showed that the community organizations were operated in a variety of ways. First, many consisted of individual members, whereas some were umbrella organizations whose members were other organizations. Second, the organizations were structured differently, with some holding annual congresses to elect their officers and others appointing their officers. Third, the organizations varied in their basic objectives. Some attempted to deliver services, often establishing an affiliate structure for each service; others were issue oriented, attempting to marshal public support for neighborhood causes; yet others were oriented toward improving neighborhood life by helping city government improve the quality and quantity of its services. Lastly, the organizations varied in the types of neighborhoods they served. Some operated in poverty areas; others served predominantly working-class populations; yet others operated on a citywide basis, and did not necessarily concentrate on a target neighborhood.

In spite of this diversity, the case studies showed that the work of a community organization can directly benefit its participants and the neighborhood (or area) being served. Time and again in the case studies participants reported their own self-satisfaction that concrete changes had been made, that the very operation of the organization created greater confidence in the future of the neighborhood, and that there was individual self-fulfillment from the participatory experience. These benefits cannot be overlooked, even though in many cases they may be difficult to assess; the opportunities afforded by being able to participate in an organized effort provide individual rewards and improve attitudes toward good citizenship that eventually have impacts far beyond the immediate activity of the organization.

At the same time, there was also ample evidence of neighborhood improvements instigated by these community organizations. In some cases the community organizations had engaged in more readily accomplishable tasks, for example, street beautification or street cleaning. In numerous cases, however, the community organizations were operating substantial services—health clinics, family service centers, housing services—and were often confronting major issues such as discriminatory real estate practices and use of redlining tactics.

Detailed analysis of these case studies, yet to be conducted, should nevertheless show how the operational differences among the organizations may be related to some of the observed outcomes. For instance, a service-oriented organization should be structured and operated differently from an issue-oriented organization. Similarly, there may be lessons to be learned about the sequence of neighborhood problems to be confronted, with early problems requiring some visible and quick result before support can be generated for dealing with other problems. Finally, there may be some practices to be avoided, such as allowing a single service to dominate the resources of the organization or allowing a single federal grant to be the dominant source of financial support. In sum, the case studies provide a rich and lasting source of documentation about the community-organizing process.

POLICIES TOWARD COMMUNITY ORGANIZATIONS

In the long run, it may be unrealistic to expect that any single community organization, in spite of the ample evidence of these concrete benefits, should survive on a permanent basis. On the contrary, community organizing and the work of the community sector are dynamic enterprises in which specific organizations may come and go because of changing needs and clienteles. What is essential is that, at any given time and place, residents have the opportunity to join together and create their own organizations.

In a like manner, no single organization should be the sole representative of a single neighborhood area. There may be several different organizations in the same area, each serving a different constituency and set of needs. Again, the goal should be to facilitate the emergence of as many organizations as citizens will support.

Under these conditions the role of the federal government is to stimulate and facilitate the development of community organizations in a manner that

- Permits the *diversity* of structures and operations seen, through the case studies, to be important for serving the diversity of local needs
- Gives a community organization the *flexibility* to adapt to changing conditions and to focus on different problems or issues over the time span of its life history
- Promotes *voluntarism* in the form of sweat equity, in-kind contributions, continued use of donations and membership dues, and support from private organizations such as churches and business groups

These should be viewed as the three objectives for federal policy. Can such policies be designed? They can—if creative and innovative approaches are pursued.

In particular, the federal support of community organizations up to this point has overemphasized the use of funds to support *programs*. Too often a community organization can only receive federal funds if it will hire and train staff to operate a specific array of programs (e.g., crime prevention programs). The case studies showed that, too frequently, community organizations had to undertake the elaborate and costly process of preparing grant proposals, many of which were subsequently not funded. Even when funds were awarded, the organizations often had to sacrifice other priorities to implement the federal program, and then had to cope with a myriad of federal regulations and red tape in operating the program. All of the efforts required to obtain federal funding had the indirect effect of diverting an organization's resources, both financial and leadership related, from other productive activities.

In contrast, the essential ingredient in community organizations is *people, not programs. Federal support must therefore be designed to help people help themselves,* a theme that is fundamental to the tenets of our democratic state. The assistance need not be given in large amounts or merely to the standard array of "established" organizations. The main goal should be that the funds serve the three features previously noted—diversity, flexibility, and voluntarism—and that they be awarded efficiently so that they involve minimal administrative cost and delay. Furthermore, assistance should be available, under conditions of equal opportunity costs, to a wide variety of organizations and not just those that are already large or well established. Because no such federal assistance program presently exists, a demonstration or experimental federal effort should be initiated.

A TEST PROGRAM

One possible design for such a demonstration or experiment could be implemented along the following lines. The theme of the test would be *revenue sharing with the community sector,* a program that would mimic some of the administrative benefits that have already been proven with existing federal revenue-sharing programs with state and local governments.

Most community organizations are eligible for, and have established themselves as nonprofit organizations under, Sec. 501(c)(3) status. (This was the case, for example, for a majority of the case study organizations, which generally established such status in the first or second year of their life histories.) In operating under this status, an organization is obligated to report certain financial information to the Internal Revenue Service on an annual basis. Most community organizations are therefore already "registered" with a federal agency and can be monitored or audited for basic managerial practices by that agency. Community organizations wishing to obtain federal assistance can be drawn from those organizations that have either registered as a 501(c)(3) organization or are eligible to do so in the future.

Eligible organizations, defined in this manner, could receive two types of federal assistance: a one-time-only, *startup grant;* and an indefinite series of *annual allotments.* Both types would be administered in a manner analogous to the way that revenue-sharing funds are presently administered. Thus an eligible entity (in this case a community organization) would, on establishing its eligibility and satisfying certain requirements outlined below, receive a check from the United States Treasury without formal proposals being prepared and without any strings being attached to the use of the funds (other than satisfaction of responsible managerial practices, of the sort subject to audit by accountants).

Startup Grants

For the startup grant, the requirements would be of the following nature. First, the startup grant could *not* be awarded in the first year of registered 501(c)(3) status. This provision would help assure that the actual initiation of the organization was based on private and voluntary contributions rather than on government funding. Only in its second or subsequent years of operation could an organization apply for a startup grant. The application would be simply signified as a checkoff in the appropriate space in the form submitted annually by the organization to the IRS; when such a checkoff had been made, the IRS would need only to note that this year was not the first one of registered status and that the organization had not previously received a startup grant. If these conditions were satisfied, a check would be disbursed to the community organization.

Second, the startup grant could only be used for equipment, other capital expenditures, or purchased items (including utilities), but not for salaries. Such a provision would again assure that, although federal funds were being used to support an important part of the infrastructure of the organization, the organization itself would have to support, in its own ways, the basic human resources. (The restriction would also reduce the possibility that organizations would be formed just to receive startup grants and pay the salaries of a few individuals, only to be disbanded at the end of the startup grant.)

Third, the amount of the startup grant would be the same for every eligible organization. This amount would be based on some prior analysis, not unlike the Census Bureau's consumer-oriented marketbasket analysis, indicating the types and extent of costs needed by the average community organization in its initial phase. The amount should be updated annually, based on subsequent marketbasket analyses, to account for inflation and other shifts in the availability and costs of resources. The establishment of a standard amount for the startup grant would both reflect a more equitable position and allow for more streamlined administrative procedures.

Fourth, the startup grants would not be intended to cover all the non-personnel costs, but only a portion of them. Thus these startup grants would not be large, but might fall in the $10,000 to $25,000 range. Keeping the startup grants at a modest amount would assure that, with limited federal resources, more community organizations could be supported and that the overall costs of the federal program might not be prohibitive. A modest amount might also reduce the incentives for using or abusing the program on the part of wealthy communities.

Annual Allotments

An organization that had already received its startup grant would then be eligible, in the following year, to begin receiving an indefinite series of annual allotments. The disbursement of these allotments would only be based on the organization's continued registration as a 501(c)(3) organization and on annual submission of its routine financial information as presently required. Disbursement would be automatic and streamlined: An eligible organization would simply get a check from the Treasury without a formal proposal and without any programmatic strings attached. (Again, these are the same conditions under which state and local governments receive their revenue-sharing funds.)

The amount of the annual allotments would be determined on the following basis. A formula would be established so that some fractional contribution would be made by the federal government as a function of the number of dues-paying members in the organization. The amount of the dues could be nominal; the main concern would be the existence and maintenance of a formal, dues-paying membership roster. The federal contribution should be established at a sufficiently low rate so that the annual allotments would again not be sizable; at the same time, the contribution should be set at a sufficiently high rate to give an organization an incentive to increase its membership base. The amount of the fractional contribution, as well as the formula on which it would be based, would have to be established through prior analysis and the proposed demonstration test. The key feature, however, is that the contribution be based on membership. This requirement would again make the program like the existing revenue-sharing programs (whose formulas generally account for the number of citizens in a jurisdiction as well as other indexes of income). But more important, the contribution would be made in such a way as to reward organizations that have attracted increasing membership bases.

There are many reasons for associating the contribution to the size of an organization's membership base. Some of these were apparent in the case studies. For example, where organizations had failed to serve neighborhood needs, the membership base began to erode. The ability to attract members, in effect, is a useful index of the value of a community organization. That is because residents may have time and energy to devote to community participation, but if they perceive no payoffs from such participation, they will be the first to acknowledge the situation and drop out. Similarly, emphasis on a large or increasing membership base also helps avoid those situations in which organizations have been formed only to serve the narrow interests of a small clique of residents. There were such examples among the case studies, but these types of organizations would have received very small annual allotments under this hypothetical demonstration test. Finally, because citizen participation should be viewed as an end in itself if democratic values are to be espoused, a formula entitlement linked to the membership base would connect federal support directly to the most relevant activity of a citizen organization.

The annual allotments would continue on an indefinite basis in this manner. At some point an organization might cease to serve a useful purpose for any significant number of residents, and at this point, if membership had dropped below some minimal threshold, the allotments would be suspended (but would start again if the membership base later increased). Thus the overall design of annual allotments would be aimed at accommodating the dynamic nature of the community-organizing enterprise, whereby organizations continually emerge, grow, decline, or cease operating.

Costs and Benefits

The main purpose of the demonstration test would be to determine the costs and benefits of a full-scale, national program of this sort. In addition, many questions need to be answered regarding the extent of desirable and undesirable second-order effects. At the outset, however, it should be noted that the program design potentially involves minimal bureaucratic costs. The administration of the existing revenue-sharing program again provides a guideline: The Treasury Department has a staff of about 200 people to administer the entire state and local government revenue-sharing program, and there are no federal field office costs nor is there any bureaucratic "prime sponsor" needed at the local level to operate the program.

The substantive costs and mechanics of operating the program, of course, can only be uncovered by the demonstration test. How many eligible organizations exist, how much each should get for startup grants or annual allotments, and whether the formulas will be able to target the program to low-income residents all remain to be seen. However, the tasks are not difficult and can be managed within the context of a demonstration test.

The substantive benefits will also be uncovered by the test. Here, the key criteria for judging benefits should be: whether the funds were able to support the required diversity of activities that appear to reflect local needs; whether the funds enabled organizations to operate flexibly over time; and whether the funds stimulated increased voluntarism. These categories, in short, appropriately return us to the three major objectives in supporting community organizations.

OTHER POLICY INITIATIVES

The preceding demonstration test is but one example of the creative and innovative policies that need to be developed. Other demonstration tests, aimed at other conceptualizations of the relationship between the federal government and the community sector, can and should be initiated. Where there is confidence that a program is ready to be implemented on a national basis, such implementation should follow with all due speed.

Whatever the initiatives, federal policy makers should envision themselves as part of an exciting frontier. In this frontier, a new relationship is being forged between the federal government and the community sector. The relationship acknowledges that some lessons have been learned from past experience. No party is served, for instance, where federal support for the community sector results in increased dependence by that sector. The design of any new program will surely be aimed at increasing the *independence* of residents to act in a collective manner. Similarly, no party is served by federal assistance that incurs great bureaucratic costs. The goal should thus also be to provide assistance in as efficient a manner as possible.

APPENDIX: CASE STUDIES

1. Adams Morgan Organization (AMO)
   Washington, D.C.
2. Birmingham Neighborhood Coalition
   Toledo, Ohio
3. Blue Hills Homes Corporation
   Kansas City, Missouri
4. Broadmoor Improvement Association, Inc. (BIA)
   New Orleans, Louisiana
5. Brooklyn Assembly
   Wilmington, North Carolina
6. Buckeye Woodland Community Congress
   Cleveland, Ohio
7. Calhoun Community Action Agency, Inc.
   Battle Creek, Michigan
8. Cherry Hill Coalition
   Seattle, Washington
9. Chinatown Neighborhood Improvement Resource Center
   San Francisco, California
10. Citizens for Community Improvement of Waterloo (CCI)
    Cleveland, Ohio
11. Citizens to Bring Broadway Back, Inc.
    Cleveland, Ohio
12. Communities Organized for Public Services (COPS)
    San Antonio, Texas

13. Detroit Shoreway Community Development Organization, Inc.
    Cleveland, Ohio
14. Eastlake Community Council
    Seattle, Washington
15. Elyria Community Council Association
    Denver, Colorado
16. Fillmore Leroy Area Residents, Inc. (FLARE)
    Buffalo, New York
17. Five Points South Neighborhood Citizens Committee
    Birmingham, Alabama
18. Greater Jacksonville Economic Opportunity, Inc.
    Jacksonville, Florida
19. Greenpoint Williamsburg Coalition of Community Organizations, Inc.
    Brooklyn, New York
20. Heights Community Congress
    Cleveland, Ohio
21. Historic Pullman Foundation, Inc.
    Chicago, Illinois
22. Inquilinos Boricuas en Accion (IBA)
    Boston, Massachusetts
23. Interfaith Adopt-a-Building, Lower East Side
    New York, New York
24. Jeff Vander Lou, Inc.
    St. Louis, Missouri
25. King William Association
    San Antonio, Texas
26. Lake View Citizens Council
    Chicago, Illinois
27. Missouri Delta Ecumenical Ministry (MDEM)
    Bootheel Region, Missouri
28. Neighborhood Uniting Project (NUP)
    Prince Georges County, Maryland
29. Nineteenth Ward Community Association, Inc.
    Rochester, New York
30. North Portland Citizens Committee
    Portland, Oregon
31. Northside Community Council
    Cincinnati, Ohio
32. Ohio City Blockclub Association
    Cleveland, Ohio
33. The Patch, Inc.
    Atlanta, Georgia
34. People Acting through Community Effort (PACE)
    Providence, Rhode Island
35. Sherman Park Community Association
    Milwaukee, Wisconsin
36. South Community Organization (SCO)
    Milwaukee, Wisconsin
37. Southwestern Oregon Community Action Committee, Inc.
    North Bend, Oregon

38. St. Ambrose Housing Aid Center
    Baltimore, Maryland
39. St. Clair–Superior Coalition
    Cleveland, Ohio
40. Tri City Citizens Union for Progress
    Newark, New Jersey
41. Union Sarah Economic Development Corporation
    St. Louis, Missouri
42. United Manchester Redevelopment Committee
    Pittsburgh, Pennsylvania
43. United West End Citizens Organizations Acting Together (UWE-COACT)
    Duluth, Minnesota
44. Youth, Education and Health in Soulard
    St. Louis, Missouri

II
Government Initiatives

Government initiatives are by definition the direct tool of public policy. The impact of such initiatives on neighborhood life was dramatized in the 1960s, when several major federal programs were first initiated or became more visible. Among these were the Community Action and Model Cities programs, which called attention to the impoverished conditions in inner-city neighborhoods. Also in this category were such policies as the tax deduction for mortgage loan interest, which accelerated the development of suburban neighborhoods.

In spite of the attention given to federal policies, however, the continuing, day-to-day policies most relevant to neighborhood life are the actions taken by local governments, both municipalities and counties. The quality and quantity of neighborhood services, though indirectly influenced by federal policies, are largely matters of local initiative. How a local government organizes these services and deals with the inevitable problems that arise ultimately affects neighborhood life substantially. For instance, residents' decisions to relocate to specific neighborhoods are determined first by housing preferences but second by the quality of schools, crime prevention, and other services provided by the local government.

Part II deals primarily with these local government initiatives. Chapter 5 presents a broad historical picture, indicating some of the nineteenth-century roots for providing neighborhood services. The chapter is especially helpful as a perspective for understanding the numerous initiatives to decentralize services in the 1960s and 1970s—that is, attempts that were made to bring services closer to those being served. The chapter also discusses a topic closely related to the overall theme of this book: that neighborhood initiatives, unlike other aspects of public policy, may work best when there is a "social symmetry" between servers and served. In short, neighborhood services may be most successful when they are perceived to be part of neighborhood social life, rather than as having been imposed on it.

Chapter 6 deals with a politically sensitive issue: How can services be provided equitably? The equity problem is examined using examples from educational services. In some cases, as with the television program "Sesame Street," a publicly funded enterprise may benefit all population groups but still increase the gap between advantaged and disadvantaged groups, and thereby increase the inequities between them. How this dilemma is produced, and what can be done about it, are the topics of this chapter.

Chapter 7 discusses a governmental initiative that has been prevalent in virtually every major American city: the public housing project. Although the initiatives emanate from the federal level, these projects are developed and maintained by local public agencies and represent a responsibility of local government. The chapter reviews research on public housing conditions and the impact of such housing on its residents.

Finally, Chapter 8 raises the possibility of taking new initiatives with a neighborhood service long taken for granted—the branch library. The chapter suggests that such libraries can assume a new function: the provision of neighborhood information and referral services, thereby filling a growing void in many urban neighborhoods. This type of government initiative may be one way of conserving the old while meeting new needs.

5
Neighborhood Service Delivery

HISTORICAL DEVELOPMENT AND THE CRISIS OF THE 1960s

NEIGHBORHOOD SERVICE PROBLEMS

The basic role of urban government is to provide police and fire protection, operate schools and hospitals, and clean the streets.[1] Presidents may focus on and be judged by their breakthroughs in foreign policy, and governors may emphasize their new highways and community colleges, but the men in city hall are the custodians of the sidewalks; they are the "dirtyworkers" of American government (Rainwater, 1967) who must deal with the most ordinary and intimate needs of their constituents. Moreover, the success or failure of service delivery is judged on a neighborhood basis, with different neighborhoods having different reputations for police protection, schools, sanitation, and housing.

Some urban governments try to improve street conditions by redeploying

---

This chapter is a slightly revised version of Robert K. Yin and Douglas Yates, *Street-Level Governments: Assessing Decentralization and Urban Services* (Lexington, Mass.: Lexington Books, 1975), Ch. 1. The original research was supported by the National Science Foundation, although none of the views reflects those of that agency.

[1] Urban services are distinctive because they are highly visible, tangible, and direct. They may also be allocated differentially by government to serve the needs of different individuals, local blocks, and communities. For these reasons the realm of urban service delivery is a natural political battleground. For a discussion of the distinctive characteristics and implications of urban service delivery, see Yates (1973, Ch. 1).

police, sanitation workers, or repair crews. Other urban administrators try to improve the reading skills of poor children by adopting one or more of a bewildering array of new educational techniques and technologies. Municipal executives in general try to increase the responsiveness and accountability of their "street-level bureaucrats"[2] by adopting new personnel procedures and by trying out a variety of organizational strategies: sometimes centralization of control and reliance on "professional" bureaucrats; sometimes decentralization and citizen participation; and sometimes the extensive use of new planning, budgeting, and evaluation techniques. In short, urban governments are constantly looking for better answers to the historical problem of how to organize and deliver urban services.

In searching for answers to service delivery problems, urban administrators are, in fact, dealing with the full range of social policy issues—not at the level of lofty debate but at the point where those broad policies impinge on specific individuals in specific neighborhoods. Criminal justice policy is ultimately about the way policemen behave on the beat and how judges operate in night court; educational policy reflects what is being done in a particular classroom; housing policy is what is built and torn down in a given neighborhood; and welfare policy often reduces to the relationship between social workers and their clients.

The dominant public theme for dealing with the service crisis of the 1960s was *decentralization*. Although new technology and the use of the computer were producing managerial reforms of a centrist nature, the greater attention—and greater hopes—were invested in a myriad of urban decentralization programs. Many of these programs aimed for ultimate decentralization by attempting to involve neighborhood residents in governmental affairs. Whatever the program, decentralization meant an attempt to place more decision making functions at the lowest level of service delivery, or at the point of contact between citizens and government. Often it did not seem to matter that these programs did not have attainable goals, for decentralization represented first and foremost the attempt to "do something" about cities.

Decentralization did not suddenly appear as a gimmick in the urban world of the 1960s. Instead, its roots are deeply embedded in the history of service delivery; and, in fact, decentralization has special prominence today because of the way the historical tensions between bureaucratic-professional control and citizen involvement have worked out in the development of city

---

[2]The concept of "street-level bureaucracy" is usefully developed in Michael Lipsky's "Toward a Theory of Street-Level Bureaucracy" (Paper delivered at the 65th annual meeting of the American Political Science Association, New York, September, 1969). A short version of the paper has appeared as "Street-Level Bureaucracy and the Analysis of Urban Reform" (Lipsky, 1971) and a revised longer version appears in Hawley and Lipsky (1976).

services. To understand decentralization in the context of this relationship between the "servers and served" (Reiss, 1970) requires a brief examination of the historical evolution of urban services.

THE EVOLUTION OF NEIGHBORHOOD SERVICES

Nineteenth-Century Foundations

In the eighteenth and early nineteenth centuries, the typical American city had only the most primitive public facilities and services. The streets of these early cities—many of which were unpaved—were the domain of pigs, dogs, cows, horses, and pedestrians. Garbage collected on the streets along with manure and human waste, and the job of garbage collection was left to itinerant scavengers and to the pigs. With few exceptions, there was no public water supply, and sellers of "tea water" from the few wells with fresh water did a brisk business of peddling their precious commodity from door to door (Duffy, 1968, pp. 30, 48–49). Firefighting was the preserve of volunteer companies who often compared with one another more than they fought fires and, in any case, were effective only when they could find sufficient water. With the development of crude wooden water mains, firefighting improved as firemen were able to tap into the mains through wooden "fireplugs."

In the mid–nineteenth century, police protection was equally haphazard since it was still emerging from the era of the night watch and the rattle. Public schooling was a halting experiment in New York's free schools and merely an idea in most cities (Kaestle, 1973; Lazerson, 1971; Ravitch, 1974). Various epidemics often swept through the typical city, and the only organized health and hospital care took place in the almshouses (Duffy, 1968, p. 232). The almshouses themselves were beginning to replace "home care" and the alleys and cellars where the poor and mentally ill were sequestered. Public transportation was limited to the omnibus—a kind of horse-drawn jitney—and later to the horse-drawn streetcar. There were almost no parks and recreation areas in the city (Conkling, 1904, p. 52).

In short, at the beginning of the great immigrations, American cities had hardly achieved a high standard of urban amenities and service delivery. An undeveloped, disorganized urban system was forced to respond to the enormous pressures created by immigration. Put another way, urban problems were running far ahead of the capacity of city government to deal with them even before the modern city began to rise. Even in a simpler urban past, the service delivery problem was already out of control.

Bargaining for Services in the Immigrant City

One does not have to read Jacob Riis or Lincoln Steffens at great length to get a flavor of the poverty and chaotic growth of the larger cities in the 1900s. Edward Banfield (1970, p. 19) would like to point out that present urban conditions—however bad they may be thought to be—simply cannot compare to conditions in immigrant neighborhoods at the turn of the century. In terms of comparative levels and quality of service delivery, Banfield's view is certainly correct, but it begs many far more important questions about urban service delivery.

Specifically, Banfield's view misses the point that for the past 100 years certain fundamental urban service problems have persisted in an apparently intractable way. Then as now, widespread police corruption was a constant embarrassment, if not a disgrace, to city governments. This pattern of corruption would be of interest only to crusading journalists and an occasionally aroused public if it did not reveal the intrinsic difficulty of establishing tight central control over the foot soldiers of city government: policemen, teachers, social workers, and garbage collectors. Because these public employees work on their own (or in small teams) out on the streets (or in classrooms) and must react rapidly to uncertain and ambiguous situations, it has always been hard for top-level urban administrators to supervise the actual delivery of service and thus enforce uniform standards of behavior. The police, in particular, present a vivid example of the tenuous control that administrators hold over foot soldiers. When city police were first established, policemen on the beat communicated with superior officers only in "face-to-face meetings or by messengers" (Rubinstein, 1973, p. 15). In later years, according to Rubinstein:

> Once the men were dismissed from roll call, their supervisors had no certain way of controlling what they did during their tour of work. The sergeants, who were called roundsmen in Philadelphia and Brooklyn during the early nineteenth century, frequently assigned men "meets," prearranged times and places where the supervisors could visually check on them. The only way a roundsman had of discovering what his men were doing was to follow them around and make inquiries among the people who lived and worked on the beats. If he wanted to watch a man at work, he could, and frequently did, accompany him, but this obligated him to neglect other duties. The men were also isolated from each other, and their only way of attracting attention in moments of distress was by swinging the large rattles which city policemen had been carrying since the sixteenth century. (p. 15)

Even with new communications technology, the problem of police supervision persisted and indeed made widespread corruption possible. Call boxes followed telegraph networks, and radio cars followed both. Various "pulling" systems have been adopted; and horns, colored lights, and bells have been used to "attract a patrolman to his box for special messages"

(Rubinstein, 1973, p. 17). But no amount of communication could place the policemen under direct, constant supervision. So policemen have continued to "coop" (sleep on duty), take bribes, react to dangerous situations, beat up suspects, and occasionally be assaulted; and police officials can still do precious little to regulate these encounters.

It is not only because of their inherent freedom and discretion that the mayor's foot soldiers are so hard to supervise and control. The foot soldiers have also always had strong incentives to treat the relationship between the servers and the served as a form of free market exchange. In a classical bureaucracy, employees are supposed to follow and apply simple rules and procedures about which there is little disagreement. But the street-level world of urban foot soldiers provides little clarity or agreement about the nature of the service "problem" or its appropriate solution. What is an intolerable vice to one segment of the community may be a pleasurable pastime or a means of employment for others. And so policemen have to deal with numbers runners, prostitutes, and owners of after-hours bars, with the knowledge that citizen demands and preferences are sharply divided, and that the practitioners of "vice" are willing to pay a great deal for a covert police license to do business.

Similarly, what may seem to be a serviceable if shabby home to a landlord and his tenants may seem a dangerous firetrap to neighbors or merchants on the block. Whose subjective appraisal should the inspector listen to in deciding whether or not to issue code violations? Consider, too, the local neighborhood carry-out bar. What may seem a valued hangout to teen-agers and unemployed men may be an unacceptable public nuisance to other residents of the neighborhood. In these cases, as in so many others, the policemen must mediate conflicting interests and apply an ambiguous law in deciding how to act or, for that matter, whether to act at all.

Given the complexity and ambiguity of these service problems, the lack of clear rules for dealing with them, and the absence of a controlling hierarchy that removes his discretion, the urban foot soldier deals with many service demands by means of *mutual adjustment and bargaining* (Lindblom, 1965). Instead of arresting the drunk or the rowdy adolescents, the policeman tells them to move on. Instead of reporting the delinquent student to the principal, the teacher extracts a promise of good behavior. Instead of closing down a "dirty" restaurant or a deteriorating house, the health or housing inspector issues only minor complaints on the promise that improvements will be made. Add the element of cynicism and greed on the part of public employees, and the willingness of offending citizens to buy indulgences, and one can easily see how a full-scale exchange system developed in American cities. Thus, in the history of American cities, services have often not been *delivered* so much as they have been *bought, sold,* and *negotiated*. This system of mutual adjustment and bargaining over services was an effective method of coordinating the supply and demand for services and an ingenious adaptation to the conflicting demands and chaotic circumstances of urban service delivery.

In the immigrant city, certain critical factors help to explain why the delicate social relationship between the servers and the served could work. Before the advent of the automobile, police walked the beat, and teachers and urban employees were likely to live near where they worked. Thus, although it is hard to demonstrate, urban foot soldiers at the turn of the century were almost certainly more visible, better known, and more rooted in the neighborhoods they served than their successors today. The living conditions of citizens and public employees tended to be roughly similar. That is, teachers, policemen, and garbagemen were likely to understand from their own living experiences what was going on in urban neighborhoods. The streets, housing, and people of the neighborhood were in this sense recognizable and familiar. Moreover, the urban foot soldiers often had ethnic ties with the people they served. That is manifestly true of the Irish policeman working in a predominantly Irish neighborhood; but if the demand for new urban employees was filled generally by recent immigrants, it must have been true for other ethnic groups as well.

What emerges from this depiction of the immigrant city is a kind of *social symmetry* in service delivery. The relationship between servers and served was roughly symmetrical when the former shared the same neighborhood, living conditions, and ethnic ties with the latter. This social symmetry was obviously supportive of the personal, even intimate role that existed between citizens and urban service deliverers. With the emphasis on bargaining for services, *trust* became a central ingredient in effective service delivery. If urban foot soldiers were to operate effectively in a close, personal relationship with clients, they could not be distrusted. And they were more likely to be distrusted if they were seen as alien, prejudiced, and ignorant of their clients' living conditions.

The Trend toward Centralization

It should be obvious that there are dramatic differences between this picture of service delivery in the immigrant city and the currently held picture of rigid, racist bureaucracies and deteriorating or nonexistent service delivery. The most widely favored explanations of these differences emphasize (1) the poverty of present-day urban immigrants; (2) the sudden deluge of new demands for service; (3) racial prejudice against nonwhites; (4) inadequate fiscal resources; and (5) at least, in Banfield's view, the social pathology of the new urban poor. However, if we submit these familiar explanations to close scrutiny, they turn out to be highly arguable.

In the first place, it is by no means clear that today's urban poor are worse off than their predecessors. Comparisons are difficult at best, but given rising levels of affluence, it seems likely that today's poor are considerably better off than their nineteenth-century counterparts (Banfield, 1970, pp. 19, 117). Second, it is even less clear that the scale of current immigration will impose a new order of magnitude of burden on city services. In fact, the growth rate in most large central cities began to decline in the second or third decade of this century, and the sharpest rates of growth (and hence of new demands) had already taken place by the 1960s. It can be argued in reply that although urban growth has slowed, the combination of middle-class outmigration and lower-class in-migration produces a net effect of service-demanding residents that is historically unique. Although we would be foolish to dismiss the scale and importance of this influx, it is hard to see how it compared to the net effect of immigration during the decades in the nineteenth century when the size of some cities doubled. Third, although it is clear that prejudice against blacks is deep-rooted, it is not obviously of a sufficiently different order of magnitude from Yankee prejudice against the Irish to explain large differences in service delivery. Fourth, cities obviously find themselves in serious financial straits today, but it is instructive to note that cities have frequently been on the verge of financial collapse ever since colonial times. For example, the tax drain caused by educational improvement and the resistance to that fiscal burden are noted by Lazerson (1971, p. 242); that new services caused severe financial strains and drove cities close to bankruptcy is documented by Bridenbaugh (1955, p. 9) and Wade (1964, p. 77).

Finally, the argument that the present urban poor are, through various forms of antisocial behavior, destroying their cities and their services is simply untenable. On this point, Banfield's account of criminality, immorality, violence, and drunkenness in the nineteenth-century urban populace serves as a stark reminder that in many ways, the nineteenth-century city was a much rougher and nastier place than the city we know today. Historical accounts of the nineteenth-century city indeed bring to light many kinds of urban poverty and squalor: For an account of infant mortality and outbreaks of epidemics, see Duffy (1968, pp. 119, 259); for a description of streets that were open sewers and littered with dead horses and cats, also see Duffy (1968, pp. 117, 191); for early incidents of rioting and racial discrimination, see Bridenbaugh (1955, pp. 299, 305); for drug addiction, see Musto (1973, p. 5); for air pollution caused by chimney smoke and for the absence of parks and other recreational facilities, see Hodges (1939, pp. 333, 363); and for the absence of garbage collection (and the use of hogs and vultures as scavengers), see Bellan (1971, p. 215).

If the familiar explanations for present-day urban problems are at least mildly suspect, where do we look to find a more satisfactory set of answers?

Our contention is that given the bargaining nature of urban services, three interrelated forces can account for the development of service delivery to its present state: the search for power and control in the city, the professionalization of urban service employees, and the rise of new technology. Each of these forces led to the increased *centralization* of service delivery, which in turn threatened to destroy the street-level relationship between the servers and the served.

The evolution of urban power and control throughout the last 100 years has been of a centrist nature. For instance, in establishing a new political order in cities, the great machines sharply centralized power and control of service delivery (Mandelbaum, 1965, pp. 364–365; Merton, 1957, p. 72; Scott, 1973). In most successful machines, even though neighborhood-based political organizations remained crucial, the focus of political attention moved away from the neighborhood to city hall—following the path of power. Later, reform mayors further centralized power by building larger bureaucracies, often with mandates from newly passed revisions of the city charter. The power changes have occurred at different rates in different cities, but the trend, up until the 1960s, had always been in the same direction—toward city hall (Banfield and Wilson, 1965).

The second factor that led to centralization was the growth in urban services of a professional ethos—emphasizing scientific management, training, specialization, and meritocratic criteria of recruitment and promotion. The rise of professionalism among teachers, social workers, or policemen can be understood in part as a strategy for increasing the status of these occupations. But, even more important, professionalism implies that service delivery should not be based on exchange or mutual adjustment with citizens but on the authority and expertise of those who deliver services. This emphasis means that the system of service delivery should be governed hierarchically and not be left to the vagaries of joint determination with citizens. And so public managers, preaching professionalism, reached for methods that worked in industry and sought to replicate the beguiling system of strong hierarchical administration through the progressive centralization of power and control (Katz, 1973, pp. 56–104). That police departments and schools were not simply factories with clear-cut production functions, technologies, and divisions of labor did not deter the prophets of scientific management.

The third major factor leading toward centralization was the rise of new technology. The earliest urban services, such as police and fire protection, water supply and garbage collection, road paving and street lighting, had originally developed in an ad-hoc, disconnected way. In many cases services were provided privately with each resident taking care of his own service needs. Even when city government began to provide services directly, service delivery was loosely organized and often chaotic as city government tried to keep up with the demands of a fast-growing urban population. One reason for this fragmentation, as we have seen, was the simple weakness of government organization. But, more fundamentally, the poor technology involved in early services reinforced the centrifugal pattern of service delivery—that is, when policemen lacked devices for communicating with central headquarters, when the streets were cleaned by wandering public scavengers, and when fire companies had limited mobility and limited communications, it was intrinsically difficult to establish centralized control of municipal operations.

As service technology developed, so did the extent of centralized bureaucratic control. Basic technological improvements like the telephone increased the possibility of central surveillance; similarly, the introduction of public reservoirs, almshouses, and hospitals all served to consolidate previously atomized services. The development of record-keeping technologies, culminating in the computer, gave central managers extensive control over their bureaucratic systems. Finally, nowhere was the centripetal effect of technology more evident than in the nineteenth-century development of urban transportation (Holt, 1972). The first transportation "system" was, of course, completely private and decentralized. People walked or drove their own horse-and-buggies. The first "public" conveyances, the omnibus and the horse-drawn streetcar, replaced self-service with a consolidated service but only to a slight extent. The omnibuses still wandered around the city along highly erratic routes, were run by a great number of different small companies, and attracted only a few riders. Thereafter, with each advance in transportation technology (before the automobile), services were consolidated further until private or public monopolies arose to run centralized traction systems. In transportation, technology tied the city together and gave rise to a highly centralized system of operation.

What makes the evolution of service delivery so interesting is that from the turn of the century to the 1960s, these centralizing forces were working indirectly to destroy the social symmetry of the older street-level structure. In addition, other changes brought about by the reformers and the rise of a national social welfare system worked directly to attack the street-level system.

The reformers sought to dismantle the neighborhood-based political patronage and exchange system, which they viewed as the cornerstone of machine politics and thus of political corruption. The reformers believed that the way to rescue service delivery from the depredations of political self-interest and especially from venal bosses was to create a centralized civil service and to place political power in the hands of a small number of "neutral" administrators serving on boards and commissions that were insulated from street-level politicals (Lubove, 1969, pp. 2–6). Whether or not the reform tradition achieved its positive goals of good government, it did in many cities achieve its negative purpose of taking authority and autonomy away from neighborhood-level service administrators, and the result was to further weaken (but not destroy) the system of local allocation and adjustment in service delivery. Finally, the growth of federal social programs, which began before 1932 but was powered by the large-scale interventions of the New Deal, further centralized the design and fiscal control of service delivery. That was especially the case with the urban renewal and public housing programs begun by federal initiatives. Service arrangements that were once negotiated by street-level employees and citizens were now often redefined by directives from Washington and were expanded, reorganized, or superseded by new service delivery mechanisms as a result of more distant bargaining processes among federal, state, and local officials.

In the face of changes in the urban power structure, professionalism, centralizing technologies, reform movements, and federal intervention, the street-level world of service delivery was largely transformed. Some street-level arrangements continued to slip through the new central controls. The persistence of police corruption, erratic garbage collection, and highly differentiated teaching methods and welfare regulation is proof of this point, with the widely reported police corruption scandals in New York (which led to the Knapp Commission), Philadelphia, and Chicago only the most recent examples. What bureaucratic centralization could and did do, however, was make the service delivery system more cumbersome, rigid, and remote. Put another way, centralization could ensure that service delivery was not intentionally hand-tailored to varied neighborhood interests and not explicitly based on ad-hoc exchanges and accommodations. Professionalism tended to increase the distance between foot soldiers and citizens by making policemen and teachers less members of the neighborhoods they served and more members of a separate, professional guild. Bureaucratization increased the complexity and formality of procedures and of communication channels between city government and its citizens (see Martin, 1965).

THE NEIGHBORHOOD SERVICE CRISIS OF THE 1960s

The service crisis of the 1960s emerged at a time when urban bureaucracies were overly centralized, inflexible, and removed from the neighborhoods. The crisis consisted of a sharp rise in the demand for services that was reflected by runaway crime and fire alarm rates, overloaded sanitation systems, and schools that produced large numbers of dropouts and failures. The crisis also consisted, it should be rememberd, of entirely new types of tensions: harassment of service employees by residents, vandalism of public property, and complete disrespect for city government's bureaucracy. And the crisis was neighborhood based: Poor and "transition" neighborhoods suffered the most, whereas residents of upper-middle-class, white neighborhoods often remained oblivious of conditions in the rest of the city.

The Loss of Social Symmetry

Over and above the debilitating effects of centralization on the server–served relationship, the population turnover in most cities by the 1960s threatened destruction of the street-level bargaining, mutual trust, and social symmetry that characterized the immigrant city. Policemen, teachers, firemen, and other public employees tended to be white and working-class, and not to be residents of the port-of-entry neighborhoods where the new immigrants arrived. The social bond between servers and served was thus to a large extent broken, and it is no surprise that feelings of distrust, hostility, and alienation grew rapidly among nonwhite urban residents. From another point of view, the city's foot soldiers also suddenly were forced to live in an unfamiliar, hostile, and threatening urban world. Policemen and teachers who knew their way around the old white neighborhoods because they grew up in them (or ones like them) were now faced with angry demands and protests and with the loss of neighborhood support and approval. They often became "dirtyworkers" to their families and sympathetic observers—and "pigs" to their bitter clients (Wilson, 1968). The incipient movement toward public service unionization, begun in the early 1960s for valid economic and occupational reasons, now gained an emotional, almost paranoid source of support from these changed social conditions (Cole, 1969; Connery and Farr, 1970; Stanley, 1972; Wellington and Winter, 1971).

The decline in social symmetry also took more subtle forms. The accounts in urban textbooks about the policemen, teachers, or social workers who could tell a "good" kid from a "bad" one presumed an intimate understanding on the part of the foot soldier, not only of particular individual residents but also of the appearances, life styles, and attitudes of residents. But when residents became unfamiliar, even alien to the deliverers of services, the capacity of policemen and teachers to make careful distinctions on the basis of subtle cues was vastly reduced. In the extreme case, all sixteen-year-old black males wearing apple hats come to look like "probable assailants" to the policeman unfamiliar with a neighborhood and the people in it. Equally, with increased social distance, residents are less able to interpret the behavior and attitudes of public employees. What the foot soldiers may think of as tough but fair conduct may appear to be blatant racism to nonwhite residents. Indeed, charges of police brutality do not primarily involve physical force, but instead stem from residents' perceptions that police behave in an insulting way, make implicit racial slurs, or fail to treat nonwhites with due respect. On the other hand, policemen, teachers, and other foot soldiers easily take strongly expressed demands, grievances, and protests about services to be hostile acts and direct personal attacks on them and their institutions.

Renewal Problems and Social Problems

At the same time, it is important not to try to explain too much by the loss of social symmetry and the resulting breakdown of social communication, for clearly there were other aspects of the service crisis. For one thing, many cities were no longer young or fast-growing, nor were they mounting large-scale services for the first time. Instead, the cities were old, their physical plant was deteriorating, and they were suffering an increasing rate of decay. Although urban governments had been successful in laying out new services as their cities grew, few governments have been very successful in renewing or restructuring old services. One reason is that it is less costly to produce new goods and services than to rehabilitate old ones. With new construction or the creation of new programs, one does not have to worry about clearing away outdated equipment or methods of operation; one does not have to worry about dealing with intricate interdependence (among services or programs); and one does not have to worry about challenging entrenched interests and disrupting established patterns of behavior. On this logic, it was clearly easier to build a new service system in response to the demands of the immigrant city than it was to restructure and reform an established service system. Thus the institutionalization of services was an administrative triumph that came as a reaction to the nineteenth-century growth of the city. But, in the 1960s, the same phenomenon of institutionalization took on a very different meaning: It was a source of persistence and inflexibility and therefore an obstacle to responsiveness and adaptation to new demands.

Second, urban government was grappling with a different and more difficult class of services in the 1960s than it had been fifty years earlier. Then, the main task of government was to build the physical city: street paving, street lighting, water and sewage systems, parks, and large-scale capital projects such as bridges and public works. Aside from debilitating graft, cities had little trouble in actually delivering these goods.

By contrast, the services demanded in the 1960s were intrinsically difficult to deliver. The typical urban "problems" were crime in the streets, drug addiction, unemployment, and delinquency. No one knew the solutions to these "social" problems. (For more on the difficulty of the social problems approach in urban research, see Yin, 1972, pp. ix–xvii.) Even trivial problems, such as the sending of false fire alarms, baffled administrators. The array of potential solutions, which remained similar to those tried for decades, included:

> [A] siren to attract attention to the firealarm box and provide for apprehension of the false alarmist. Another patent contains a camera which takes a snapshot of the individual setting off the alarm. The best idea, from the human-interest standpoint, includes a pair of handcuffs which manacle the "culprit" the instant he sets off the firealarm. (Hodges, 1939, p. 501)

More important, urban administrators had simply never known how to prevent widespread family breakdown in poor neighborhoods, ensure that health and housing regulations were enforced,[3] prevent high rates of welfare dependence among new immigrant groups (black or white), or educate low-income children (Greer, 1972, p. 108).

Reactions to the Crisis: Centralization and Decentralization

When faced with the service crisis of the 1960s, urban administrators came up with many remedies: Some called for further centralization, but others espoused a new theme—decentralization. The centrist strategies were extensions of what had occurred in the past, now packaged under such labels as program budgeting, operations research, and service efficiency. Mayors moved to increase central bureaucratic control by creating "super" agencies, strong budget bureaus or city planning agencies, and specialized staff functions at the very top. Cities turned desperately to new applications of space-age technology for other potential solutions. The evaluation of the success of these centrist strategies, however, must be left for another occasion.

In cities across the country, a wide array of decentralization strategies have been tried. The move to decentralize is potentially of great significance in the continuing evolution of neighborhood service delivery. For the first time, in the late 1960s and early 1970s, cities tried at last to turn the tide and to reform the point of contact of service delivery; for decentralization, above all else, has meant the enhancement of the functions of both the servers and the served. The innovations that were attempted are by now well-known: police–community relations and team policing programs, districtwide and citywide decentralization of schools, new neighborhood health and mental health centers, neighborhood councils or little city hall facilities for multiservice programs, and community development corporations (Schmandt, 1972).

The research need is to assess these various decentralization efforts as they occurred in different services and in different cities (e.g., Altshuler, 1970; Fantini, Gittell, and Magat, 1970; Farr, Liebman, and Wood, 1972; Kotler, 1969; Nordlinger, 1973). Investigators need to review the record that de-

---

[3]Schlesinger (1933, p. 110) notes that the first tenement housing laws were enforced sporadically, if at all; Green (1965, p. 116) adds more generally that most of the early tenement and plumbing laws and building codes were all but unenforceable.

centralization has amassed, and to explain the outcomes of these decentralization efforts in terms of the inherent differences among urban services and the decentralization strategies tried in each service.

REFERENCES

Altshuler, Alan. *Community Control.* New York: Pegasus, 1970.
Banfield, Edward. *The Unheavenly City.* Boston: Little, Brown, 1970.
Banfield, Edward, and Wilson, James Q. *City Politics.* Cambridge: Harvard University Press, 1965.
Bellan, Ruben C. *The Evolving City.* Toronto: Copp Clark, 1971.
Bridenbaugh, Carl. *Cities in Revolt: Urban Life in America 1743–1776.* New York: Oxford University Press, 1955.
Cole, Stephen. *The Unionization of Teachers.* New York: Praeger, 1969.
Conkling, Alfred. *City Government in the United States.* New York: Century, 1904.
Connery, Robert H., and Farr, William V., eds. *Unionization of Municipal Employees.* New York: Academy of Political Science, Columbia University, 1970.
Duffy, John. *A History of Public Health in New York City, 1825–1866.* New York: Russell Sage Foundation, 1968.
Fantini, Mario; Gittell, Marilyn, and Magat, Richard. *Community Control and the Urban School.* New York: Praeger, 1970.
Farr, Walter, Liebman, Lance, and Wood, Jeffrey. *Decentralizing City Government.* New York: Praeger, 1972.
Green, Constance McLaughlin. *The Rise of Urban America.* New York: Harper & Row, 1965.
Greer, Colin. *The Great School Legend.* New York: Basic Books, 1972.
Hawley, Willis, and Lipsky, Michael. *Theoretical Perspectives on Urban Politics.* Englewood Cliffs, N.J.: Prentice-Hall, 1976.
Hodges, Henry. *City Management.* New York: Crofts, 1939.
Holt, Glen. "The Changing Perception of Urban Pathology." In *Cities in American History,* edited by Kenneth Jackson and Stanley Schultz. New York: Alfred A. Knopf, 1972.
Kaestle, Carl F. *The Evolution of an Urban School System.* Cambridge: Harvard University Press, 1973.
Katz, Michael. *Class, Bureaucracy, and Schools.* New York: Praeger, 1973.
Kotler, Milton. *Neighborhood Government.* New York: Bobbs-Merrill, 1969.
Lazerson, Marvin. *Origins of the Urban School.* Cambridge: Harvard University Press, 1971.
Lindblom, Charles E. *The Intelligence of Democracy.* New York: Free Press, 1965.
Lipsky, Michael. "Street-Level Bureaucracy and the Analysis of Urban Reform." *Urban Affairs Quarterly* 1971, 6, 391–406.
Lubove, Roy. *The Professional Altruist.* New York: Atheneum, 1969.
Mandelbaum, Seymour. *Boss Tweed's New York.* New York: Wiley, 1965.
Martin, Roscoe. *The City in the Federal System.* New York: Atherton Press, 1965.
Merton, Robert K. "The Latent Functions of the Machine." In *Social Theory and Social Structure,* rev. ed., edited by Robert K. Merton. New York: Free Press, 1957.
Musto, David. *The American Disease.* New Haven: Yale University Press, 1973.
Nordlinger, Eric. *Decentralizing the City.* Cambridge, Mass.: MIT Press, 1973.
Rainwater, Lee. "The Revolt of the Dirtyworkers." *Trans-Action* 4 (November 1967): 35–40.
Ravitch, Diane. *The Great School Wars.* New York: Basic Books, 1974.

Reiss, Albert, Jr. "Servers and Served in Service." In *Financing the Metropolis,* edited by John P. Crecine. Beverly Hills, Calif.: Sage Publications, 1970.
Rubinstein, Jonathan. *City Police.* New York: Farrar, Straus & Giroux, 1973.
Schlesinger, Arthur M. *The Rise of the City.* New York: Macmillan, 1933.
Schmandt, Henry J. "Municipal Decentralization: An Overview." *Public Administration Review* 32 (October 1972): 571–588.
Scott, James. *Comparative Political Corruption.* Englewood Cliffs, N.J.: Prentice-Hall, 1973.
Stanley, David T. *Managing Local Government under Union Pressure.* Washington, D.C.: Brookings Institution, 1972.
Wade, Richard. *The Urban Frontier.* Chicago: University of Chicago Press, 1964.
Wellington, Harry H., and Winter, Ralph K., Jr. *The Unions and the Cities.* Washington, D.C.: Brookings Institution, 1971.
Wilson, James Q. "The Urban Unease." *The Public Interest* 12 (Summer 1968): 25–39.
Yates, Douglas. *Neighborhood Democracy.* Lexington, Mass.: Lexington Books, D. C. Heath, 1973.
Yin, Robert K., ed. *The City in the Seventies.* Itasca, Ill.: Peacock, 1972.

6

The (In)equity of Information Systems in Education

INTRODUCTION

The primary mission of the U.S. National Institute of Education is to seek ways of providing *equal opportunity* for education of *high quality* to all persons, regardless of race, color, religion, sex, national origin, or social class (National Institute of Education, 1978). Thus the achievement of equity in education has been deemed as important as the achievement of high quality in education. The purpose of this chapter is to review the problems, experiences, and prospects for achieving equity in the use of information, as implied by the current array of information delivery systems available in education. Because educational services—at the primary and secondary levels—impinge directly at the neighborhood level, this inquiry is another illustration of the policy-making problems in dealing with neighborhood life.

By *information delivery systems* is meant: *the communications network, both human and technological, through which educational information is transmitted to users, who may be school administrators, teachers, or students.* There is a variety of such delivery systems currently in place. In most cases, the goal of these systems is either: (1) to provide information about new R&D knowledge, or (2) to teach lessons about substantive topics in education.

This chapter was originally presented as a paper at a Conference on Equity in Educational Information Dissemination, sponsored by the National Institute of Education, in Washington, D.C., February 1979.

THE (IN)EQUITY OF INFORMATION SYSTEMS IN EDUCATION

Whichever the case, problems may be said to exist regarding any improvement in educational equity. Briefly, the line of reasoning is as follows:

1. Most information delivery systems have been designed to promote *equal access* to educational information.
2. The equality of access, however, generally benefits information-rich (or advantaged) populations to a greater degree than information-poor (or disadvantaged) populations; although both populations will gain in absolute terms, there is a differential gain that appears to increase the inequity between these populations.
3. To the extent that federal policy is concerned with increased equity, new systems must be designed to provide *unequal* access—that is, systems that favor utilization by disadvantaged populations.
4. The support of such new systems is not likely to be feasible, because they will rightly be interpreted as exclusionary and discriminatory, even though the result may be increased equity. Moreover, those excluded will be members of the majority population, and it may be politically infeasible to use significant national resources for activities in which the majority population is deliberately excluded.

EXISTING EXPERIENCES WITH INFORMATION DELIVERY SYSTEMS: THREE EXAMPLES

Formal information delivery systems can take a variety of forms.[1] Although it is not the purpose of this chapter to develop a typology of such systems, a useful dimension along which they may be arrayed is from passive-user to active-user systems. In general, *passive-user* systems are designed and controlled by some central organization, and information is disseminated to users in the classic marketing sense. In contrast, *active-user* systems are designed and controlled in part by the user groups themselves, so that users assume more of a proactive role in consuming information. In between these two extremes there may be any number of *mixed* systems.

In education, all three types of systems exist. Thus Table 9 lists some of the major information delivery systems according to whether they are passive-user, mixed, or active-user. This list could be expanded, and numerous other comparative dimensions could be developed to achieve a more sophisticated

---

[1] No attempt has been made here to cover the characteristics of informal systems, typically involving direct practitioner-to-practitioner communication. Even though such systems may be significant conveyors of information, they are not usually susceptible to federal intervention programs.

Table 9
Information Delivery Systems in Education

Type of system	Illustrative examples
Passive-user	1. ERIC Clearinghouse 2. Over-the-air television programs (e.g., "Sesame Street") 3. Support of newsletters, journal publications, and research reports
Mixed-user	4. National Diffusion Network (OE) 5. R&D Utilization Network (NIE)
Active-user	6. Closed-circuit television in schools 7. Urban cable television

typology of systems. However, the immediate purpose of having this crude typology is to indicate the extent to which the systems do vary, as well as to provide the rationale for selecting three illustrative systems for further discussion in relation to equity. In addition, the author has some direct research experience with at least one example of all three types,[2] and the conclusions from all, regarding the achievement of equity, appear to be similar. Thus, to the extent that the crude typology is valid, the conclusions to be drawn may be said to be generalizable to the whole population of information delivery systems.

A Passive-User Illustration: "Sesame Street"

No single informational effort in education has achieved the success of the television program "Sesame Street" (Lesser, 1974). The program was developed by a nonprofit company, the Children's Television Workshop, and is aired on public television to virtually all communities in the United States. The goal of the program has been to increase the educational skills of preschool children, and existing evaluations have definitively shown positive effects on individual learning (Yin, 1973b). Moreover, the program has also been an artistic success, has received numerous accolades in the performing arts, and has spawned a variety of foreign-language versions that are broadcast in other countries.

Although "Sesame Street" has attained success in serving the needs of user populations, the program nevertheless represents a passive-user system

---

[2]See Yin (1973a, 1973b, and 1978) for an analysis of "Sesame Street" and urban cable television. The author is currently engaged in research on an example of the third type, the R&D utilization network.

THE (IN)EQUITY OF INFORMATION SYSTEMS IN EDUCATION

in that the main user role is in receiving the information. The design of the program, distribution system, and subsequent informational lessons are all centrally controlled by a single organization and its federal government sponsors (mainly the Corporation for Public Broadcasting and the United States Office of Education). Home users are active only to the degree that they must know when the program is available and they must turn on their television sets; school users are somewhat more active in that teachers may select specific programs, tape them, and integrate their viewing with other classroom activities.

As regards equity, the existing evaluation data have shown that "Sesame Street," although producing positive outcomes for preschoolers of all backgrounds, differentially benefits children from advantaged families over those from disadvantaged families (e.g., Cook, 1975). In essence, "Sesame Street" has increased the *inequity* among social groups. The reasons for this outcome are not difficult to understand. The availability of attractive over-the-air programming on an equal-access basis—that is, any viewer who wishes to watch the program can do so—has meant that more children from advantaged families view the program more repetitively and hence obtain greater exposure to it; and that these children learn more from their viewing experiences. The increased inequity that is produced has been one of the major criticisms of the program, and the issue continues to draw controversy.

A Mixed-User Illustration: NIE's R&D Utilization Program

In 1976 the National Institute of Education (NIE) initiated a new program to increase the utilization of R&D knowledge by school systems and teachers. In this program seven project sites, mainly state departments of education, were given awards to develop special networks consisting of the following components:

- An organization to develop an R&D product base to provide information on new educational practices
- A linkage network system, involving intermediary service agencies, to facilitate communication among the product base, state departments of education, and local school systems
- Practitioners in local school systems, who would themselves undertake needs assessments and implement new classroom practices to alleviate educational problems

Each of the seven projects serves an average of thirty schools, sometimes all located within the same state but other times in several states (see Table 10). The program has mainly focused on improving the teaching of basic skills

Table 10
Organizational and Geographic Setting of Each RDU Project

	Project characteristics		
		Geographic location of:	
Name of RDU project	Host organization	Project headquarters	Operating sites, by state
Northwest Reading Consortium (NRC)	Washington State Department of Education	Olympia, WA	Alaska Idaho Oregon Washington
Georgia RDU Project	Georgia Department of Education	Atlanta, GA	Georgia
Pennsylvania School Improvement Program (PSIP)	Pennsylvania Department of Education	Harrisburg, PA	Pennsylvania
The Consortium	The Network (nonprofit organization)	Andover, MA	California Connecticut Kansas Massachusetts Minnesota Washington
NEA/NIE Inservice Education Project	National Education Association	Washington, D.C.	12 states
Florida Linkage System (FLS)	Florida Department of Education	Tallahassee, FL	Florida
Career Education Dissemination	Michigan Department of Education	Lansing, MI	Michigan

(reading and mathematics), but some of the seven sites have also emphasized the teaching of career education.

The R&D Utilization (RDU) program may be regarded as a mixed-user system because state and local officials, including the users or teachers, participate actively in the design and implementation of the program. Both the overall organization at each project site as well as the specific educational practices to be implemented in the classroom are determined with considerable participation by these user groups. Although centralized sources of financial and R&D support are involved, and although the ultimate decisions

THE (IN)EQUITY OF INFORMATION SYSTEMS IN EDUCATION

regarding the program are made by a federal agency (the NIE), users do carry out a more active role.

The RDU program has been undergoing extensive evaluation, both at the national level and by the local sites themselves (Chabotar and Kell, 1978). Although there are no evaluative data yet available from which to judge the impact of the group, the implementation of the program suggests that certain outcomes are likely. First, there may very well be differentially positive gains made by underachieving students. The reason is that the target schools have been those in which students have performed more poorly than statewide norms; to this extent the program may be differentially assisting disadvantaged students. Second, however, because the seven project sites have tended to be state departments of education, which tend not to have strong relationships with schools in large cities, the schools participating in the RDU program have tended to be located in rural or suburban school districts. Only a small percentage of the students being served are black, and to this extent the RDU program does not serve disadvantaged populations (although no data are available on family income).

As regards equity, the RDU program may therefore increase the equity among student populations, but only to the extent that disadvantaged populations are synonymous with students who have below-average achievements in rural and suburban schools. One potential lesson is that federal strategies that attempt to create networks in the most efficient and equitable fashion—for example, through the fifty state departments of education—may produce inequities of results because large, urban school districts generally fall outside these networks. Yet to establish a program dealing only with large, urban school districts would be much more uneconomic and fragmented, and would produce a decentralizing rather than a networking impact.

To the extent that the RDU program is successful, other sites may be expected to develop similar approaches (with or without federal support), and ultimately a larger population of students would be covered. What remains unclear is whether, with such increased coverage, it can be expected that disadvantaged students will eventually benefit more from the program than will advantaged students (again, even though both groups might obtain positive gains in an absolute sense). In short, unless the program were directly targeted to school districts in large central cities, and other participants were specifically precluded from participating, the long-term results are likely to be equality of access but inequity of outcome.

An Active-User Illustration: Urban Cable Television

Cable television systems have traditionally existed in rural areas throughout the country. Such systems have primarily been used to allow homes to receive commercial television in areas where over-the-air reception was poor. In such areas a cable television system included a large, master antenna that would receive distant, over-the-air signals, and these signals were then transmitted to individual homes through a wire or cable network that physically entered each individual home.

Over the last ten years, public interest in cable television has grown because of the potential development of such systems for urban areas (e.g., Yin, 1973a). The motivation for such urban cable television systems has been entirely different from that in rural areas. Of course, homes in urban areas generally already have acceptable access to over-the-air commercial programs. The promise of urban cable television, instead, has been the possibility that the existing program offerings can be increased through

- The addition of numerous channels beyond the six or seven typically available over-the-air (cable capabilities allow for the reception of twenty, thirty, and even more channels in which the picture reception is much better than the UHF broadcasts over-the-air)
- The development of new programs, oriented toward the needs of specific neighborhoods that can be served by separate cable systems (which are technically capable of being discrete systems rather than having to serve an entire metropolitan area)
- Local program production, utilizing community studios and other facilities that can be developed for individual cable systems

Moreover, FCC regulations regarding urban cable systems, passed in 1972, specifically required that one cable channel be set aside for educational use.

Urban cable systems may be regarded as active-user systems for several reasons. First, existing technology makes it possible for cable systems to carry signals in both directions—upstream as well as downstream. To this extent viewers can provide feedback or otherwise participate actively during, say, a two-way video training session. Second, user groups can contribute to the design and production of programs, either by providing tapes or by operating a community studio (one channel was also set aside for community-originated programs). Third, the entire cable system may be owned and operated on a community basis. Thus the promise of urban cable television has been the possibility of minority ownership of an entire media system, leading to political, financial, and programming benefits.

The promise of urban cable television has been thwarted, however, by local television stations and mixed bureaucratic directives from the FCC (Yin, 1978). In urban places, the over-the-air stations are threatened by a declining viewer base attributable to cable television (no such threat exists in the rural areas served by cable television). Moreover, although there have been suc-

THE (IN)EQUITY OF INFORMATION SYSTEMS IN EDUCATION 87

cessful experiments and demonstrations with two-way systems, these types of urban cable systems have simply not been developed with the vigor and in the quantity that was once expected. Ironically, new cable systems have continued to emerge, but these have been suburban versions of the traditional rural systems: High user fees are charged for the opportunity to obtain improved picture reception or a more diverse array of commercial programs (or both).

Urban cable television may be seen as a case in which the proposed information network was potentially more exclusionary than the existing one (over-the-air television). As a result, local television stations lobbied the FCC, which resulted in a set of regulations generally unfavorable to the development of cable systems in disadvantaged, urban areas. Although the cable television saga is much broader than the educational concerns covered by the present chapter, the urban cable experience does suggest the difficulty of using public policy to develop exclusionary systems. In contrast, where financial markets are allowed to operate alone, as in the emergence of suburban cable systems, cable systems may thrive.

ISSUES RAISED BY EXISTING EXPERIENCES

This review of three illustrative cases appears to support at least three general propositions about equity and information delivery systems. On an individual basis, the three cases appear to support two propositions: (1) Equality of access produces inequity of outcomes, but (2) inequality of access, which might be needed to produce equitable outcomes, is a difficult public policy position. Across cases, a third proposition may be entertained: Centralized, passive-user systems may be more effective than decentralized, active-user systems. All of these general propositions have potential implications for the design of future federal policy, and therefore are worth reviewing. Rather than considering the propositions as definitive conclusions, the reader should imagine the types of research that might be designed to test these propositions further.

Proposition 1: Equality of Access Produces Inequity of Outcomes

Among the three, the "Sesame Street" case was the only one in which there was substantial equality of access. Under these circumstances, the evidence suggested that inequities increased because the benefits derived by advantaged populations were greater than those derived by disadvantaged populations. In the second case, the R&D Utilization program, the fragmentary implementation pattern suggested that equality of access—as defined by the development of networks through state departments of education—produces inequities because large urban school districts are not properly served. In the third illustration, urban cable systems, there has been little access by any group because such systems have not been developed to any significant degree.

In spite of the diversity of these experiences, a general proposition supported by all would be that: *As equality of access to information delivery systems increases, there will be increasingly inequitable results—that is, the benefits to advantaged populations will be differentially greater than those to disadvantaged populations.* The proposition may also be true in its reverse form—that is, that as access is made less equitable and targeted to special populations, those special populations will be the only beneficiaries, and hence inequities may be reduced. This first proposition, whether argued in either direction, is consistent with other observations concerning communications technology and equity. Katzman (1974), for instance, has noted that information-rich (and hence advantaged) populations will always derive differentially greater benefits than information-poor (and hence disadvantaged) populations from effective information systems.

Proposition 2: Inequality of Access Is a Difficult Public Policy Position

To the extent that equality of access is inversely related to equity of outcome, there are several serious implications for future federal policy. First, highly targeted but necessarily exclusionary information delivery systems need to be developed in the future if equity of outcome is desired. Although such compensatory activities have been supported by federal programs in other areas—for example, food stamps or school lunches are only available to those in need, and not on an equal-access basis—it may be more difficult to support such exclusionary programs where information delivery systems are involved.[3] The reason is that *equality of access to information* appears to be a special value embedded in our democratic state. One need only cite the extensive debate and evolution of the FCC's Fairness Doctrine to suggest the pervasive nature of this social value. Thus the urban cable television illustration, which showed the difficulties of establishing exclusionary information delivery systems through public policy, may be expected to be repeated whenever a similar issue arises.

---

[3] A counterexample is the U.S. Department of Education's support for bilingual television programs, but the majority population is not excluded from viewing such programs.

THE (IN)EQUITY OF INFORMATION SYSTEMS IN EDUCATION

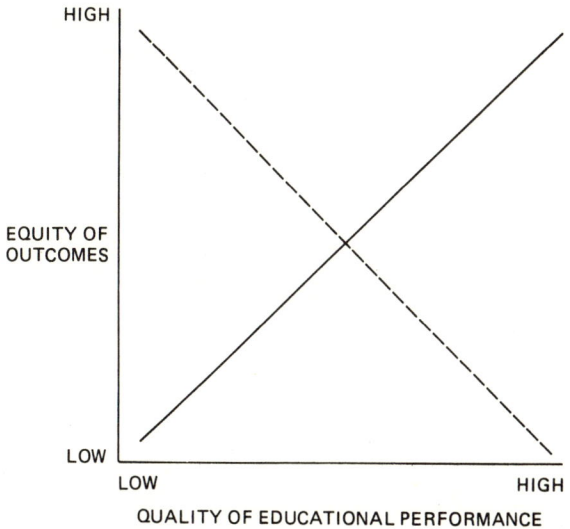

Figure 3. Possible relationship between educational performance and equity.

Second, there is an interesting secondary implication: namely, that the most equitable outcomes may be achieved where the overall quality of performance is low, rather than high. The reasoning is based on the observation that overall educational performance does appear to increase as access to information delivery systems increases. Thus all students do perform better after watching "Sesame Street." However, if one advocates reduced access to such systems, as one must in order to promote equity, fewer students will have the opportunity to participate in such systems. Indeed, this point is the crux of the exclusionary principle previously described. With decreased participation, the overall benefits will decline; extrapolating this trend further, the most equitable situation may very well be the one where every part of the population is performing rather poorly. Although such an extreme situation should obviously be avoided, the main point of this observation is that the general shape of the curve between equity and quality may be an inverse rather than direct relationship (see Figure 3).[4] To the extent that the relationship is inverse, federal policies that attempt to pursue quality education as well as equity of educational outcome may be flawed in their basic design.

---

[4]The inverse relationship was also suggested in a study of street sanitation, where it is possible that all streets are most likely to achieve equity when all are dirty (Yin, 1974).

Proposition 3: Centralized Information Systems May Be More Effective than Decentralized Systems

The evidence for this proposition is drawn from the general pattern across the three illustrative cases. In general, the most effective information delivery system was also the most centralized one, "Sesame Street." As systems become increasingly user controlled and decentralized, the systems may be said to be more tentative and have mixed outcomes (e.g., the R&D Utilization program) or even not implementable without considerable conflict (e.g., urban cable systems). Furthermore, there is little evidence concerning the effectiveness of completely decentralized systems, partly because such systems would, at least in the information field, contradict the major substantive benefits from centralized data bases and information technologies.

As a result of the preceding observations, it would seem foolhardy for minority groups to attempt to develop their own information systems on any decentralized basis. User control and active-user systems are simply not necessary for effective information delivery (although there may be other psychological or political benefits from such systems). At the same time, even though centralized systems may be functionally more effective, it is generally more difficult to develop political support for such systems where they are also to be exclusionary. In other words, there may be greater political tolerance for exclusionary systems when they are also decentralized.

The observation that *centralized, exclusionary* information systems may be the most desirable for reducing inequities poses yet further complications for federal policy. There is no clear basis on which such systems could be politically supported when the majority population was the primary population being excluded, but federal resources were being used because a centralized system was the most effective. Again, although federal programs of this compensatory nature do exist in other fields—for example, the Community Services Administration does selectively support community development corporations in low-income neighborhoods but not all neighborhoods—such programs in the information field would appear to be less likely.

IMPLICATIONS FOR FURTHER RESEARCH

The major mission of the NIE is to improve educational quality and equity. The major method available to the NIE to pursue its mission, however, is to support research, development, and dissemination of knowledge. Thus one may rightfully wonder about the research implications of this chapter. These implications would seem rather obvious, for the discussion has revolved around three major propositions that clearly deserve further testing and ver-

THE (IN)EQUITY OF INFORMATION SYSTEMS IN EDUCATION

ification. For information delivery systems, this chapter has also suggested a fourth proposition concerning the potentially inverse relationship between quality and equity.

Not all of these propositions are equally testable in a scientific sense. Thus, for a research agenda on equity and information delivery systems, the following three topics (omitting proposition 2) should be included:

1. The greater the equality of access to information delivery systems in education, the greater the inequity of outcomes.
2. Centralized information delivery systems are more effective than decentralized systems.
3. Equitable outcomes and quality of education are inversely related.

If research shows that these propositions are essentially correct, then the federal policy implications have already been raised in the form of several potential dilemmas in seeking support for systems that provide equity but poor performance or for centralized, exclusionary systems. However, if research shows that these propositions are incorrect, then new alternatives may be created that can expand the policy options. The latter outcome would clearly become a classic example of research playing a constructive role in expanding the potential array of political choices and social benefits.

REFERENCES

Chabotar, Kent, and Kell, Diane. *Linking R&D with Schools.* Cambridge, Mass.: Abt Associates, 1978.

Cook, Thomas. *"Sesame Street" Revisited.* New York: Russell Sage Foundation, 1975.

Katzman, Natan. "The Impact of Communications Technology: Promises and Prospects." *Journal of Communications* 1974, *24*, 47–58.

Lesser, Gerald. *Children and Television: Lessons from Sesame Street.* New York: Random House, 1974.

National Institute of Education. *Summary of the Reorganization Plan.* Washington, D.C.: U.S. Government Printing Office, June 1978.

Yin, Robert K. *Cable Television: Applications for Municipal Services.* Santa Monica, Calif.: Rand Corporation, 1973a.

Yin, Robert K. *The Workshop and the World: Toward an Assessment of the Children's Television Workshop.* Santa Monica, Calif.: Rand Corporation, 1973b.

Yin, Robert K. "On the Equality of Municipal Service Outcomes." New York: New York City–Rand Institute, 1974.

Yin, Robert K. "Cabling the City: A Federal Urban Innovation." In *Innovation and Implementation in Public Organizations,* edited by Richard Nelson and Douglas Yates. Lexington, Mass.: Lexington Books, 1978, pp. 175–186.

7
Can Public Housing Help?

THE CONTINUING CONTROVERSY

Public housing is the oldest subsidized housing program in the United States, having been established by the Housing Act of 1937. In the program, federal funds are administered by a local housing authority, which acquires a site, prepares plans, and supervises the construction of new housing units. The units are intended to provide low-rent housing for low-income families. In most cities, public housing has been a controversial program (Bauer, 1957; Bellush and Hausknecht, 1967). Proponents argue that the housing is needed by low-income families and compares favorably to the alternative housing units usually available to those families. Opponents point out that public housing projects often become centers of dangerous and unhealthy living conditions, and that these conditions also adversely affect the surrounding neighborhood.

In the early 1970s support for public housing was especially threatened by the publicity over the demise of the Pruitt-Igoe project in St. Louis, Missouri (Wilson, 1973). The project had been a social eyesore and had produced images of a "vertical ghetto" (e.g., Rainwater, 1967, 1970). Such experiences led to vehement objections to new projects—for example, in Forest Hills, New York (Glazer, 1972; Goodman, 1972)—as well as a search for alternative approaches to low-income housing programs.

This chapter is excerpted from an unpublished paper coauthored with Georges Vernez, "Social Aspects of Federal Low-Income Housing Programs" (Santa Monica, Calif.: Rand Corporation, 1973). The original research was supported by the U.S. Department of Housing and Urban Development; none of the conclusions or statements in this chapter is a reflection of the official position of that agency.

In spite of the controversy, information on the housing preferences of low-income families themselves is rare. A frequently cited study found that in one area of San Juan, Puerto Rico, 65 percent of those living in the slums preferred the slums, whereas about 75 percent of those living in a two- to four-story public housing project *disliked* living in the projects (Hollingshead and Rogler, 1963). An apparently important factor was the effect of public housing in isolating the nuclear family and imposing many official restrictions, such as prohibiting livestock, for project life. A similar survey of a southwestern city also found that a majority of black ghetto residents preferred not to live in public housing; however, this city was dominated by single-family housing units, and it was subsequently found that residents found multiunit dwellings more acceptable if more private space and an option to own existed (Williams, 1971).

However, in comparison to these results of attitude surveys, the waiting lists for new occupants of public housing projects have generally been long, and vacancy rates have been low (Joint Economic Committee, 1972, p. 576). The vacancy rates vary for different projects, of course, but to the extent that eligible families continue to apply for public housing units, this fact presumably reflects some preference for public housing relative to other housing.

Because of the continuing differences of opinion over the merits and desirability of public housing, two general questions are worth further examination:

- What has been the apparent impact of public housing on the social conditions of residents?
- What are the ways, in managing public housing units, that project life might be improved?

IMPACT OF PUBLIC HOUSING ON OTHER SOCIAL CONDITIONS

Most of the popular notions about public housing life have been derived from intensive participant-observation in projects that have been, unfortunately, the worst examples of public housing (Freedman, 1969, pp. 115–122). Rainwater's (1970) well-known study, for instance, took place in a housing project that consisted of 33 11-story buildings, with a high (over 20 percent) vacancy rate just preceding the time of study. Similar biases may be found in research on a midwestern housing project, in which the elevators were not designed to stop on every floor, the project accounted for the bulk of that city's public housing deficit, and the vacancy rate was 20 to 30 percent (Moore, 1969); and in research on Boston housing projects, deliberately chosen to reflect the worst of public housing conditions (Peattie, 1971). Despite these experiences, it is worth recalling Rainwater's own observation: "No matter what criticisms are made of public housing projects, there is no doubt that the structures themselves are infinitely preferable to slum housing" (Rainwater, 1966).

One of the few systematic surveys of the social impact of public housing was a longitudinal study conducted in Baltimore (Wilner et al., 1962). This study compared families in a public housing project with comparable families living outside public housing over a three-year period. The results were modest, but the public housing families showed better health in some illness categories, improved school attendance, and greater satisfaction with housing and neighborhood conditions; no differences were found in the other illness categories, family relations, school performance, or attitudes toward education, occupation, or homeownership. The results of this study, together with its exhaustive review of prior research, suggest that for most residents until 1960 public housing represented a positive experience, with distinct if modest social benefits.

Since that time research on the general impact of public housing has been limited primarily to the participant-observation studies previously cited (Moore, 1969; Peattie, 1971; Rainwater, 1966, 1967, 1970). These studies, focusing almost entirely on problem projects, have shown that certain housing projects can result in an inordinate concentration of social pathology. Projects dominated by families on welfare and with large numbers of children, especially in combination with high-rise architectural designs, can result in high rates of crime and illness. The same projects tend not to attract new applicants and thus have high vacancy rates, with life in the project appearing to be worse than life in the surrounding slum area. In addition, one study has shown that, by virtue of the site and architectural characteristics alone, project residents can become quite isolated from residents in the surrounding area, unless many of the project residents were originally drawn from that area (Kriesberg, 1968).

One of the few studies to examine public housing conditions in many projects simultaneously, however, has produced a slightly different picture. This study analyzed crime rates in public housing projects for the whole city of New York in 1967 (Fairley and Liechenstein, 1971). On the average, the crime rates were *lower* than the crime rates of the surrounding precinct; the rates were also *lower,* with the exception of robberies, than the citywide rates. The investigators further found that the project crime rates were most highly correlated with the crime rate of the surrounding precinct, and also positively correlated with the number of families and the number of broken families in the project, and negatively correlated with the income of project families.

These results may be unique to New York City, where public housing has possibly enjoyed better maintenance, greater public support, and greater police protection (the public housing authority has its own police force) than in other cities. In addition, there may be a methodological bias, in that much more crime may normally occur in the streets and in commercial areas than in residential areas, making the low public housing crime rates less surprising. Nevertheless, the results do suggest that the conclusions from individual participant-observer studies may not be representative of public housing projects in general.

In sum, except for problem projects, public housing may offer a better alternative to other types of housing. Residents may derive better housing opportunities, which in turn lead to improved social conditions in comparison to other ghetto housing. The clear exception to this pattern is the problem project, where for any number of reasons severe socially undesirable conditions are the result. A major policy issue is thus to avoid the creation of such problem projects. Are there managerial initiatives that can be taken in this regard? We shall now turn to the research bearing on this question.

MANAGEMENT OF PUBLIC HOUSING

The relevant managerial initiatives fall into three categories: *site selection, architectural design,* and *tenant selection.* These types of initiatives appear to determine the social conditions in public housing projects, and particularly whether a project will be successfully operated and attractive to prospective residents. In dealing with these initiatives, one potential problem, however, is that the needed policies may be the most politically unpalatable ones, from the point of view of both the public in general and public housing residents themselves.

Site Selection

The area in which a new project is located appears to have an important impact on the nature of the project. Not surprisingly, the site selection process has often been the focus of local controversy and thus the subject of major studies of local politics, especially in major cities such as Chicago (Meyerson and Banfield, 1955). There is also a considerable legal literature concerning site selection (Genung, 1971).

The major impact of site selection appears to be on the racial composition of a project (Freedman, 1969; Ledbetter, 1967; Peattie, 1971). The project's residents are likely to reflect the racial composition of the neighborhood in which the project is located, and because most urban areas are heavily segregated (Taeuber and Taeuber, 1970), the selection of a site generally makes the difference between a segregated or integrated public housing facility, and may ultimately have a strong bearing on the type of families that occupy the project.

In Newark, New Jersey, for instance, a project was built in a predominantly Italian neighborhood, and the housing authority attempted to give first preference to Italian residents who had been displaced by the project (Kaplan, 1963). That policy displeased the black community, which felt that black families had a greater need for new public housing. In the second year of operation greater priority was given to black families, but that displeased the Italians. Similar problems have been faced by housing authorities in other cities (Roshco, 1960). The main dilemma stems from three somewhat contradictory factors: (a) It is difficult to create a project whose racial and income composition does not reflect that of the surrounding neighborhood; (b) there are not many racially integrated neighborhoods in cities in general, much less ones willing to accept new public housing projects in their area; and (c) most community and political leaders will not support new public housing projects if there is a strong likelihood that they will become segregated facilities. Moreover, the dilemma persists in spite of the fact that there have been some notable successes in integrating families of different race and income in some projects (Boeschenstein, 1971).

A second issue related to site selection is the question of the size of a public housing project. Disenchantment with the social impact of large projects has created a preference for scatter-site housing. The presumption is that smaller projects will have less impact on the surrounding neighborhood, and hence be less obtrusive. Little research has been carried out on this topic, with a few documented experiences—such as New Yorkers' resistance to scatter-site housing in the early 1970s—thus receiving disproportionate attention. However, the limited experiences with scatter-site housing in Forest Hills, New York should not be misinterpreted: The proposed project involved 840 units in three buildings, a scale quite large by scatter-site standards (Glazer, 1972; Goodman, 1972).

Architectural Design

Public housing projects vary considerably in their design characteristics. For instance, some buildings are walk-ups, others are elevator buildings, and yet others have elevators that do not stop at every floor. As another example, the number of units per project and the number of rooms per unit also vary from project to project. In spite of the design variations, and in spite of the known effect of design on social interaction (the classic study, dealing with campus housing, is Festinger and Back, 1950), there has been only one notable study of the effects of public housing design on public housing life—that of Newman (1972).

A general conclusion from earlier research had been that large projects, though necessary for maintaining a certain level of density (and hence to provide the desired number of units), produced undesirable social consequences: vandalism, garbage and ill-kept hallways, elevator accidents, and general resident dissatisfaction (Freedman, 1969; Ledbetter, 1967; Yancey, 1971). Newman (1972), in his study of housing design, corroborated the general relationships and carried the research much further. He examined housing projects in New York City, comparing two neighboring projects similar in tenant composition and density, but different in that one was a high-rise and the other a low-rise.

The high-rise design produced many open spaces that fell outside of the area of residential surveillance: Building entrances were too far from the street and led to unprotected paths; building grounds were too extensive to allow activities to be closely seen from windows; the concept of superblocks led to reduced vigilance on the part of normal passersby on streets; building lobbies, corridors, stairways, and elevators served too many people and were not adequately cared for; and the high-rise itself meant that children playing outside were often beyond the visual and shouting distance of adults. As a result Newman found that high-rise buildings, even when matched for other characteristics with low-rise projects, produced a more socially undesirable environment, primarily gauged in terms of crime rates. Not surprisingly, public housing residents' own preferences for architectural design are consistent with Newman's conclusions (Committee on Housing Research and Development, 1971, 1972).

One of the major tradeoffs in constructing low-rise projects is the cost of maintenance. Allowance for adequate maintenance appears to be a critical element in successful public housing (Lowry, 1971). Research on the maintenance costs for public housing in New York City has shown, for example, that such costs increase 1 percent as project size (the total number of dwelling units per project) decreases by 10 percent (Rydell, 1970). Maintenance costs do, however, decrease as dwelling unit size decreases. In other words, although smaller projects appear to require higher expenditures for maintenance, the inclusion of smaller dwelling units in the project may offset this increase.

Tenant Selection

Until the early 1960s public housing authorities played a strong role in determining application priorities and evicting unruly families, and hence in controlling the demographic composition of projects. One investigator has described in some detail his own participant-observer experiences with a housing authority office, and how the housing official fulfilled the "gatekeeper" function often found in public bureaucracies (Deutcher, 1968).

The housing authority's role has traditionally been exercised through the use of three criteria regarding tenant composition. One important criterion used by housing managers has been the racial composition of the projects (Jahoda and West, 1951). The maintenance of an integrated project appears to require a white–black ratio in which whites are a clear majority (sixty to seventy percent). If a project has a lower proportion of white tenants, it is likely to become completely occupied by black families (Freedman, 1969, pp. 140–144; Silverman, 1965; Spiegel, 1960). However, the precise definition of the tipping point, whether applied to public housing or to changes in the racial composition of neighborhoods, has still not been systematically investigated, and the universality of the tipping phenomenon is still not known (Wolf, 1963).

A second criterion has been the family characteristics of the tenants. Here, "successful" projects are claimed to be those that are able to maintain large proportions of the *working poor* and low proportions of the *dependent poor,* the latter defined primarily as female-headed households on welfare rolls (Starr, 1971). This claim has led to some debate concerning "problem families" (Wood, 1957), and to the notion that the exclusion of such families is necessary to minimize social chaos in a project (e.g., Scobie, 1973; Starr, 1973). However, although many observers have noted the need to minimize the number of problem families, no research has: (a) defined the important characteristics of problem families, (b) suggested the appropriate mix, or (c) identified the consequences of having too many problem families (Friedman, 1967; McEntire, 1960, p. 330).

A third criterion has been family income. Here, housing officials have had to balance the need to serve the poorest families first against the need to minimize the budgetary deficit of the housing project. One problem that appears repeatedly is that, because of the eligibility limitations on income, families with rising incomes will eventually become ineligible for continued residence in a project, even though such families can provide a socially stabilizing effect and improve the project's financial ability to support more families with very low incomes (Abrams, 1965).

During the 1960s external changes gradually reduced the ability of housing officials to use these three traditional criteria (a broad survey of the socioeconomic characteristics of housing managers and their attitudes is found in Hartman and Levi, 1973). First, the demand for public housing rapidly increased among black families. This trend meant that a housing official either had to allow projects to become entirely black, or to leave a number of units unoccupied in anticipation of new applications from white families. This artificial maintenance of a significant number of vacancies raised public objections, and housing officials had to abandon the policy (Hill, 1966; Ledbetter, 1967). Civil rights legislation also prohibited such discrimination. Similarly, the demand for public housing increased among larger families, so that the smaller dwelling units suffered higher vacancy rates. In Pruitt-Igoe, for instance, Rainwater (1967) noted that, whereas the project's overall vacancy rate was around 20 percent, the vacancy rate for two-bedroom apartments was about 35 to 40 percent. Finally, the demand for public housing increased among very poor families. In 1955 the median net income of families admitted to public housing was 46.5 percent of the median income of all families in the United States; in 1961 it was less than 40 percent, and this gap widened in subsequent years (Schorr, 1968).

In sum, public housing managers do have some control over three important sets of policies, involving: site selection (for new projects), architectural design, and tenant selection. Successful projects appear to require a mix among tenant characteristics such as race, family characteristics, and income, but these and other considerations have become less important because of external changes in the 1960s. Moreover, there is a continual tradeoff between judicious public housing management, acting in the interest of a project as a whole, and social equity, involving discrimination against individual families (whether according to race, income, or family characteristics).

REFERENCES

Abrams, Charles. *The City Is the Frontier*. New York: Harper & Row, 1965.

Bauer, Catherine. "The Dreary Deadlock of Public Housing." *Architectural Forum* 106 (May 1957): 141–142.

Bellush, Jewel, and Hausknecht, Murray. "Public Housing: The Context of Failure." In *Urban Renewal: People, Policies, and Planning*, edited by Jewel Bellush and Murray Hausknecht. Garden City, N.Y.: Anchor Books, 1967, pp. 451–461.

Boeschenstein, Warren. "Design of Socially Mixed Housing." *Journal of the American Institute of Planners* 37 (September 1971): 311–318.

Committee on Housing Research and Development. *Activities and Attitudes of Public Housing Residents in Rockford, Illinois*. Champaign: University of Illinois, 1971.

Committee on Housing Research and Development. *Families in Public Housing*. Champaign: University of Illinois, 1972.

Deutcher, Irwin. "The Gatekeeper in Public Housing." In *Among the People*, edited by Irwin Deutcher and Elizabeth J. Thompson. New York: Basic Books, 1968, Ch. 3.

Fairley, William, and Liechenstein, Michael. *Improving Public Safety in Urban Apartment Dwellings: Security Concepts and Experimental Design for New York Housing Authority Buildings*. New York: New York City–Rand Institute, 1971.

Festinger, Leon S., and Back, Kurt. *Social Pressures in Informal Groups*. New York: Harper & Bros., 1950.

Freedman, Leonard. *Public Housing: The Politics of Poverty*. New York: Holt, Rinehart & Winston, 1969.

Friedman, L. M. "Government and Slum Housing: Some General Considerations." *Law and Contemporary Society* 1967, *32*, 357–360.

Genung, George R. "Public Housing: Success or Failure?" *George Washington Law Review* 1971, *39*, 734–763.

Glazer, Nathan. "When the Melting Pot Doesn't Melt." *New York Times Magazine*, 2 January 1972.

Goodman, Walter. "The Battle of Forest Hills: Who's Ahead?" *New York Times Magazine*, 20 February 1972.

Hartman, Chester W., and Levi, Margaret. "Public Housing Managers: An Appraisal." *Journal of the American Institute of Planners* 1973, *38*, 125–137.

Hill, Herbert. "Demographic Change and Racial Ghettos: The Crisis of American Cities." *Journal of Urban Law* 1966, *44*, 231–285.

Hollingshead, August, and Rogler, L. H. "Attitudes towards Slums and Public Housing in Puerto Rico." In *The Urban Condition*, edited by Leonard H. Duhl. New York: Simon & Schuster, 1963, pp. 229–245.

Jahoda, Marie, and West, Patricia Salter. "Race Relations in Public Housing." *Journal of Social Issues* 1951, *7*, 132–139.

Joint Economic Committee, U.S. Congress. *The Economics of Federal Subsidy Programs*. Pt. 5, 92nd Congress, 2d Session, 9 October 1972.

Kaplan, Harold. *Urban Renewal Politics: Slum Clearance in Newark*. New York: Columbia University Press, 1963.

Kriesberg, Louis. "Neighborhood Setting and the Isolation of Public Housing Tenants." *Journal of the American Institute of Planners* 1968, *34*, 43–49.

Ledbetter, William H., Jr. "Public Housing: A Social Experiment Seeks Acceptance." *Law and Contemporary Problems* 1967, *32*, 490–527.

Lowry, Ira S. *Housing Assistance for Low-Income Urban Families: A Fresh Approach*. Santa Monica, Calif.: Rand Corporation, 1971.

McEntire, David. *Residence and Race*. Berkeley: University of California Press, 1960.

Meyerson, Martin, and Banfield, Edward C. *Politics, Planning, and the Public Interest: The Case of Public Housing in Chicago*. Glencoe, Ill.: Free Press, 1955.

Moore, William, Jr. *The Vertical Ghetto: Everyday Life in an Urban Project*. New York: Random House, 1969.

Newman, Oscar. *Defensible Space*. New York: Macmillan, 1972.

Peattie, Lisa. "Public Housing: Urban Slums under Public Managements." In *Race, Change, and Urban Society*, edited by Peter Orleans and William Ellis. Beverly Hills, Calif.: Sage Publications, 1971, pp. 285–310.

Rainwater, Lee. "Fear and House-as-Haven in the Lower Class." *Journal of the American Institute of Planners* 1966, *32*, 23–30.

Rainwater, Lee. "The Lessons of Pruitt-Igoe." *The Public Interest* 1967, No. 8, 116–126.

Rainwater, Lee. *Behind Ghetto Walls*. Chicago: Aldine, 1970.

Roshco, Bernard. "The Integration Problem and Public Housing." *The New Leader*, 4–11 July 1960, pp. 10–13.

Rydell, C. Peter. *Factors Affecting Maintenance and Operating Costs in Federal Public Housing Projects*. New York: New York City–Rand Institute, 1970.

Schorr, Alvin L. *Slums and Social Insecurity*. Washington, D.C.: U.S. Department of Health, Education and Welfare, 1963.

Schorr, Alvin L. "Housing the Poor." In *Power, Poverty, and Urban Policy*, edited by Warner Bloomberg, Jr. and Henry J. Schmandt. Beverly Hills, Calif.: Sage Publications, 1968, pp. 115–150.

Scobie, Richard S. "Problem Families and Public Housing." *The Public Interest* 1973, No. 31, 126–129.

Silverman, Abner D. "The Low Rent Housing Program and the Great Society." Address to the annual meeting of the Pennsylvania Association of Housing and Redevelopment Authorities, January 1965.

Spiegel, Hans B. C. "Tenants' Intergroup Attitudes in a Public Housing Project with Declining White Population." *Phylon* 1960, *21*, 30–35.

Starr, Robert. "Which of the Poor Shall Live in Public Housing?" *The Public Interest* 1971, No. 23, 116–124.

Starr, Robert. "A Reply" (to Scobie). *The Public Interest* 1973, No. 31, 130–134.

Taeuber, Karl, and Taeuber, Alma. *Negroes in Cities*. Chicago: Aldine, 1970.

Williams, J. Allen, Jr. "The Multifamily Housing Solution and Housing Type Preferences." *Social Science Quarterly* 1971, *52*, 543–559.

Wilner, Daniel M. et al. *The Housing Environment and Family Life*. Baltimore: Johns Hopkins University Press, 1962.

Wilson, Andrew. "St. Louis Set to Shut Big Housing Project as Colossal Failure." *Washington Post*, 17 June 1973.

Wolf, Eleanor P. "The Tipping Point in Racially Changing Neighborhoods." *Journal of the American Institute of Planners* 1963, *29*, 217–222.

Wood, Elizabeth. *The Small Hard Core: The Housing of Problem Families in New York City*. New York: Citizens' Housing and Planning Council of New York, Inc., 1957.

Yancey, William L. "Architecture, Interaction and Social Control: The Case of a Large-Scale Public Housing Project." *Environment and Behavior* 1971, *3*, 3–22.

8
The Neighborhood Library as an Information and Referral Center

THE TRADITIONAL INFORMATION NETWORK

Most neighborhoods have an informal network that transmits information within the neighborhood. The traditional network consists of the people in the neighborhood: (1) the residents themselves; (2) those—such as the druggist, the apartment house superintendent, the retail store proprietor, or the locally elected government official—whose neighborhood roles bring them into frequent contact with many of the residents; and (3) local institutions such as the settlement house, the church, and the school, whose primary activities are neighborhood oriented.

In most residential neighborhoods, this informal network plays a significant role in maintaining the neighborhood. The network can help acquaint residents with their neighbors and with various neighborhood resources. The network also acts to socialize newcomers to the neighborhood, informally teaching new inmigrants, for instance, about the neighborhood *norms* that help define desirable and undesirable behavior. The sociologist Suzanne

---

This chapter is based on excerpts from Robert K. Yin, Brigitte L. Kenney, and Karen A. Possner, *Neighborhood Communication Centers* (Santa Monica, Calif.: Rand Corporation, 1974), pp. 4–24. The original research was supported by the John and Mary R. Markle Foundation, although this chapter is in no way a reflection of that organization's official policy.

THE NEIGHBORHOOD LIBRARY

Keller perceptively noted that being a good neighbor is not necessarily a matter of specific behaviors, but is one of conforming to the norms (or expectations) of each local area. Thus the same behavior—for example, to act reservedly toward one's neighbors—can be the characteristic expectation in one neighborhood but unacceptable in another (Keller, 1968, pp. 19-22). The function of the informal network may also become more important as the rate of residential turnover increases. If a neighborhood is to maintain its cohesiveness in spite of high residential mobility, the informal network must provide a considerable amount of information in a short period of time (Fellin and Litwak, 1963).

Challenges to the Traditional Network

Two dramatic social trends during the 1950s and 1960s conspired to reduce the effectiveness of information networks in many neighborhoods. The first was a rapid increase in population turnover, marked by a massive movement of whites into the suburbs and a subsequent rise in the number of low-income blacks and ethnic minorities in the central city. For central-city neighborhoods this change meant that new urban residents, with different life styles and needs, had moved into the area in large numbers. These people often required information to deal with neighborhood services and the survival problems of urban life, including advice on personal health care, homemaking, and consumer activities. At the same time, the very foundations of the traditional information network crumbled in these neighborhoods as local stores and churches closed and as high costs made elevator operators, doormen, and other neighborhood artisans obsolete.

The second trend was the growth and specialization of public service bureaucracies. Although the increase of public programs meant higher levels of service for residents, the bureaucratic size and specialization of these programs created a new burden for the already taxed information network: A resident could benefit from the expanded public services only if he knew of their existence; knew the eligibility rules; knew where and when to go to use the service; and could cope with the forms, impersonal relations, and other bureaucratic obstacles of public agencies. For all of these tasks, information was a necessary but usually inadequate commodity.

New Neighborhood Institutions

To compensate for the decline of the traditional network, municipalities began to develop new neighborhood institutions that specialized in service information.[1] Several programs were begun with federal support. In 1966 President Lyndon Johnson initiated the Neighborhood Pilot Centers program with the hope of providing a neighborhood center for every urban ghetto in the country. These centers were to coordinate the programs of other federal agencies in a given neighborhood. In theory, the centers would provide one-stop services, thereby reducing the need for specialized information that might otherwise be required for using the services (Hallman, 1970, pp. 138–162). In practice, the neighborhood pilot centers failed to extend beyond fourteen cities, as the coordination of services for several federal agencies proved an insurmountable task (Abt Associates, 1969).

A second type of compensatory institution emerged in relation to riot prevention and rumor control. Several municipal governments initiated *rumor control centers* in 1967 following the outbreak of rioting. A subsequent study of thirty such centers found that they were never more than marginal or "intermittent" institutions, generally staffed on a part-time basis and inactive during tranquil periods (Ponting, 1973). The study also pointed out a major flaw in the formal communications role of these centers: They operated from within city government and hence had difficulty establishing credibility among neighborhood residents; yet the centers were not well connected with the appropriate governmental agencies such as the police department either.

Riot prevention was also the main impetus for a third type of institution, the Neighborhood Action Task Force. The task forces assumed a more diverse array of functions than rumor control centers and hence evolved as a separate institution. Initially described in the *Report of the National Advisory Commission on Civil Disorders* (1968), the task forces were to be located in neighborhood storefront offices, each the responsibility of a prominent city official, and were to emphasize communications of all sorts, including riot prevention information, grievances concerning local services, and information about neighborhood events. Other than these information or "helping" services, the task forces provided little service. In New York, Milwaukee, and other cities, task force offices operated in many neighborhoods for several years. However, these offices have been linked to specific political figures and have not necessarily continued after an incumbent has left office.

In recent years two other innovations have been explored in an effort to serve neighborhood information needs: the *little city hall* and the *multi-service center* (Grollman, 1971; Yin, Hearn, and Shapiro, 1974). The little city hall goes beyond the task force by providing more information to the

---

[1]Although there are many new types of neighborhood institutions (e.g., health centers, community development corporations, and Head Start centers), this discussion focuses on those institutions whose main commodity is information, particularly in providing help or assistance for using other services. For a general description of neighborhood service institutions, both past and present, see Hallman (1973) and Post (1973).

citizen about city services. In some cases, routine functions (filing forms for licenses) can also be carried out in the little city hall (National League of Cities, 1973; Nordlinger, 1972). The little city hall deals mainly with information, but the multiservice center may provide substantive services as well. The multiservice center may be part of some federal program (e.g., the Model Cities and Neighborhood Facilities programs of the Department of Housing and Urban Development), and its range and quality of services may vary considerably from center to center. In spite of these variations, information and referral services tend to be the dominant activity of both types of facilities.

The degree of success of these new neighborhood institutions has not been established. There has generally been inconclusive evidence concerning the costs of these innovations, their permanence, and the amount of residential satisfaction they produce. And in general, how one assesses either the amount or kind of information needed is a difficult question. The National Commission on Urban Problems, after its series of hearings, suggested that cities build neighborhood information and referral centers "to orient low-income residents and migrants to the opportunities, demands, and responsibilities of an urban society" (1968, p. 353). The commission recommended that these centers provide such information as a family budgeting course, hints on housekeeping techniques, and tenant education. Recent studies have also focused on the information needs of disadvantaged urban populations such as the elderly, the poor, the handicapped, the undereducated, and the non–English speaking. The results have been as one might expect: These people do not see their problems in terms of information needs, are not active information seekers, rely more on informal than formal channels, and are locked into deficient information networks (Bourne, 1973; Childers, 1975; Warner et al., 1974). The urban poor in particular make only marginal use of existing information sources (Greenberg and Dervin, 1970), and urban blacks have more difficulty making contact with government services than urban whites, even when one controls for differences in income (Jacob, 1972).

The emergence of new neighborhood institutions raises a major policy issue. If municipal governments find that neighborhoods need better information systems, either to replace or to complement the traditional information network, two basic strategies are feasible:

- Promote the development of new neighborhood institutions, such as pilot centers, task forces, little city halls, and multiservice centers.
- Utilize existing neighborhood institutions, such as schools, community centers, and branch libraries.

The first strategy is ultimately the more costly of the two. The most comprehensive system of little city halls, for instance, involves fourteen facilities throughout the city of Boston at an annual cost of over $1.2 million (Nordlinger, 1972). To the extent that existing facilities with *their current staffs* can serve as neighborhood information centers, cities may be able to provide better information services with a more modest outlay of new expenditures. One obvious existing facility, found in virtually every urban neighborhood, is the branch library.

THE BRANCH LIBRARY

On the surface, the library appears to have many of the desirable qualities of a local information and referral center. These include: (1) potentially relevant staff expertise, (2) accessibility to residents, (3) service to all residents, and (4) linkage through the library system to resources beyond the scope of the immediate neighborhood.

The potentially relevant expertise stems from the fact that libraries, unlike most other neighborhood institutions, specialize in providing information. Librarians are trained in the use of reference works and in referring inquiries to the appropriate source for answering specific questions.

Second, the library is easily accessible to residents in both a spatial and a temporal sense. Spatially, although few cities have built enough libraries so that all residents are within the half-mile walking distance that has been the traditional distance used by city planners for determining access to neighborhood facilities (Grundt, 1968), the majority of residents in older cities can usually walk to a branch library. That a neighborhood network of branches already exists can be seen in Table 11, which lists the number of branch libraries in the twenty largest central cities. The branches are generally located in residential neighborhoods and serve an average population of 50,000 people. In terms of temporal accessibility, the library has longer hours of service, including evenings and weekends, than any other public service or private welfare agency, except for emergency services.

Third, the library has the explicit charter of serving all residents in a community, covering all age, income, and occupational groups. Although library users tend to come from certain subgroups of the population (e.g., students), the library is open to all residents.

Finally, even though the branch library operates within a specific neighborhood, all branches are part of a citywide system. Individual branches are not limited to the information resources of a single neighborhood, but can draw from a broader resource base. If the system has adequate interbranch communication, the individual branch librarian can benefit from the experience of the entire library system.

Thus, by these four criteria, the existing branch library offers a potentially

Table 11
Number of Branch Libraries in Twenty Largest Central Cities

City	1970 census population (000)	Number of branch libraries[a]	Population per branch (000)
New York	7,895	194	40.7
Chicago	3,367	63	53.4
Los Angeles	2,816	62	45.4
Philadelphia	1,949	42	46.4
Detroit	1,511	29	52.1
Houston	1,233	18	68.5
Baltimore	906	25	36.2
Dallas	844	12	70.3
Washington, D.C.	757	20	37.9
Cleveland	751	37	20.3
Indianapolis	745	21	35.5
Milwaukee	717	14	51.2
San Francisco	716	29	24.7
San Diego	687	20	34.4
San Antonio	654	9	72.7
Boston	641	28	22.9
Memphis	624	18	34.7
St. Louis	622	20	31.1
New Orleans	593	11	53.9
Phoenix	582	6	97.0

[a] Library Surveys Branch, U.S. Office of Education, *Statistics of Public Libraries Serving Areas with At Least 25,000 Inhabitants, 1968* (Washington, D.C.: U.S. Government Printing Office, 1970).

attractive facility for developing a local information and referral service. Urban libraries themselves, however, have already been undergoing certain changes that are worth reviewing.

The Urban Public Library at the Crossroads

The suggestion of an addition of an information and referral service within the library comes at a time when the role of many urban libraries has been declining, especially in older cities. An examination of service activity patterns, in fact, suggests that if libraries are to continue to serve the public, they must diversify and adopt new services.

Although there are no readily acceptable measures of library utilization, one measure that has been traditionally used has been the number of transactions involving library materials.[2] The older central cities, themselves sites of declining populations, have tended to suffer the sharpest declines in transactions. Table 12 divides all cities of over 400,000 population into three population groups. Within each of the three groups, the cities are ranked by the order of population increase from 1960 to 1970. Cities with the greatest increases have been those with significant annexations—Jacksonville, Nashville-Davidson (Tennessee), and Indianapolis. The cities with the greatest declines are the older ones such as St. Louis, Pittsburgh, Cleveland, Buffalo, and Detroit.

Along with the data on overall population changes for each city, Table 12 also shows (1) the percent change in library transactions from 1962 to 1971, and (2) the amount of municipal government support for the public library, divided by the number of transactions. Not surprisingly, there is a tendency for cities with declining populations also to show declines in transactions, creating a situation in 1971 in which the same cities were also paying more in municipal government support per transaction. Detroit, for instance, showed a decline of 41.4 percent in library transactions and a $2.57 rate per transaction, which is the highest rate of any of these cities. Cities in a similar situation are Boston, Cleveland, and Buffalo, and to a lesser extent Baltimore, San Francisco, New York, and Chicago.

New Alternatives for the Urban Library

The declining importance of public librarianship and the declining rates of library activity have already attracted considerable attention. Many people have proposed new plans for changing the role of the library, and some of these options have already been tried. In general, they have been aimed at expanding the user base of the library. Most urban library surveys have shown that students and people of middle-income backgrounds have been the main library patrons. The middle-class nature of library users was noted as early as 1949 in Berelson's (1949) famous study of the public library, and this pattern has become even more accentuated since then.[3] Because the income distribution of the central-city population has changed, and because schools themselves have developed better library facilities, the pool of the traditional

---

[2]This measure obviously leaves much to be desired, as it does not account for in-library use, reference activities, or the value of the library service to its clients. The measure has been the subject of much controversy, and major efforts are now under way to develop more effective measures. See Hamberg et al. (1969), Goddard (1970), Crowley and Childers (1971), and DeProspo et al. (1974).

[3]Similar results, based on a survey of 306 libraries, are reported in Martin (1972). For examples of local surveys, see Bundy (1968), Coughlin et al. (1972), and Newhouse and Alexander (1972).

Table 12
Public Library Activity in Central Cities over 400,000 Population

Population of central city	Percent population change, 1960–1979	Library activity	
		Percent change in library transactions, 1962–1971	Municipal government support divided by transactions, 1971
Over 800,000			
Houston	31.4	94.2	$ .81
Dallas	24.1	57.6	1.01
Los Angeles	14.7	6.2	.81
New York	1.5	−13.0	1.39
Philadelphia	−2.7	−6.9	1.31
Baltimore	−3.5	−29.0	1.58
Chicago	−5.2	−11.1	1.30
Detroit	−9.5	−41.4	2.57
600,000–799,999			
Indianapolis[a]	56.5	34.1	.89
Memphis	25.3	−37.1	.82
San Diego	21.6	119.5	.67
San Antonio	11.2	67.5	.57
Washington, D.C.	−.9	4.5	2.07
Milwaukee	−3.2	2.5	1.24
San Francisco	−3.3	−8.5	1.45
Boston	−8.0	−25.4	2.51
Cleveland	−14.3	−40.4	1.73
St. Louis	−17.1	−10.0	.95
400,000–599,999			
Jacksonville	163.2	48.2	.89
Nashville-Davidson	162.0	53.6	.89
San Jose	118.6	45.7	.75
Phoenix	32.6	65.9	.77
Atlanta	28.4	8.7	1.08
Columbus	14.6	16.3	.90
Kansas City, MO	6.5	−27.6	.85
Denver	4.3	8.3	1.11
Seattle	−4.7	2.5	.93
New Orleans	−5.6	1.1	1.17
Cincinnati	−9.9	7.6	.89
Minneapolis	−10.1	−1.8	1.19
Buffalo	−13.1	−54.3	1.46
Pittsburgh	−13.9	31.9	1.68

Source: Library Surveys Branch, U.S. Office of Education, *Statistics of Public Library Systems Serving Populations of 35,000 or Above, 1962* (Washington, D.C.: U.S. Government Printing Office, 1965). The 1971 data were unpublished and were obtained directly from the Library Surveys Branch.
[a]The library figures are for 1962–1968 and 1968.

user population for public libraries has diminished, and most of the new options for expanding library use have attempted to attract new types of users.

One option promoted by a small minority has been for the library to develop into an elitist institution, serving the serious reader (Banfield, 1973). According to the logic underlying this option, school libraries are increasingly able to serve the student; paperback books and rental libraries are increasingly able to serve the light readers; and the low-income urban families simply do not have any use for the traditional library. In fact, the poverty of the low-income groups in the city

> consists not so much of a lack of income (although they lack that) as of a lack of the cultural standards and of the motivations, including the desire for self-improvement and for "getting ahead," that would make them more productive and hence better paid. (Banfield, 1973).

By this reasoning, the library, says Banfield, should aim to serve the serious reader by providing soundproof cubicles, purchasing and maintaining a large supply of books for such readers, and offering the services of a personal shopper to take book orders on the telephone and even arrange for home deliveries.

The most prevalent options regarding the increased use of the public library, however, have really been the opposite of this elitist course. Branch libraries in central-city neighborhoods have felt the effects of changing neighborhood populations, usually from middle- to low-income and from white to black, and have seen their challenge as trying to serve the new neighborhood populations (e.g., Nyren, 1970). This challenge is seen as parallel to the original purpose of the public library system, which was to serve the needs of non-English-speaking urban immigrants during the early twentieth century. The subsequent innovations in library services have been twofold: those dealing with improved dissemination of books and other multimedia materials, and those dealing with the development of new types of services, such as information and referral.

Improved Dissemination of Books and Related Materials

The focus on new ways of disseminating books and related media has been the theme of several federally funded projects. Typically, individual branch libraries have explored some of the following innovations:

- Expanding the use of paperback books, including a no-checkout-needed policy
- Providing mobile services, or locating satellite libraries in highly visible, storefront facilities

- Hiring library aides who are neighborhood residents
- Using the appropriate mass media to publicize library services
- Developing new reading programs for preschool children (in conjunction with Head Start programs) and for slow-reading adults
- Providing services to staff of service agencies and other neighborhood institutions
- Developing participatory, multimedia activities such as the use of art and music, emphasis on the crafts, and the presentation of films and guest speakers

The common goals have been to change the traditional image of the library, to increase the accessibility of the library and its materials, and to emphasize activities in which users can participate.

These projects have generally followed an *a priori* assumption held by library staff regarding the need for books. Although many of the assumed needs appear to have been reaffirmed by some studies (e.g., Clift, 1969), and although the changes have received some favorable publicity (e.g., "As Libraries Go All Out," 1973), there has been some criticism of this approach because of the predisposition of librarians to think in terms of the dissemination of books rather than of information. Lipsman (1972), for instance, surveyed more than 3,000 residents in fifteen cities that had library programs aimed at serving low-income residents. Although she found the programs to be fulfilling some needs, the libraries had generally made little attempt to assess residents' needs beforehand, and the programs gave little emphasis to the dissemination of information about such community matters as: opportunities for employment, education, and housing; application procedures for social service programs; and references to existing regulations on local building codes, tenants' rights, or related legislative matters.

Information and Referral Services

A second approach to improving library services, and the one most relevant to a neighborhood's networking needs, is to develop new information and referral (I&R) services within the existing library system. *Information and referral service connotes an active, intervening activity, in which the intervenor may serve, if necessary, as an advocate for the individual seeking assistance.* This service differs from the traditional library reference service, which consists of directing inquiries to reference works, bibliographies, directories, and other materials but rarely includes the communications function of putting an inquirer in touch with people from other agencies. As previously noted, the need for information services has already helped produce such new neighborhood institutions as little city halls and multiservice centers. What will be traced here is the implementation of plans to provide such services within the public library.

One of the important models for an information and referral service is the Citizens' Advice Bureau (CAB) in Britain. These offices were opened during World War II to deal with war-related community problems, but the operations have continued to the present and include over 450 outlets that receive more than one million inquiries per year. Kahn (1966, pp. 16–36) helped publicize the CABs in a study in the mid-1960s, describing the functions of the offices and analyzing the nature of the inquiries. The offices provide information, advice, referral, assistance, and emotional support; they do not deal, however, with emergency calls and make no attempt to follow up the initial inquiries. The vast majority of inquiries cover issues related to family needs (e.g., finding day-care assistance or making a will); information about civil, local, and national events; and legal problems related to property and land. Kahn compares the British experience with a parallel operation in New York City, and he recommends a design for a national network of neighborhood information centers in the United States (pp. 55–59, 74–97).

Although no national network has been considered, the last few years have seen the initiation of several local information and referral projects, both within and outside the library system (Bolch et al., 1972). Among those outside the system, one statewide project, the Wisconsin Information Service, has operated since 1972, with fourteen centers serving the information needs of senior citizens on a county basis (Long, 1973). The Wisconsin Information Service is operated by the state social services department, with financial support from the U.S. Department of Health, Education and Welfare (predecessor to Health and Human Services). The service involves a resource file on available services, the provision of information to inquirers, the arrangement of appointments with an agency on the inquirer's behalf (occasionally providing escort service for the inquirer's trip to the agency), and outreach programs publicizing the availability of various services and their eligibility requirements. Other projects were begun as part of the neighborhood service centers supported by the U.S. Office of Economic Opportunity. Even before the eventual reductions in support of national antipoverty programs, however, the information and referral activities appeared to have encountered major difficulties. According to one critic the activities were based more on advocacy on behalf of the inquirer than on expertise about the appropriate referral, and hence never established a credible, full range of services (Kopecky, 1972).

Within the library system, there have also been several innovations, with a few notable false starts. An ambitious project, for instance, was begun in the central library of Baltimore's public library system in collaboration with members of a nearby school of library science. The center suffered through

Table 13
Number and Nature of Inquiries for Neighborhood Information Center Project, First Five Months of Operation (1973)

City	Number of inquiries	Dominant subject matter
Atlanta	510	Employment General reference services
Cleveland	670	Employment Food stamps and welfare services
Detroit	478	Legal aid and consumer information Sanitation Public health
Houston	652	Employment General reference services Food stamps and welfare services
New York (Queens Borough)	439	General reference services

a series of staffing and funding problems, however, and eventually closed (Donohue, 1972; Donohue and Kochen, 1974). The most innovative series of projects within the library system began in 1972, when five major library systems formed a consortium to administer neighborhood information centers in five cities: Atlanta, Cleveland, Detroit, Houston, and New York City (Queens Borough). The overall project, known as the Neighborhood Information Center project, was initially coordinated by the Cleveland Public Library, and has been supported by the United States Office of Education (under the Higher Education Act of 1965, Title II). Each city developed its own version of information and referral services, and all began operating in at least one or two branch libraries by early 1973 (Turick, 1973). Table 13 shows the number of inquiries and their dominant subject matter for the first five months of operation of this project. The services are similar to the other information and referral services already discussed, but each city has had different operational experiences. The significance of the Neighborhood Information Center project, besides the initiation of five information and referral services, is that it is one of the few occasions on which different municipal library systems in different regions of the country have collaborated on a single coordinated project.

The use of libraries to provide information and referral services is important for two reasons. First, it means that neighborhood information needs may indeed be adequately served through an existing institution rather than through a new institution. Second, the information and referral activity may eventually help to increase the overall use of the urban branch library and thereby enhance the justification for its continued support.

REFERENCES

Abt Associates. *A Study of Neighborhood Pilot Center Programs.* Cambridge, Mass.: Abt Associates, 1969.

"As Libraries Go All Out to Shed a Stodgy Image." *U.S. News and World Report,* 24, December 1973.

Banfield, Edward C. "Some Alternatives for the Public Library." In *The Metropolitan Library,* edited by Ralph W. Conant and Kathleen Molz. Cambridge, Mass.: MIT Press, 1973, pp. 89–100.

Berelson, Bernard. *The Library's Public.* New York: Columbia University Press, 1949.

Bolch, Eleanor et. al. *Information and Referral Services: An Annotated Bibliography.* Minneapolis: Institute for Interdisciplinary Studies, 1972.

Bourne, Charles P. "Preliminary Investigation of Present and Potential Library and Information Service Needs." Paper prepared for the U.S. National Commission on Libraries and Information Services, Washington, DC, February 1973.

Bundy, Mary Lee. *Metropolitan Public Library Users.* College Park, Md.: School of Library and Information Services, University of Maryland, 1968.

Childers, Thomas. *Knowledge/Information Needs of the Disadvantaged.* Metuchen, NJ: Scarecrow Press, 1975.

Clift, Virgil A. "A Study of the Library Services for the Disadvantaged in Buffalo, Rochester, and Syracuse." School of Education, New York University, June 1969.

Coughlin, Robert E. et al. *Urban Analysis for Branch Library System Planning.* Westport, Conn.: Greenwood Press, 1972.

Crowley, Terence, and Childers, Thomas. *Information Service in Public Libraries: Two Studies.* Metuchen, NJ: Scarecrow Press, 1971.

DeProspo, Ernest R. et al. *Performance Measures for Public Libraries.* Chicago: American Library Association, 1974.

Donohue, C., and Kochen, Manfred. *Information for the Community.* Chicago: American Library Association, 1974.

Donohue, Joseph C. "Planning for a Community Information Center." *Library Journal* 1972, 97, 3284–3288.

Fellin, Phillip, and Litwak, Eugene. "Neighborhood Cohesion under Conditions of Mobility." *American Sociological Review* 1963, 28, 364–376.

Goddard, Haynes C. "A Study in the Theory and Measurement of Benefits and Costs in the Public Library." PhD. dissertation, Department of Economics, Indiana University, 1970.

Greenberg, Bradley S., and Dervin, Brenda. *Use of the Mass Media by the Urban Poor.* New York: Praeger, 1970.

Grollman, Judith. "Decentralization of Municipal Services." *Urban Data Service Reports* 3 (February 1971): 1–9.

Grundt, Leonard. *Efficient Patterns for Adequate Library Services in a Large City: A Survey of Boston.* Urbana, Ill.: University of Illinois Graduate School of Library Science, 1968.

Hallman, Howard W. *Neighborhood Control of Public Programs.* New York: Praeger, 1970.

Hallman, Howard W. "The Neighborhood as an Organizational Unit: A Historical Perspective," In *Neighborhood Control in the 1970s,* edited by George Frederickson. New York: Chandler, 1973, pp. 7–16.

Hamberg, Morris et al. "A System Analysis of the Library and Information Science Statistical Data System." Philadelphia: Wharton School, University of Pennsylvania, 1969.

Jacob, Herbert. "Contact with Government Agencies." *Midwest Journal of Political Science* 1972, *16*, 123–146.

Kahn, Alfred J. *Neighborhood Information Centers: A Study and Some Proposals*. New York: Columbia University School of Social Work, 1966.

Keller, Suzanne. *The Urban Neighborhood*. New York: Random House, 1968.

Kopecky, Frank J. "Office of Economic Opportunity Community Centers: A Critical Analysis." In *Libraries and Neighborhood Information Centers*, edited by Carol L. Kronus and Linda Crowe. Urbana, Ill.: University of Illinois Graduate School of Library Science, 1972, pp. 61–72.

Lipsman, Claire. *The Disadvantaged and Library Effectiveness*. Chicago: American Library Association, 1972.

Long, Nicholas. "Wisconsin Information Service: An I&R Network." *RQ* 12 (Summer 1973): 356–359.

Martin, Allie Beth. *A Strategy for Public Library Change*. Chicago: American Library Association, 1972.

National Commission on Urban Problems. *Building the American City*. Washington, D.C.: U.S. Government Printing Office, 1968.

National League of Cities/US Conference on Mayors. *Little City Halls*. Washington, DC: 1973.

Newhouse, Joseph P., and Alexander, Arthur J. *An Economic Analysis of Public Library Services*. Santa Monica, Calif.: Rand Corporation, 1972.

Nordlinger, Eric. *Decentralizing the City: A Study of Boston's Little City Halls*. Cambridge, Mass.: MIT Press, 1972.

Nyren, Dorothy, ed. *Community Service: Innovations in Outreach at the Brooklyn Public Library*. Chicago: American Library Association, 1970.

Ponting, J. Rick. "Rumor Control Centers." *American Behavioral Scientist* 16 (January–February 1973): 391–401.

Post, Joyce. "Background Reading on Total Community Service." In *Total Community Library Service* edited by Guy Garrison. Chicago: American Library Association, 1973, pp. 98–121.

Report of the National Advisory Commission on Civil Disorders. New York: Bantam Books, 1968.

Turick, Dorothy A., ed. "The Neighborhood Information Center." *RQ* 12 (Summer 1973): 341–363.

Warner, Edward S. et al. *Information Needs of Urban Residents*. Regional Planning Council and Westat, Inc., 1974.

Yin, Robert K., Hearn, Robert W., Shapiro, Paula. "Administrative Decentralization of Municipal Services." *Policy Sciences* 1974, *5*, 57–70.

III
Research Initiatives

Research investigations have themselves become a part of the American neighborhood scene. In most cases the purpose of the research has been to produce new ideas for improving neighborhood life. The research can inquire into social processes, analyze the pattern of municipal services, or evaluate specific activities. Whatever the case, the amount and variety of neighborhood research have increased substantially over the past decade.

Nevertheless, researchers have usually found neighborhoods difficult subjects to study. The problems range from defining a neighborhood to developing consistent measures of neighborhood activity. The vulnerability of the craft is reflected by the fact that some of the most important pieces of neighborhood "research" have, in fact, not been done by formally trained researchers. Thus the insights derived from Jane Jacobs's ideas about urban neighborhoods have been invaluable even though Jacobs's training was in journalism and not social science.

But if journalism and nonresearch crafts can already contribute so much, cannot social science be expected to do even better? That is the challenge posed to contemporary research investigators, and it is the general topic of the final four chapters of this volume. Each chapter attempts to suggest ways in which the traditional research constraints can be alleviated—even while preserving rigor and methodological quality. The overall purpose of these chapters is to show that improvements in the research craft are indeed possible, and that such improvements can in turn lead to better ideas for improving neighborhoods.

Chapter 9 begins by establishing the basic ground for conducting research: that the search must be for an understanding of neighborhood "facts." The chapter discusses some of the obstacles to this quest, but suggests that not all of them are insurmountable.

Chapter 10 describes a comprehensive experience in applying participant-observation to the study of neighborhood *policy*. This particular field method is shown to have both qualitative and quantitative possibilities in addressing many of the common problems of urban neighborhoods.

Similarly, Chapter 11 provides an illustration of the use of urban and neighborhood indicators—that is, proxy measures for important social phenomena that cannot be measured directly. In this illustration the pattern of urban fire alarms is analyzed and shown, among other things, to be sensitive to important neighborhood conditions. To any municipal official wanting a neighborhood indicator system, continued monitoring of fire alarm patterns would be a good start.

Finally, Chapter 12 addresses a chronic problem in neighborhood research—the inability to conduct satisfactory evaluations of neighborhood programs. The chapter shows how such programs actually pose special problems for evaluators, unlike what might be found in education, health, and income supplement programs. In fact, neighborhood programs cannot be evaluated with the traditional evaluation designs that may work satisfactorily with these other topics. The chapter indicates why that is the case and suggests some alternatives.

Overall, Part III attempts to broaden the reader's notion of how neighborhoods can be studied. It is hoped that future research will not only be more diverse but also more responsive to the needs for information, whether these are the needs of residents or of policy makers. In this way research initiatives can also improve American neighborhoods, thus forming an important supplement to citizen and government initiatives.

9
Neighborhood Fact-Gathering
HOW CAN WE STUDY NEIGHBORHOODS BETTER?

THE NEIGHBORHOOD AS A TARGET OF RESEARCH

No set of facts is as elusive as neighborhood facts. For the researcher who analyzes census data, one set of conclusions appears to emerge. For the researcher who talks to longtime residents, there may be a different picture. And finally, for the researcher who lives in the neighborhood for a few years, yet another set of facts may appear most pertinent. Thus what most researchers know about neighborhoods may be a mixture of their personal experiences, their aspirations regarding living conditions in America, and their research evidence.

For some vocations (getting elected to public office, running a neighborhood business or real estate agency, or being an active participant in neighborhood affairs) an uncertain knowledge base may be acceptable. However, for other vocations, particularly any that are based on the principles of empirical research, we need to know whether any methodological improvements are possible. In other words, can neighborhood fact-gathering become a process that is susceptible to empirical social science? This chapter identifies three types of obstacles to achieving such an objective:

- False obstacles (which are often used as excuses for not pursuing further work)

This chapter is an edited version of a paper by the same title that appears in Robert Hollister and Phillip L. Clay, eds. *Neighborhood Policy and Planning* Department of Urban Studies and Planning, Massachusetts Institute of Technology, Cambridge: 1978.

- True obstacles that most people generally recognize
- True obstacles that have been generally overlooked

The examination of these obstacles is premised on one basic assumption—that the neighborhood is a valid target of research. Some have claimed, on the contrary, that neighborhoods are only artifacts of life, representing everyone and no one (e.g., Goering and Rogowsky, 1978). There is, however, a strong line of argument that eminently justifies neighborhoods as a target of research (e.g., Reuss, 1977).[1] The primary justification is that there are certain phenomena that involve neighborhood or *proximity-based dynamics* that cannot be covered by analyses of individuals, individual jobs, households, or citywide phenomena.

At least six types of characteristics can be enumerated:

- *Neighborhood relationships,* those instances of assistance and friendship induced by physical proximity and primary-group, face-to-face communications (Cooley, 1909/1956; Gist and Fava, 1971, p. 405)
- Homogeneity of *housing submarkets* on a geographic basis, generally a result of zoning and construction patterns, and leading to certain cycles of physical aging and residential turnover
- *Historic districts,* often marked by geographically distinctive terrain, that have led to certain small-area identities generally characterized by neighborhood "names"
- The existence of small-area *districts for municipal services* (e.g., Yin and Yates, 1975), especially catchment areas for schools or political representation
- *Intrametropolitan location* within the larger context of urban development, strongly influencing the specialization of neighborhood functions—for example, various types of bedroom suburbs, commercial and industrial neighborhoods, and the central business district or CBD (Burgess, 1925)
- *Neighborhood norms,* whereby social control, neighborhood defense, and networking patterns exist (Jacobs, 1961; Morris and Hess, 1975; Suttles, 1972)

The enumeration of these characteristics is not meant to imply that the same small area will always satisfy each characteristic. Indeed, one of the challenges for neighborhood research is that neighborhoods may need to be defined

---

[1]The statement by Congressman Reuss is mainly intended to cover urban policy, but the discussion is also one of the most sensitive and compelling descriptions of neighborhood policy (pp. 44–56).

NEIGHBORHOOD FACT-GATHERING

differently, depending on the functional issue being addressed. However, the enumeration does suggest that specific phenomena are different from (though not necessarily independent of) those at the citywide level, the household level, or the individual level.

Thus, if one assumes that the neighborhood is a valid target of research, the importance of gathering facts about neighborhoods emerges more clearly. We need to develop an empirically based craft in order to study neighborhoods better.

FALSE OBSTACLES

To examine the positive side first, there are at least two obstacles that commonly emerge but that in fact are false obstacles: the problem of *defining* neighborhoods, and the problem of *evaluating outcomes* from neighborhood activities.

Defining Neighborhoods

Most students begin their dissertations with a long chapter on the problems of defining what is meant by "neighborhoods." After reviewing the same stale literature, they invariably conclude that no viable definition has emerged. Either the experts need to get together and come to some agreement, or various terms and labels need to be redefined in a consistent manner. In spite of a lack of definition, the student goes on with the subsequent chapters and substantive issues of the dissertation. Nevertheless the dissertation usually ends under a cloud. If only a standard definition existed, other issues might have been addressed differently.

The student most certainly should not be blamed for this state of affairs, for it is the student's job to finish the dissertation, and this task has been accomplished rather well. Researchers, in fact, are the real culprits, for they have failed to inform the rest of the world that *there is no standard definition of "neighborhood."* And there never will be, because the notion of a standard definition is empty. Thus the real answer to the definitional problem, "What is a neighborhood?" is, "It depends." It depends on the subject of inquiry. For studies on service problems, for instance, the neighborhood might be a geographic district; for research on community organizations, the neighborhood might consist of the residents who can potentially serve or be served by such organizations; for studies of neighborhood politics, the neighborhood might consist of those persons who influence key decisions. Given the research context, each of these different definitions is the "right" one.

In short, the search for the all-purpose definition of "neighborhood" should cease. The nonexistence of such a definition should not be considered an obstacle to further work. Persons doing studies of neighborhoods should use the definition that is most appropriate for the inquiry, recognizing that different definitions need to be used on different occasions (Yin, 1977).

Evaluating Outcomes from Neighborhood Activities

A second obstacle to further research is cited by certain skeptics. Neighborhood activities (e.g., volunteer block groups, boosterism, or even governmental decentralization), they say, need to be subjected to evaluation, especially if any public policy is involved. This obstacle most certainly is false, for the evaluation results are likely to be negative, not because of any inherent shortcoming in neighborhood activities, but because of the inappropriate nature of the traditional evaluation paradigm.[2]

One task of the researcher, therefore, is to create a different climate for viewing neighborhood activities—one in which the burden of evidence is placed on those who would like to show that the activities are *ineffective*. Note that ineffectiveness measures are not merely the observation of null effects for effectiveness measures. For a citizen crime prevention activity, ineffectiveness measures might include errors (e.g., false arrests, unnecessary injuries), low participation rates, complaints by participants, complaints by residents, or failure to gain cooperation from the police. Most of these ineffectiveness measures are more easily monitored and assessed than the typical array of effectiveness measures. Yet no evaluation has deliberately assumed the burden of demonstrating ineffectiveness.

Other tasks may be considered as well. First, methodological research should be encouraged so that neighborhood activities might be more accurately assessed in the future.[3] Second, the ultimate limitations of the evaluation paradigm may still have to be recognized. Here it is important to remember that evaluation research is only one mechanism (and a fairly unimportant one, at that) for setting public priorities. The political process, as reflected in voting behavior and the priorities of legislators and other elected officials, is in fact the more common way of setting public priorities. The worthiness of a neighborhood activity might thus have to be judged simply by input measures—for example, how many participated (or were employed) at what cost, and how the activity was received by other residents and local service officials. Until such alternatives are fully developed, and until the state of the art of evaluation is improved, further promotion of other neighborhood research

---

[2]See Chapter 12 for a fuller treatment of this topic.
[3]An agenda for such research based on the need for *practical methodologies* is presented in Chapter 12.

should not be hindered by this false obstacle posed by the "effectiveness" issue.

TRUE OBSTACLES (THAT ARE GENERALLY RECOGNIZED)

What Is Changing when Neighborhoods Change?

A common motivation for studying neighborhoods is that an observer feels a neighborhood has radically changed, and that a study is needed to understand these changes and their reasons. Usually, however, if one asks such an observer to enumerate the specific changes that would ultimately serve as the dependent variables in the proposed study, great difficulties arise. Data for specific variables, such as racial composition or housing deterioration, are difficult to obtain; moreover, the observer usually feels that what has changed is much more than the aggregate nature of these variables. Somehow the neighborhood milieu has changed, and that is what is important.

This difficulty in assessing neighborhood change is but one example of a common and true obstacle for conducting neighborhood research: the problem of disaggregating neighborhood phenomena so that a feasible study can be done. For the study of neighborhood change, one alternative is to design single studies in a more fragmented manner, with only a series of studies, conducted over time, resulting in the development of an overall picture. Take, for example, the apparently straightforward research topic of household composition and residential turnover. This topic has become an increasingly important concern to policy makers because residential turnover is a primary basis for neighborhood change (whether in an upgrading or declining situation), and residential turnover is essentially a matter of mobility by individual households, and not individual persons (e.g., James, 1977).[4] To investigate these issues, several different studies might be designed.

The first deals with the basic question of how households are to be defined. The important problem here is that, with changes in American life styles, the nuclear family as a model household is no longer as dominant as it once was; the most rapidly increasing households consist of either single parents or unrelated individuals. In fact, the social change is significant enough that the United States Census Bureau did not even attempt to identify the

---

[4]One recent work (Goetze, Colton, and O'Donnell, 1977) concerned with residential turnover, however, only provides data on birth cohorts and the general population, and fails to point out the difference between *individual* and *household* population characteristics. Thus, for older central cities, the fact that the population may be declining yet the number of households may be increasing is often misunderstood.

"head of household" in the 1980 census. Such changes in household composition and definition all have important implications for the housing market and hence for neighborhood development and stability, and the topic should become one part of research on household composition and residential turnover.

A second type of study is concerned with the development of methodologies for enumerating households on a small-area, timely basis. At this time no such methodology exists, whether based on sample surveys or on neighborhood indicator systems. Such a methodology would help to distinguish, for instance, between gentrification (where newcomers are moving into a neighborhood) and upgrading (where neighborhood conditions are also improving, but as a result of efforts by the original residents). In a thirty-city survey of neighborhood change, Clay (1978) noted that these two phenomena tended to occur in different kinds of neighborhoods with different architectural, market, and social characteristics. A workable methodology could be very helpful in allowing policy makers to make assessments of residential turnover in individual cities.

Additional studies are needed to focus on specific public programs and their effects on residential turnover.[5] When assessing federal programs such as the Community Development Block Grants, for instance, federal agencies usually need to know whether their programs have produced excessive turnover rates or have created socially undesirable displacements.

Neighborhood Typologies

Spiro Agnew once remarked, "Once you've seen one ghetto, you've seen them all." Maybe he or some other nonresearcher would be more successful than researchers have been in creating neighborhood typologies.

The need for such typologies is self-evident. Most studies of a single neighborhood or of a small group of neighborhoods always raise issues of external validity. That is not surprising, for without a typology, one cannot even claim to have a sampling procedure. Yet it is impossible to study all neighborhoods, even though we might want to generalize to such a universe. As a result, almost every neighborhood study develops its own unique rationale for selecting the neighborhoods to be studied and for inferring the other (nonstudied) neighborhoods to which the results can be generalized.

The problem of developing a neighborhood typology is a true obstacle to further research. There have been a few attempts at developing such typologies, but the results are still less than satisfactory. Some typologies are based on purely cross-sectional characteristics and account for differences,

---

[5]For a listing of the major evaluation efforts regarding federal programs for neighborhoods, see Public Technology, Inc. (1978).

for instance, among central-business-district, working-class residential, and upper-income residential neighborhoods. Other typologies are based on neighborhood change over time, which can be depicted as a five-stage process of decline and upgrading (e.g., Hoover and Vernon, 1959/1962, pp. 183–198; Public Affairs Counseling, 1976) or in terms of other stages (e.g., Birch, 1974). However, the most promising typologies may have to be formulated to include *both* cross-sectional factors and changes over time. Thus Goetze (1976), for instance, has appropriately suggested that different housing and revitalization policies are relevant for different neighborhoods defined according to both of these dimensions (see Figure 4).

Other approaches might also be explored. The first is to borrow from other fields that have similar problems, for example, clinical medicine. Medical practitioners have to typologize patients even though the underlying theories and measurement problems have not been fully articulated. The approach used by that profession is to use *standardized protocols*. With such protocols, scientific communication can at least be promoted, and better theories can ultimately be developed. Thus, for neighborhoods, one approach might simply be for a professional association to establish the ground rules for neighborhood protocols. Empirical studies would thus be required to follow such protocols in identifying their neighborhoods in the broader context of an admittedly arbitrary typology. The studies could, of course, also go beyond these protocols and develop more refined typologies; the main objective, however, would be that, in the short run, the results of different studies could then more readily be compared and better typologies might emerge.

A second approach is to take some existing research technique—for example, social area analysis—and to conduct the necessary validation steps to establish better typologies. Social area analysis has made one significant achievement: Through the use of factor analysis on census tract variables, it has shown that most census tracts can be characterized by their placement on a three-way dimensional matrix consisting of familism, ethnicity, and income factors. One untested notion has been to take the results of social area analysis and, for statistically similar tracts within and between cities, to make systematic field observations. Would tracts with equivalent factor scores "look" alike in the field? Or the procedure could be reversed. What if neighborhoods that bore subjective similarities were then compared on an array of census or municipal data? Again, this or some similar approach seems a promising way of readdressing the problem of creating neighborhood typologies.

Lack of Contiguity of District Boundaries

A third true obstacle has been encountered by numerous researchers. Even after they have defined neighborhoods in terms of geographic units,

Market Perception

	Rising	Stable	Declining	Rapidly Declining
Good / Minor Repairs Required	**G/R** —rising values —rising rents	**G/S** —ideal neighborhood		
Fair / Moderate Repairs Required	**F/R** —reverse filtration —absentees taking over —existing tenants being displaced —speculation	**F/S** —greying —low turnover	**F/D** —blockbusting —*un*realistic expectations —arterial or industrial blight —racial fears	
Poor / Major Repairs Required		**P/S** —market "bottomed out" —some abandonment —realistic expectations	**P/D** —abandonment —foreclosures —multi-problems	**P/RD** —firebombing —disaster wholesale

Housing Condition

Figure 4. Illustrative neighborhood typology. (Source: Goetze, 1976.)

they then find that much of the information about small geographic units does not follow the same geographic boundaries. Thus census tracts, police precincts, health catchment areas, school districts, and the like do not coincide. The woes created by this obstacle are all too familiarly captured in the now-standard overlay map, showing the lack of boundary contiguity.

However, there is some long-term hope. With the development of improved computational capabilities, it is becoming increasingly possible to use geocode routines and to break down all the original data according to street address. The researcher can then establish some minimal geographic unit (e.g., a city block or blockface), from which any areal unit reflecting a neighborhood can then be constructed. Yet, as anyone who has tried to use geocoding routines knows, we cannot be too optimistic. The procedures are tedious, they do not work easily, and the original files often have to be manually searched for their address information.

TRUE OBSTACLES (THAT ARE GENERALLY OVERLOOKED)

A final set of obstacles is also difficult to overcome. Unlike the previous set, however, these obstacles have not always been recognized by most researchers.

Neighborhood versus Individual Units of Analysis

Neighborhoods, by definition, involve group activities and phenomena. These phenomena are captured by such concepts as "tipping," "neighborhood confidence," and "community conflict." In contrast to these *collective* phenomena, much of behavioral science is oriented to the collection of information from and about *individuals*. That is especially true of experimental and quasi-experimental designs, as well as of surveys. However, even field research begins by getting "into the neighborhood," an activity that, when operationalized, actually means gaining access to a specific neighborhood organization or clique. Thus some of the most highly regarded studies of urban neighborhoods—for example, *Street-Corner Society* and *Tally's Corner*—are not actually neighborhood studies. Instead, they are studies of small groups in urban neighborhoods; little is known about the representativeness of these groups or about the characteristics of the neighborhood settings within which these groups exist. Such research deserves its critical acclaim as small-group research; but too often the efforts have been regarded as neighborhood studies.

A similar problem arises with survey research techniques, where an investigator believes he will increase the sampling size and hence boost the quantitative potential of a neighborhood study by interviewing residents. No matter how large and well chosen the sample of residents, this approach is limited in its ability to cover neighborhood phenomena. For instance, a survey covering neighborhood confidence can legitimately result in an overall assessment of the degree of confidence existing in a neighborhood. Such confidence is nevertheless a collective phenomenon, for which only a single, summary statistic is relevant. In short, no matter how large the sample of residents within the neighborhood, the sample size for the collective phenomenon is still "1"(Yin, 1981).

Assessing Events outside of the Neighborhood

A second common difficulty is that neighborhood conditions and change may be strongly influenced by events that occur outside of the neighborhood. That is especially the case, for instance, in understanding housing markets and residential turnover. In conducting such studies it is insufficient merely to account for factors within a neighborhood. Residential turnover rates, and hence housing prices, are necessarily responsive to market conditions in other neighborhoods. Dramatic "pull" effects may occur, as in the development of Coop City in the Bronx Borough of New York, where the availability of 17,000 new housing units enhanced intracity migratory patterns and led to the further abandonment of other Bronx neighborhoods.

The problem of dealing with such external factors is that the relevant ones are difficult to identify or assess. In the case of events in a geographically contiguous neighborhood, the researcher may devote some attention to these factors. However, the relevant events may also occur in distant areas, including other locations in the metropolitan area, regional trends, and even changes in distant cities. Overriding all these factors, of course, are some of the macroeconomic changes such as federal fiscal, energy, and housing policies. Similarly, changes in municipal service policies, as in the deployment of police or the opening or closing of schools, can affect neighborhood conditions (Yin and Yates, 1975).

All of these examples are intended to convey the fact that neighborhoods are notoriously "open" systems, and any focus on specific neighborhoods without accounting for these external conditions can lead to mistaken conclusions. There have been few attempts to deal with the assessment of these external factors in conjunction with a neighborhood study, but to do so is clearly an enormous task. The only guidance that can be suggested is that researchers need to be explicit about their theoretical approach to the study of neighborhoods, and the propositions to be investigated should identify salient external events, even if these events cannot be included in the scope of study. Such an approach will at least forewarn the casual reader regarding premature conclusions about the neighborhood under study.

Comparative Studies

Because of the large size and historic importance of many neighborhoods, especially those in large cities, there has been a strong tendency for researchers to conduct neighborhood studies by focusing only on a single neighborhood. Dissertation shelves are replete with these kinds of case studies, but even some of the most well-known books, such as Jane Jacobs's *Death and Life of Great American Cities,* are also based on inquiries into single neighborhoods.

Except where a case study has been purposely identified as the critical case (similar to the "critical experiment"), single case studies are generally a weak basis from which to generalize about neighborhood phenomena. It may be recalled that many of Jacobs's conclusions about neighborhood life were challenged because her observations tended to be limited to the Greenwich Village area in New York. Her insightful comments about the role of streets and sidewalks in promoting surveillance behavior and public safety, for instance, were considered findings typical of that neighborhood but not necessarily applicable elsewhere. For this reason researchers should try to design comparative neighborhood studies, where the same phenomena are studied in at least two neighborhoods if not more.

The logic underlying the design of comparative neighborhood studies is not different from the general logic of comparing the results from different experiments (Yin, 1981). Yet single case studies, even if the data that are assembled are highly quantitative, continue to be common. Because there appears to be no justification for such solo case studies, our suspicion is that the problem is another example of a true obstacle that has generally been overlooked.

SUMMARY

Research on neighborhoods is an important endeavor, from the point of view of both social science theory and public policy. We know too little about neighborhood phenomena even though they affect our everyday lives and pose serious dilemmas for public policy.

To enhance our understanding of neighborhoods, however, requires an explicit attempt to improve the craft with which neighborhoods are studied. This craft, at a minimum, demands that greater attention be paid to neighborhood fact-gathering and the fact-gathering process. In other words, we need to have more information about neighborhoods, but we must also set explicit rules by which such information is gathered. Too often, what passes for neighborhood research are advocacy statements and assertions that reflect a prior ideological commitment. The development of new knowledge about neighborhoods will not be well served under such circumstances.

In contrast, although totally value-free social science does not exist, there are nevertheless certain basic procedures that can be followed that will create a more robust knowledge base. The purpose of this chapter has been to identify some of the obstacles that have precluded the development of such procedures. No magical or easy solutions have been proposed, but the hope is that neighborhood fact-gathering and the quality of neighborhood research will be improved.

REFERENCES

Birch, David L. *Models of Neighborhood Evolution*. Cambridge, Mass.: Harvard–MIT Joint Center for Urban Studies, 1974.

Burgess, Ernest W. "The Growth of the City." In *The City*, edited by R. E. Park and E. W. Burgess. Chicago: University of Chicago Press, 1925, pp. 47–62.

Clay, Phillip L. "Neighborhood Revitalization: Issues, Trends, and Strategies." Department of Urban Studies and Planning, Massachusetts Institute of Technology, 1978.

Cooley, Charles Horton. *Social Organizations: A Study of the Larger Mind*. 1909. Reprint. Glencoe, Ill.: Free Press, 1956.

Gist, Noel P., and Fava, Sylvia Fleis. *Urban Society*. 5th ed., New York: Thomas Y. Crowell, 1971.

Goering, John M., and Rogowsky, Edward T. "The Myth of Neighborhoods." *New York Affairs* 1978, 5, 82–86.

Goetze, Rolf W. *Building Neighborhood Confidence*. Cambridge, Mass.: Ballinger, 1976.

Goetze, Rolf W.; Colton, Kent W.; O'Donnell, Vincent F. *Stabilizing Neighborhoods: A Fresh Approach to Housing Dynamics and Perceptions*. Cambridge, Mass.: Public Systems Evaluation, 1977.

Hoover, Edgar M., and Vernon, Raymond. *Anatomy of a Metropolis*. Garden City, N.Y.: Doubleday, 1962. (Originally published, 1959.)

Jacobs, Jane. *The Death and Life of Great American Cities*. New York: Vintage Books, 1961.

James, Franklin J. *Back to the City: An Appraisal of Housing Reinvestment and Population Change in Urban America*. Washington, D.C.: Urban Institute, 1977.

Morris, David, and Hess, Karl. *Neighborhood Power: The New Localism*. Boston: Beacon Press, 1975.

Public Affairs Counseling. *The Dynamics of Neighborhood Change*. Report prepared for the U.S. Department of Housing and Urban Development, Washington, D.C., 1976.

Public Technology, Inc. "Summary Review of HUD-Sponsored and HUD-Related R&D of Relevance to Boston/Urban Consortium Study of Neighborhood Resource Allocation." Draft report, Washington, D.C., 1978.

Reuss, Henry S. "To Save a City." Subcommittee on the City, United States House of Representatives Committee on Banking, Finance, and Urban Affairs, Congress, 1st Session, 1977.

Suttles, Gerald D. *The Social Construction of Communities*. Chicago: University of Chicago Press, 1972.

Yin, Robert K. "What a National Commission on Neighborhoods Could Do." *Journal of the American Real Estate and Urban Economics Association* 1977, 5, 255–278.

Yin, Robert K. "The Case Study Crisis: Some Answers." *Administrative Science Quarterly* 1981, 26, 58–65.

Yin, Robert K., and Yates, Douglas. *Street-Level Governments: Assessing Decentralization and Urban Services*. Lexington, Mass.: Lexington Books, 1975.

10
Using Participant-Observation to Study Urban Neighborhoods

TRADITIONAL AND MODIFIED PARTICIPANT-OBSERVATION

The urban neighborhood, long of interest to city planners and sociologists, has in recent years become of increasing concern to public policy makers. The reasons have been painfully obvious: The urban riots of the 1960s, the continued ethnic and racial changes in the city, and the feared abandonment of the central city have all had their greatest impact at the neighborhood level.

The concern with urban neighborhoods has called attention to a large gap, however, in the policy maker's information resources. The consideration of any alternative courses of action requires the establishment of a neighborhood "early warning system" (Jacoby, 1970), or development of some new program for neighborhood improvement. There is simply no system conveying relevant and timely information regarding neighborhood conditions or providing feedback about any governmental actions. Such information would seem extremely important, especially in the light of the often

---

This chapter is based on two previous works by the author: *Participation-Observation and the Development of Urban Neighborhood Policy* (New York: New York City–Rand Institute, 1972); and "Towards an Urban Neighborhood Policy," *Urban Analysis* 1972, *1*, 3–16.

rapid changes that occur in contemporary urban neighborhoods. These changes involve population turnover as well as the turnover of local institutions like retail stores, churches, and community organizations, and can result in new demands on municipal services.

The provision of such information would at first glance seem to be difficult and prohibitively expensive to establish. Some types of information, like the results of routine housing inspections and the daily amount of garbage collected, are readily available through municipal records, but are not necessarily accurate. Other types of information, like the ethnic composition of a neighborhood or the use of parks and other public facilities, can only be collected through residential surveys. In the past such surveys have been routinely conducted in just a few cities (e.g., Boston, Detroit, and Dayton), with the number of surveys per year and the total sample of residents both limited by the high cost per interview. Typically, the result is that a survey is conducted annually and for a sample size of less than a thousand residents for a whole metropolitan area, making neighborhood-level analyses extremely difficult. Furthermore, certain important constituents of a neighborhood, especially its young and teen-age population, are rarely if ever surveyed.

Participant-Observation: The Traditional Approach

Yet social scientists have employed another field method, participant-observation, that can potentially provide some of the types of information sought by the policy maker. Historically, the investigators with the earliest experience in participant-observation used it as an anthropological field technique. The term "participant-observation" was probably first coined by Eduard Lindeman (see Bruyn, 1966), and the first detailed statements about the method were written by Lohman (1937) and Kluckhohn (1940) although, of course, many important participant-observation studies had already been completed by then, including those of the Chicago school (see Burgess and Bogue, 1967) and the Lynds' study of Middletown (Lynd and Lynd, 1929, 1937). Perhaps the most famous participant-observer study was Whyte's (1955) work on streetcorner gangs in Boston's North End during the 1940s. In recent years there has been a strong revival of interest in that study, because students of poverty areas and deviant subgroups in the city have increasingly found that strong social barriers exist that cannot be penetrated by any other method. As one result, there are now several firsthand accounts by participant-observers of their unique experiences in a contemporary urban setting (e.g., Gans, 1972; Hannerz, 1969; Jacobs, 1970; Liebow, 1967; Vidich et al., 1964).

As a research method, the classical dilemma posed by participant-observation is that it calls on the researcher to fulfill two roles, participating and observing, and these roles often conflict with each other. As a participant, an investigator becomes privy to many interpersonal relationships otherwise unavailable to an outsider, but these tend to be *subjective* experiences. As an observer, the investigator attempts to emulate the natural scientist, dealing with the *objective* world of events. Whereas in other investigations the aim is to minimize one role and maximize the other, the well-trained participant-observer tries to maximize his opportunities in both roles.

Stemming from the duality of the participant-observer role are many important problems. For one, the participant-observer collects data about events of which he may be a part, creating a reactive situation. Second, the participant role may become so dominant as to threaten the whole enterprise, either by preventing the pursuit of logical inquiries because they may threaten the rapport that has been established (see Miller, 1952), or because the information obtained is so sensitive that public availability of the data may lead to the injury of particular persons or groups. Third, the investigator constantly faces the problem of checking the credibility of his informants and the views they express (Becker, 1958).

At the same time, the role also has some well-established advantages. Despite its potential lack of representativeness, participant-observation is the preferred method in any exploratory study, where the relevant variables and questions are not known, and where the researcher needs a flexible framework so that he can follow any number of new developments. Even after a project is fully under way, the relative freedom can lead to completely unanticipated phenomena, such as Whyte's observations about the role of bowling in reinforcing the status hierarchy of the streetcorner gang (Whyte, 1964). In addition, participant-observation can provide the appropriate context for the phenomena being studied, and thereby help the investigator understand the local meaning of events, customs, and language. Such benefits are usually unavailable to the survey researcher or the interviewer.

Modifying Participant-Observation

The traditional application of participant-observation has been on a case study basis, with a single investigator generally spending several years in the field studying a single neighborhood group. This traditional application needs to be modified, however, in order to be useful to the policy maker. In general, the policy maker needs a comparative framework, in which most if not all neighborhoods of a city can be covered; also needed are some clearly objective measures of neighborhood conditions, as might be included as part of a series of neighborhood indicators, in which certain key observations could be made in a timely manner and at relatively low cost by a special team of observers.

More specifically, four kinds of modifications in the traditional use of participant-observation have to be tested. First, several neighborhoods have to be studied simultaneously, using the same general research procedures.[1] Such standardization can be imposed with a minimal sacrifice of the traditional strength of participant-observation, where an investigator must be free to operate according to his own progress in uncovering new information and informants; it only demands that a few of the same specific assignments be carried out in each neighborhood. With this approach, not only can neighborhoods be compared, but the study of common urban problems can also be enriched by the fact that observations have been made in a variety of natural settings. In either case, the comparative approach may reveal some of the important and unanticipatable categories for organizing field observations, as suggested by Glaser and Strauss (1967).

Second, more than one investigator should study the same area. Ideally, there should be at least two participant-observers operating in the same neighborhood. However, because such an effort may require an excessive commitment of research resources, a more economical approach is to have a field worker operate primarily in one area and secondarily in another. In the primary area, the field worker would act in the full capacity as a participant-observer; in the secondary area, he could act more as an alternate observer of neighborhood conditions. Thus a group of participant-observers would rotate so that every neighborhood would have more than one field worker, even though the total number of neighborhoods and field workers was identical.

Third, the participant-observer's work can be designed to emphasize the quantification of observable events. Such a task has only seldom been systematically incorporated into academic field work (e.g., Molotch, 1969; Suttles, 1968).[2] For policy-making purposes, the main goal would be to determine whether neighborhood or street indicators exist in the form of "unobtrusive" measures (Webb, Campbell, Schwartz, and Sechrest, 1966), reflecting neighborhood activity and condition. Such indicators might help the policy maker in managing the delivery of municipal services; more ambitiously, such indicators might serve as the basis for assessing the quality of neighborhood life, and complement any effort to develop a comprehensive set of social indicators.[3]

---

[1]Some of the early Chicago studies actually did develop a rudimentary comparative approach, in that the studies covered more than one small area within the same city (e.g., McKenzie, 1923; Zorbaugh, 1929). However, this theme has not been further elaborated in subsequent participant-observation research.

[2]For a brief outline of the different variables that might be subject to quantification, see Valentine (1968).

[3]See Chapter 11 for an illustrative example of such indicators.

Fourth, small-area data, whether available through the census, special surveys, or municipal records, can be used in close conjunction with the field work. In previous studies where such data have been used, they have generally been integrated only after the field work has been completed and in order to test specific hypotheses. With adequate preparation, however, the data can also be used to guide the field work as it is being carried out, directing the participant-observer's attention to specific neighborhood events while he is still in the field.

To test these four modifications, a field study of seven New York City neighborhoods was designed, with seven participant-observers working in these neighborhoods for a three-month period. Because the period of study was so short, there was little hope of developing the highly intimate relationships usually established by participant-observers. The main goal of the study, however, was to test these four modifications, and thus this shortcoming was not deemed critical, the assumption being that it could be overcome in the future simply by lengthening the period of work.

OVERVIEW OF THE FIELD STUDY

The field study involved the following New York City neighborhoods: Highbridge and Morrisania in the Bronx; Harlem, East Harlem, and the Lower East Side in Manhattan; and Bushwick and Brownsville in Brooklyn (areas A though G, respectively, in Figure 5). The neighborhood boundaries do not represent political boundaries, but instead reflect the areas covered by each field worker. This group of neighborhoods was not chosen out of any experimental design; it was simply selected on the basis of the individuals available for field work and the location of their prior field experiences. The neighborhoods included

- An all-black neighborhood (Harlem)
- A predominantly Puerto Rican neighborhood (East Harlem)
- A predominantly white middle-class neighborhood (Highbridge)
- Several mixed neighborhoods (Morrisania, Lower East Side, Bushwick, and Brownsville)

The group also included some of New York City's well-known poverty areas (Harlem, East Harlem, Lower East Side, and Brownsville), neighborhoods experiencing significant deterioration (Bushwick and Morrisania), and a neighborhood undergoing the initial stages of large-scale ethnic change (Highbridge).

The participant-observers were graduate students recruited from local

Figure 5. The New York City–Rand Institute small-area studies.

universities. All had either some formal training in field work or some experience in the neighborhood they were studying; for the three-month period of the study, most lived in or near that neighborhood. Four of the observers were black and three were white, including one Puerto Rican; one was female.

The normal routine for each participant-observer was to spend most of the time in the neighborhood, with weekly meetings at some central location for group discussions. During the first six weeks the participant-observers all worked alone in their own neighborhoods. Later, however, trips were systematically made by each participant-observer to the other neighborhoods as well. The participant-observers all kept diaries of their activities, noting the people they had contacted as well as the most interesting and most noteworthy events that happened to them during the day. They also filled out data sheets and made maps to complete specific assignments.

The general orientation of the participant-observer was to participate in the neighborhood's street activities (e.g., playing sports, talking in bars, hanging around the streetcorner). Little effort was made to contact or interview in any orderly fashion the dominant community organizations operating in each neighborhood. Such organizations exist in amazing quantity, and would themselves be ample material for an entire study. Instead, with the focus on street life, the major tasks of the participant-observers were: (a) to determine the kinds of events that could be readily observed and that had bearing on the physical and social conditions of the neighborhood, and (b) to study certain municipal problems that exist in varying degrees in many neighborhoods, for example, the illegal opening and use of fire hydrants. Throughout the study, the emphasis was on developing an appreciation of the neighborhood from the point of view of the residents and their use of the streets.

THE PARTICIPANT-OBSERVER IN THE FIELD

First Days in the Field

Each participant-observer was initially assigned an intersection in his or her neighborhood that had a firebox with a high rate of alarms (though each knew nothing at the outset about any of the alarm history in his area). For the first three weeks the participant-observers were to use this intersection as a center from which to radiate and to talk with people, determine hangouts, and participate in any street activities. The observers were also asked to carry out two assignments. The first was intended to help them become aware of the streetcorner environment, and called for them to map the types of buildings or functional uses of the four corners of twenty intersections, and to count the number of people loitering on the corners or passing through the intersections at a given hour of the day. The second was related to a municipal service, and involved estimating the amount of garbage on 100 blockfaces by using a five-point rating scale. In addition, the observers had to try to determine some of the causes of undue garbage accumulation in their areas, and it was in the course of the garbage survey that the boundaries of each observer's area were established (in a special survey of this kind, a field worker can cover about a thirty- to forty-block area on a typical week's assignment, though not without some exhaustion at the end of each day).

The first days in the field were also interesting in that the observers all had to develop very quickly some kind of daily routine. This task not only involved establishing contacts, but also finding someplace to go to write notes or to avoid getting rained on, places to eat and rest, and someplace where they could be contacted. The routine-seeking seems remarkably similar, in retrospect, to that reported about the new cop on the beat or other street workers.

Finally, and more important methodologically, during the first few days most participant-observers reported clear perceptions about the psychological boundaries of their new roles. As an inhabitant of an area or a tourist going through it, one could feel relatively secure and content. As soon as one tried to be a participant-observer, especially by approaching strange people and asking questions, one would become ill-at-ease and wary. During the very first days, the boundary between personal self and participant-observer could easily be encountered, as if it physically existed, like Goffman's description of the front- and backstages of the waiter and of "regional" behavior (Goffman, 1959, pp. 106-140). For instance, one of the field workers could watch a local fire with many others and be perfectly satisfied at one moment, but then might take the initiative by making comments or asking questions and become alert and uncomfortable in the next; or, he could try to meet people on the street and feel frustrated at the lack of conversational material at one moment, but then decide to call it a day and feel happy again in the next. Related to these perceptions of their new role were some tendencies to be overly aware of being an outsider; in a few cases the participant-observers even thought they were being followed. Only gradually did such perceptions disappear, and only with those participant-observers who successfully became an integral part of the neighborhood's street life.

Rotation of Participant-Observers

After the first six weeks a new routine was added to the participant-observers' regular activities, whereby each spent a day visiting colleagues in the other neighborhoods. This rotation proved to be one of the high points of the summer's work, with both negative and positive effects. The negative aspects were that the observers had to abbreviate the work in their own areas and endanger some of their own rapport, first because they would be away visiting other areas, and second because, as hosts to other observers, they could not follow the same activities they would have if alone. For instance, black–white pairs of participant-observers were especially conspicuous in dominantly black or dominantly white neighborhoods, and were thus limited to general tours of the area rather than any more serious interactions.

Such negative effects, however, tended to be outweighed by the new perceptions the participant-observers felt were added to their own experiences. First, the observers felt that, in pairs, they tended to perceive more events and found their own dialogue very rewarding. Second, the visits to other areas made them more aware of certain constancies in the environment of their own neighborhoods that they had not noticed before. On returning to their own neighborhoods, in other words, they had new things to look for and were sensitized to other phenomena previously overlooked. For instance, one observer had not realized how barren his low-income neighborhood was of greenery until he visited another equally low-income neighborhood that was nevertheless filled with small parks and patches of green. Other observers immediately sensed the different levels of street activity in the neighborhoods, or the different types of people hanging around the streets.

Finally, the participant-observers had a general focus for their visits in that all were asked to observe a specific municipal service or street activity on each visit, and to report on that aspect of neighborhood life on the basis of seeing several areas in addition to having a more intimate knowledge of their own area. The topics covered in this manner were:

- The use and abuse of fire hydrants
- The adequacy of public outpatient facilities
- The street activity of police
- The role of the mayor's urban task forces (in which then-Mayor Lindsay tried to encourage neighborhood–city government interactions through the establishment of local storefront offices nominally staffed by prominent city employees)
- Children's play patterns
- Discussions with single adult (and presumably unemployed) men

These topics were in addition to the garbage ratings (done by all field workers), and met with a variety of success. For instance, with the hydrants, where the phenomena were readily observable and limited in scope, the participant-observer was able to produce a fairly complete report. With the outpatient facilities, the phenomena were available for study but too diverse and time-consuming, and the report consisted of a series of visits to clinics with few general conclusions. Finally, with the adult men, the phenomena (in this case, life histories) were not readily observable and communication was extremely difficult; the topic remained essentially intractable.

At the same time in the study, participant-observers reported and exhibited changes in their own roles. The changes were facilitated by their own progress in the field, by a general meeting in which some of the observations on garbage were reported to relevant officials in city government, and by the visits to each other's neighborhoods. In several cases the progress in the field meant the disintegration of the boundary between personal self and participant-observer. Some observers reported being unable to avoid their participant-observer roles even when not working and on their own time; other versions of the same phenomena were the expressed feeling that the work assignment had become more than a job, or a notable decline in concern over the boundary problem in cases where observations during the first few weeks had been plentiful.

A meeting with municipal sanitation officials took place in early July and was intended as an occasion for exchanging information; the participant-observers provided their field observations about the garbage conditions in their neighborhoods, and the officials provided their knowledge about problems in the delivery of service. We had hoped that such a meeting could give both sides some valuable insights. The confrontation proved quite frustrating for both sides, however, with the result that, although valuable information was exchanged, by the end of the meeting neither side fully appreciated nor understood the problems of the other. In retrospect, given the tremendous garbage problem in New York, such an outcome was probably inevitable.

The effect of the rotation compounded these events because the participant-observers not only had an opportunity to converse about their field observations but, perhaps for the first time, could also talk with each other in a more leisurely fashion about the general implications of their studies and the intricate relationships among their roles, the various neighborhoods, and significant social change.

The outcome of all these changes was that the observers themselves became community advocates, feeling confident that they now understood what was going on in the neighborhoods, and thus expressing both their views about the plight of the local residents and their own doubts about the usefulness of research or the ability of a government bureaucracy to cope with the "real problems." At this critical point, all field work had to be suspended for a few days, and we engaged in lengthy discussions in an attempt to reduce some of the conflicts. The main issues involved the observers' frustration over the unlikelihood of any short-term changes; their inability to report, to their own satisfaction, many field observations for lack of either time or appropriate channels; and the poor historical record of research and government action in making meaningful improvements at the local level. We managed to survive only by talking these issues through and, in the end, by relying on the strength of personal relationships to re-ignite a basic curiosity about neighborhoods, independent of any hope for immediate change.

Some Research Observations about Participant-Observation

The effect of having seven participant-observers operating in the field simultaneously was to clarify several important characteristics of the use of participant-observation. Although some of these have been described by previous investigators (e.g., Gans, 1962; Whyte, 1955, 1964), the limitations and benefits have not been systematically spelled out.

First, the initial contacts made by each participant-observer reflected a strong bias toward people of the same sex and age. The female participant-observer talked initially to other women on the street, and was the only one to do so; all of the participant-observers interacted at first with people of approximately their own ages (generally older teen-agers and young adults). Such experiences are consistent with previous reports (e.g., Hannerz, 1969); Whyte (1955) and Gans (1962) also mention the benefits of using their wives to gain entry into the local female communities, and the different interactions that were experienced as part of marriage dyads rather than as single males. But the limitations imposed by an observer's own sex and age have never been clearly tested, and one wonders whether an aged or female William Whyte or Elliot Liebow would not have reached entirely different conclusions about their streetcorners; they certainly would have been part of a different crowd. In general, and most importantly, if different neighborhoods have different casts of people dominating neighborhood activity, the determination of a neighborhood's condition on the basis of one participant-observer's reports will be extremely difficult. A logical solution in future studies would be to sample more systematically from the universe of potential field workers; one might employ people of at least two distinct sex and age backgrounds—for example, males in their twenties and females in their forties or fifties.

Second, the experiences of all the participant-observers confirmed the difficulties of maintaining the fully hybrid role of being both a participant and an observer. On this problem much has also been written. Bruyn (1966) has analyzed the philosophical implications of the two roles and suggests that the dilemmas created by having to fill both roles simultaneously are basically the dilemmas of being a social scientist. But it is Whyte (1955) who has described most clearly the slender path that must be followed: The investigator must be careful to avoid becoming either a nonparticipating observer or a nonobserving participant. Others have described the implications of the variant roles between these two extremes (e.g., Gold, 1958; Schwartz and Schwartz, 1955).

In the present study, one participant-observer did become highly involved in his neighborhood. As a result of a serendipitous contact early in the study, he was enlisted as a member of a black separatist organization that was prominent in the neighborhood. At first his reputation was linked to that of the initially befriended person; later, however, he rose to a more central position that was based on his own independent reputation for strong leadership and friendship. At the same time, it was this participant-observer who experienced the most difficulty in reporting his activities, having to consider whether his reports would betray his trusts with neighborhood confidants. Other participant-observers who were not as highly involved in their neighborhood's activities were able to make their reports with greater ease, but at the same time felt frustrated that they could not participate more with local residents. However, on the few occasions in which they did become actively involved with the neighborhood people, they too experienced reporting difficulties. There seemed, in other words, to be a continual conflict between the participant and observer roles. Because of the conflict, any given individual tended toward one role at the expense of the other, and no individual appeared able to maintain the complete posture of "participant-observer" for any extended period of time.[4]

APPLYING PARTICIPANT-OBSERVATION TO MUNICIPAL POLICY MAKING: TWO CASES

Participant-observation proved useful in two general ways for assessing the impact of municipal services. First, the participant-observers were able to observe and interpret the use of municipal services, yielding insights that can be highly beneficial to the policy maker. Second, the participant-observers identified various neighborhood events that could be enumerated and that were significant in describing neighborhood conditions and the potential need for services. As illustrative examples of these two uses, two aspects of the summer's field work are described below: the use and abuse of fire hydrants, and observations of streetcorner characteristics in relation to fire alarms. Be-

---

[4]Barbara Dohrenwend (personal communication) suggests that the participant-observer role is by definition a transitory one, and that it is perhaps best that no person attempt to fill the role for too long a period of time. In this light, it would be interesting to examine the "break" periods or other vacations taken by participant-observers who have spent two or three years on their studies, from the point of view of both the frequency of such breaks and the activities pursued during those times.

sides covering two service problems, these two cases also represent two contrasting approaches to data collection techniques, one being more qualitative and the other more quantitative. These cases therefore suggest the range of applications for participant-observation.

The Use and Misuse of Fire Hydrants in New York City[5]

In New York and other cities, the unauthorized use of fire hydrants has led to undue reduction in local water pressure and wasting of the city's water supply. The subsequent damage to the hydrants has made an increasing number inaccessible to the fire department. As part of my work this summer, I have observed how the hydrants are used by local residents, and have compared my observations with current attempts by the Department of Water Resources and the New York City Fire Department to prevent hydrant abuse.

The Current Situation

In order for the fire department to have quick access to water for fighting fires, hydrants are located with great frequency throughout New York City (there are about 100,000 altogether), and each of them can easily be turned on. An individual hydrant has two nozzles, one larger than the other. The large nozzle gives out 1,700 gallons of water per minute; the small one 650 gallons per minute. The water is released by removing the caps on these nozzles and turning the brass bolt on top of the hydrant with a wrench.

During the last few years, the unauthorized use of hydrants has increased rapidly. There is no systematic monitoring of the hydrants, so the precise increase is unknown. However, the frequency of resident complaints suggests that the unauthorized openings occur much more often than in the past. Another sign of the increase is the growing amount of money spent for hydrant repair. For instance, in 1964, the city replaced 500 hydrant caps; this year (1970) it will replace 12,000 of them, at a cost of eight dollars each. Aside from the loss of the caps, the main damage the hydrants sustain in being misused involves the brass threads needed for connecting the fire hoses, the inner valves of the hydrant, or the brass bolt that turns on the hydrant (the bolt is easily damaged by improper tools, or it can be sawed off altogether and sold for its intrinsic value). In any of these cases, the hydrant becomes inoperable to the fire department (the Department of Water Resources estimates that seven percent of the hydrants are inoperable). Finally, it should be noted that the misuse of hydrants is generally concentrated in a few areas

---

[5]This subsection was written in August, 1970 by the author and Linda Fraser, based on the latter's activities as a field worker.

of the city, so that the inoperable hydrants are similarly concentrated, increasing the hazards from the point of view of fighting fires.

It is normally the responsibility of the police department to close any hydrants that have been improperly opened. The uniformity with which the police carry out this responsibility varies, however, among different areas of the city. For instance, our neighborhood observers have noted that in some cases (Brownsville) the police pass open hydrants without making any attempt to close them; in other cases (East Harlem) the police may make a nominal attempt, but those who have been using the hydrant stand by and return to it as soon as the police have gone; in still other cases (Highbridge) the users may flee and exhibit more fear of the police, but still reopen the hydrant on some later occasion.

The city has also begun two programs in the last few years to prevent hydrant misuse. These two programs reveal an ambivalent attitude in city policy. On the one hand, the city has encouraged the use of hydrants by distributing spray cap attachments; on the other hand, it has discouraged hydrant use by installing hydrant harnesses that only the fire department can detach from the hydrant.

The spray cap program is based on the notion that residents should have some source of water for playing and wading, particularly in hot weather. The caps contain about three-dozen holes and fit onto the hydrant nozzle, but when in use they substantially reduce the loss of water and water pressure. The caps are distributed by two offices—the local police precinct or the mayor's urban task force—and are supposed to be signed for and returned. Along with the cap, a wrench is also given out. Thus the spray cap campaign makes two important assumptions: first, that a major use of the hydrants is similar to that provided by a local wading pool, and second, that the hydrant users should take the initiative by obtaining the caps from the local precinct or task force office.

The harness program is based on the notion that certain hydrants must be made inaccessible to the public. The harness is a thick metal belt that holds the nozzle caps in place; without removing the harness, the caps cannot be removed. So far about 25,000 harnesses have been installed. The vast majority have successfully prevented further abuse of the hydrants, but in many cases the harnesses have been broken (and the hydrants still misused), or the harnesses are still attached but the hydrants have been severely damaged. Among the damaged hydrants, most typically, the brass bolt is sawed off, but in other instances hydrants have been bent at the base or their bonnets shattered.

Other devices have been considered by the city, and indeed are being used by other cities. In each case city officials are caught between the fire department needing quick and easy access to a hydrant and some security device preventing local residents from using the hydrant. Officials are also aware that any new device (such as securing the brass bolt so that it cannot be turned) is likely to result in some retaliation on the part of residents, so that a short-run increase in hydrant damage can be expected.

The Observed Use of Hydrants

As a result of my work in Morrisania this summer and visits to the other small areas that are part of our study, I have found the following to be the main uses of hydrants by local residents.

Play. It is clear that many children do wade in the water and are generally satisfied merely by getting wet. However, this level of activity is limited mostly to very young children (up to five or six years) and to girls. For the older children and most of the boys, *the main play activity involves directing the strong hydrant flow at some object or person.* The method is to hold a cylindrical object (such as a beer can), which has been completely opened at both ends, near the nozzle of a fully flowing hydrant. The result is a powerful spray that can be aimed at different objects. People and cars are the objects most often sprayed. The people rarely get angry, as if they accept the risks in walking down a street with an open hydrant. Cars are another matter, for it may not be so easy for them to turn around and use another street, and also the children may wave the car through the street (indicating that the car will not get sprayed) and then decide to spray the car if the driver is perceived to be an outsider or of the wrong ethnicity. In general, the objects that are most often sprayed are those perceived as traveling through the area but not necessarily belonging to it. Buses (and passengers who have neglected to close their windows), for instance, are a good target. My own interpretation of this desire to spray objects is that the spray represents a powerful force that the children control, direct, and manipulate, and contrasts greatly with the many other aspects of their lives in which all of the powerful forces are out of their control. This contrast may be the reason that fire hydrants have such great attraction in low-income areas. For a change, children can manipulate their environment rather than be manipulated by it.

Games. The open hydrants provide an opportunity for all sorts of games. Two games require the hydrants to be opened full force: In one, the contest is to see who can most closely approach the hydrant by walking into its powerful spray; in the other, children ride on wooden crates that sled across or down the street, as in surfing. Other games require only a small but steady flow of water—racing hand-carved boats down the stream to some finish line and betting on the boats, or rolling wheels through the water and making water tracks with the wheels on the dry parts of the street.

Functional Uses. Many people do not remember that the hydrant's water comes from the same water main as water for houses and apartment buildings. Thus hydrant water can be safely used as a source of water for drinking, filling jars (I have seen men filling quart or gallon jars, but do not know why), cleaning cars, and even washing dishes. The hydrant water is preferable because it is cooler than the apartment water, but its use in these cases may also indicate that there is no running water in the user's household. Unfortunately, since the hydrant and apartment water are on the same main, a vicious cycle can easily be started: With the greater use of a hydrant, water pressure in the nearby apartment building will go down, and with the reduction in pressure, there is more need to use the hydrant and perhaps turn on another hydrant down the street, thus further reducing water pressure. Finally, the hydrants are used to spray the streets, either to cool them off or to clean them of debris, which often only the powerful hydrant spray can affect.

In all of these uses of hydrants, there is general cooperation within the community among neighbors and between adults and children. A local superintendent, for instance, may use his wrench to turn on a hydrant for a group of children, or mothers will bring their little children to a hydrant so they can play in the water. The unauthorized use of the hydrants, in other words, has become a *local custom,* and is by no means a surreptitious activity carried on by small groups of vandals.

Two observations regarding hydrants with spray caps may be of interest. First, where one hydrant on the street has a cap and the other is also turned on but without a cap, nobody plays at the capped hydrant. Second, water sprays (but not involving a hydrant) are also found in many of the public housing projects. That little girls are the main users of these sprays reinforces my interpretation that limited spray and merely getting wet are not the most attractive aspects of hydrant use.

Principles for Possible Solutions

Many different alternatives have already been considered in many different cities. Some, like the spray cap and harness programs, have been put into effect. Rather than consider specific solutions, however, I have chosen to emphasize some of the underlying principles that might lead to a more satisfactory solution.

First, I wish to make no judgment over whether the residents should be allowed to continue using hydrants. If it is decided that they should not, however, and an attempt is made to make the hydrants inaccessible to the residents but not to the firemen, then I strongly suggest that, whatever the change, it be made *internally,* without any obvious change to the outside of the hydrant. The harnesses, for instance, are unsightly and an open affront to the community, serving as constant reminders that the people have been denied access to the hydrant. It seems that a visible change is more likely to be interpreted by the residents as a challenge, that is, to learn how to get around the new device or to make it and the hydrant inoperable. An internal change, on the other hand, would not be conspicuous and might leave the residents more bewildered. An example of an internal change would be some sort of control of the valve system, preferably at a level higher than the individual hydrant. It has been suggested, for instance, that the hydrants be turned off as their normal state, and only be turned on when a relevant fire alarm is received.

Second, if it is decided that residents should have access to the hydrants, some basis for the open sharing of hydrants (between residents and firemen) should be established. The sharing might be very simple: Some hydrants would belong to the community, be identified as such, and not be used by the firemen; other hydrants would belong to the fire department and would be made inaccessible to the community. Unlike the use of the harnesses, no small area would be left entirely without a community hydrant; furthermore, the city and community could decide together which hydrants should be left to the residents and which to the firemen.

Third, if it is decided to solicit the community's cooperation on any of these matters, communications with the community should be initiated through local groups to which the older children are responsive, not the police precinct or task force office. The precinct, of course, has entirely negative associations for most youths in low-income areas; the task force offices mainly cater to the adult community, where they have any influence at all (a few of the worst areas with regard to open hydrants have been those with the least effective task forces). There are many indigenous youth groups in these communities, some of which already operate "street" programs, and it might be worth gaining their cooperation instead of using an existing city agency or setting up a new one.

Quantifying Neighborhood Observations: Fire Alarms and Streetcorners

Several assignments were completed in attempting to assess the ease of quantifying field observations and the usefulness of municipal records. As an illustrative example, one assignment, dealing with streetcorner observations and fire alarms, will be described.

It should be remembered that the alarm records were initially used to locate the exact streetcorner from which each participant-observer began his neighborhood work, with each participant-observer starting at a corner having a high rate of alarms (though no participant-observer knew anything at the outset about his neighborhood's alarm history, or about the reasons for the selection of the particular streetcorner). Such an assignment generally meant that the participant-observer began his field work at a very active and densely populated place in the neighborhood. Thus much time and effort were saved in locating "the action" during the first days in the field.

False Alarms

More pertinent to the delivery of fire services, specific observations were subsequently made with the goal of developing insight into the causes of the high and rapidly increasing rate of false alarms. To begin with, the total number of fire alarms in New York City had risen at a very high rate during the last ten years, having tripled from 1959 to 1969 and doubled from 1964 to 1969. As part of this overall rise, however, the proportion of false alarms had risen from 15.9 percent to 30.1 percent. Thus the number of false alarms had increased disproportionately in a period already marked by rapidly rising total alarms.

Because similar trends have occurred in other major cities, the search for effective measures to reduce false alarms has become increasingly urgent. Most typically, analyses of false alarm incidence have suggested that false alarms occur in or around schools and peak during the nonschool hours, so that preventive campaigns have largely been directed toward the school-age population. In New York City, however, such campaigns have had a diminishing impact. Other preventive measures tried or considered in various cities have been: the physical removal of street alarm boxes with high numbers of false alarms, the surveillance (by police, citizen volunteers, or cameras) of alarm boxes during periods of expected false alarms, and various mechanical alterations of the alarm box itself. In general, however, although the measures may have an initial deterrent effect, little long-term change occurs, and the short-term reduction may be accompanied by rises in false alarms at neighboring boxes.

The failure to develop adequate strategies for reducing fire alarms has resulted in part from a paucity of information. Because so few perpetrators of false alarms are apprehended, there is little opportunity to study directly the possible individual motives, as has been done, for instance, in cases of arson (e.g., Lewis and Yarnell, 1951; Macht and Mack, 1968; Vandersall and Wiener, 1970). Instead researchers have generally been limited to analyzing the false alarm incidence, and to indicating its important temporal and geographic variations. A complementary way of approaching the problem is to make field observations of alarm box locations (streetcorners) and to compare the observations with the alarm histories of each of the relevant alarm boxes. The individual motives would still be inaccessible for study, but the observations could focus on the pertinent streetcorner conditions within which false alarms occur, and might offer a different kind of insight into the false-alarm-producing process. In particular, it is not clear whether corners with disproportionately high numbers of false alarms tend to be corners with great or little activity. Some have hypothesized that false alarms occur near bars and carry-out food shops where many groups of people stand around; others, however, have countered that the false alarms occur on quiet corners, where there is little likelihood of a perpetrator being seen in action (Klatt, 1970).

In New York City, a study of streetcorners is particularly feasible because fire alarms are recorded according to the location of one of some 15,000 alarm boxes, which are generally placed at every other streetcorner. The alarm boxes are at the disposal of the public, who may use them to signal a call for fire equipment. On receiving a call, the fire department automatically dispatches fire engines to the site of the alarm box; only after arriving at the scene and dealing with the incident at hand does the department classify the original call according to one of five categories of alarms: (1) a building fire, (2) a nonbuilding (usually garbage or brush) fire, (3) a transportation fire (e.g., a fire in a vehicle), (4) an emergency (valid calls for help but not involving a fire), or (5) a false alarm. Because all alarms thus become associated with a streetcorner location,[6] there is an excellent opportunity to study the streetcorners in relation to their alarm histories.

Streetcorner Observations

Each participant-observer observed four corners in his neighborhood at different time periods, and covered

- The number of adults hanging around
- The number of children playing in the area
- The amount of garbage on the street
- The degree of residential land use of the streetcorner
- The general condition of the immediately surrounding buildings

The rankings for the number of adults and children were based on the average of the number of people observed at four time intervals. The rankings for

---

[6]Many alarms are received by telephone. In such cases, the alarm is still assigned to the nearest streetcorner alarm box for record-keeping purposes.

garbage were derived from a simple rating scheme, in which the amount of garbage on the sidewalks and streets was estimated on three different days according to a five-point scale.[7] Finally, the degree of residential land use was established by the ratio of store entrances to residential entrances, and the general condition of the immediately surrounding buildings was derived from the number of vacant buildings and a subjective impression of general building deterioration.

These observations were converted to ranks, with the four corners of each neighborhood ordered from 1 to 4 in terms of the degree to which they exhibited each of the observed street conditions (Table 14). The corners were also ranked according to the magnitude of the different types of alarms (the raw numbers for the alarms are shown in Table 14). None of the participant-observers was told of the alarm histories of the respective streetcorners until all the field observations had been completed.

Results

The rankings of the different alarm types were correlated with the rankings of the streetcorner characteristics, again within each neighborhood, but using Kendall's τ (Kendall, 1962). For any given correlation, for example, false alarms versus the number of adults, the different τ's for all seven neighborhoods were calculated and averaged.[8] Table 15 shows the τ's for all comparisons between alarm types and streetcorner characteristics.

The correlations indicated that all alarm categories were significantly related to each other. It was, therefore, expected that streetcorner characteristics related to one type of alarm were likely to be related to the others as well, and that generally was the case, with garbage (Table 15, column 8)

---

[7]This five-point scale consisted of: 1 = an essentially clean street (sidewalks and gutters); 2 = a street with garbage, but all garbage is properly contained and there is no litter; 3 = a street with garbage that is predominantly properly contained, but with litter and uncontained garbage as well; 4 = a street with garbage that is predominantly uncontained; 5 = a street in which uncontained garbage and litter dominate the entire sidewalk and gutter, to the extent that a pedestrian must deviate several times from a normal walking course.

[8]That is,

$$\bar{\tau}_{A,SC} = \frac{1}{7} \sum_{i=1}^{7} \tau_{A,SC,N_i}$$

for a comparison between a given alarm type and streetcorner characteristic, where A = alarm type, SC = streetcorner characteristic, and N_i = neighborhood i.

Table 14
Alarm Incidences and Streetcorner Rankings for Four Fire Boxes in Each Neighborhood

Neighborhood	Fire box no.	Number of alarms (1969)					Streetcorner characteristics (1 = Most, 4 = Least)				
		Bldg.	Non-bldg.	Trans.	Emerg.	False	Adults	Children	Garbage	More residential	Poor bldg. condition
Morrisania	2590	24	45	9	5[a]	28	2	1	1	3	1
	2707	16	14	3	16	35	3	3	3	2	3
	2711	44	10	6	40	15	1	2	2	4	2
	2749	6	6	0	5	2	4	4	4	1	4
Highbridge	2715	21	4	1	11	22	2	4	2	1	3
	2716	26	15	4	16	35	1	1	1	2	1
	2753	3[a]	2	0	5	2	3	2	3	4	2
	4738	3	2[a]	1[a]	0	1	4	3	4	3	4
Harlem	1376	50	28	4	28	21	2	1	1	3	1
	1385	71	55	3	35	21[a]	1	3	4	1	2
	1397	40	29	4[a]	14	25	4	2	2	2	3
	1420	23	9	0	11	16	3	4	3	4	4
East Harlem	1327	12	27	6[a]	11	19	4	1	3	1	3
	1328	16	6	3	16	17	2	3	4	2	4
	1334	78	98	26	18	29	3	2	1	3	1
	1343	32	76	6	34	42	1	4	2	4	2
Lower East Side	421	13	21	3	15	11	4	4	4	2	3
	432	87	114	56	24	27	1	1	1	4	1
	438	8	12	1	10	13	3	3	3	3	4
	439	53	39	9	26	32	2	2	2	1	2
Bushwick	808	6	5	2	5	30	2	2	2	4	4
	821	15	22	27	9	38	1	1	1	3	1
	822	34	31	9	13	51	3	3	3	1	2
	824	10	15	3	7	48	4	4	4	2	3
Brownsville	1639	22	10	1	17	14	4	4	4	3	4
	1640	151	121	20	39	132	3	1	1	2	1
	1659	96	85	14	31	83	2	3	2	1	2
	1671	30	18	1	9	32	1	2	3	4	3

[a]Tie was broken by ranking this box higher on basis of 1968 data.

Table 15
Correlation Coefficients for Alarms and Streetcorner Characteristics, Averaged Across All Seven Neighborhoods[a]

	Type of alarm					Streetcorner characteristics				
	(1) Bldg.	(2) Non-bldg.	(3) Trans.	(4) Emerg.	(5) False	(6) Adults	(7) Children	(8) Garbage	(9) More residential	(10) Poor bldg. condition
Type of alarm										
Building fire	X	0.76[c]	0.62[c]	0.86[c]	0.52[c]	0.52[c]	0.38[b]	0.57[b]	0.05	0.76[c]
Non-building fire		X	0.76[c]	0.62[c]	0.67	0.29	0.29	0.59[c]	0.29	0.71[c]
Transportation fire			X	0.43[b]	0.48[b]	0.19	0.57[c]	0.67[c]	0.10	0.71[c]
Emergency				X	0.62[c]	0.43[b]	0.14	0.38[b]	0.14	0.57[c]
False alarm					X	0.24	0.24	0.48[b]	0.24	0.48[b]
Streetcorner characteristics										
Adults						X	0.33	0.48[b]	−0.24	0.38[b]
Children							X	0.67[c]	−0.14	0.57[c]
Garbage								X	−0.19	0.71[c]
More residential									X	0.05
Poor building condition										X

[a] The values can range from −1 to +1, with zero indicating a completely random relation between the two variables in question; the significance levels indicate the probability that the value could have been obtained by chance if the variables were really unrelated.
[b] p < 0.05.
[c] p < 0.01.

and poor building condition (column 10) most closely related to all alarm categories, and residential land use (column 9) least related to all of them. Compared to other alarm types, the false alarm correlations did tend to be among the lower ones in relating to the presence of adults, children, garbage, and poor building condition, and among the higher ones in relating to residential land use. The tendencies, though not strong, were more in the direction of supporting the hypothesis that false alarms, in relation to the other alarm types, do tend to occur on the quieter corners of the neighborhood, where there are fewer people and less commercial activity.

Quantifying Field Observations: General Assessment

In general, the various tasks showed that quantification of human events is possible, but is also likely to be highly tedious and difficult. Even determining whether a person is passing through an intersection or hanging around it requires some carefully planned definitions; it entails the same difficulties encountered by investigators trying to code observations of any other complex human behavior (e.g., Weick, 1968). Mapping and counting physical structures, on the other hand, is not as difficult as dealing with human activities. For one thing, many characteristics of the physical environment, such as vacant buildings, are not as transient as human activities, and are not influenced by as many outside factors such as weather, holidays, and time of day.

Furthermore, the skills required to make quantitative assessments are different from those needed for successful participant-observation, and it may be that different individuals should carry out the two activities. In particular, once valid street indicators have been established, a future arrangement might be to have separate indicator-assessing and participant-observer teams.

CONCLUSIONS

This experience with participant-observation showed that there are several payoffs from using participant-observation as a tool for studying different urban neighborhoods, though no one should underestimate the sheer physical demand on the field worker who makes a commitment to this brand of sidewalk sociology.

First, participant-observation remains one of the few ways a social scientist or policy maker can uncover the qualitative differences among neighborhood subcultures. One of the assignments that was left uncompleted called for the canvassing of a neighborhood's recreation areas, with their location, use, and users to be noted. The reason it could not be completed was that the use of streets for recreation by kids is so intense and imaginative that it makes any distinction between recreation areas and nonrecreation areas rather meaningless. As another example, the study of sanitation conditions showed that two neighborhoods could have entirely different problems although residents would make similar complaints. In one neighborhood, garbage had accumulated over a long period of time and was a chronic problem; in another neighborhood, the first signs of poor garbage-disposal habits had appeared (a family that threw garbage out the window had just moved onto an otherwise well-kept block). In both cases the local residents were equally upset and vociferous, and might have responded similarly in an attitude survey, but the garbage "problem" and the potential solutions in the two cases were quite different.

Second, where systematically used, participant-observation can also uncover the quantitative means for assessing neighborhood conditions and change. Here the participant-observer can identify the observable signs in the neighborhood and the meaning of such signs. Out of the present study evolved several hypotheses about such signs: A shifting ethnic population is reflected by newly closed and opened stores and churches; signs of the least cared-for blocks in a neighborhood or of the least desirable neighborhoods are abandoned autos and other dumped garbage; broken family structures are reflected by the lack of dyadic groups of adult males and children (or of nuclear families) walking on the streets together; local unemployment is reflected by the incidence of male-only groups hanging around the street; and the initial vacant building on a block stigmatizes a neighborhood in the eyes of its residents, to the extent that continued residence in that area may become undesirable.

These and other hypotheses have to be fully tested in future work. Perhaps the most logical way of testing them would be to carry out a special study combining participant-observation with an area survey. It should be noted, however, that once street indicators have been identified and validated, they can be easily monitored for large sections of a city by a special team of observers or by neighborhood residents themselves (a "windshield" survey), and can provide a continual source of information about neighborhood condition and change. Furthermore, signs may be identified for some characteristics, like age, ethnicity, and income of a neighborhood's population, that otherwise remain unknown except for the diennial census and special surveys.

Finally, given such a framework for developing knowledge about urban neighborhoods, participant-observation can be used to cover neighborhoods in more than one city, and thus can form the basis for a broader comparative approach to the study of the urban neighborhood.

REFERENCES

Becker, Howard S. "Problems of Inference and Proof in Participant Observation." *American Sociological Review* 23 (1958): 652–660.

Bruyn, Severyn. *The Human Perspective in Sociology: The Methodology of Participant Observation.* Englewood Cliffs, N.J.: Prentice-Hall, 1966, pp. 1–22.

Burgess, Ernest W., and Bogue, Donald J. "Research in Urban Society: A Long View." In *Urban Sociology,* edited by Ernest W. Burgess and Donald J. Bogue. Chicago: Phoenix Books, 1967, pp. 1–14.

Gans, Herbert J. *The Urban Villagers: Group and Class in the Life of Italian-Americans.* New York: Free Press, 1962.

Glaser, Barney G., and Strauss, Anselm L. *The Discovery of Grounded Theory: Strategies for Qualitative Research.* Chicago: Aldine, 1967.

Goffman, Erving. *The Presentation of Self in Everyday Life.* Garden City, N.Y.: Anchor Books, 1959.

Gold, Raymond L. "Roles in Sociological Field Observations." *Social Forces* 1958, **36**, 217–223.

Hannerz, Ulf. *Soulside: Inquiries into Ghetto Culture and Community.* New York: Columbia University Press, 1969.

Jacobs, Glenn, ed. *The Participant Observer: Encounters with Social Reality.* New York: George Braziller, 1970.

Jacoby, Joan E. "The Neighborhood Early Warning System." *Socio-Economic Planning Sciences* 1970, *4*, 123–129.

Kendall, Maurice G. *Rank Correlation Methods.* 3d ed. London: Charles Griffin, 1962.

Klatt, James R. "False Alarms." *Fire Journal* 1970, *64*, 23.

Kluckhohn, Florence R. "The Participant Observer in Community Studies." *American Journal of Sociology* 1940, *46*, 331–343.

Lewis, Nolan D. C., and Yarnell, Helen. "Pathological Firesetting." *Journal of Nervous and Mental Diseases,* Monograph No. 82 (1951).

Liebow, Elliot. *Tally's Corner: A Study of Negro Streetcorner Men.* Boston: Little, Brown, 1967.

Lohman, J. D. "The Participant Observer in Community Studies." *American Sociological Review* 1937, *2*, 890–897.

Lynd, Robert and Lynd, Helen. *Middletown.* New York: Harcourt Brace, 1929.

Lynd, Robert, and Lynd, Helen. *Middletown in Transition.* New York: Harcourt Brace, 1937.

Macht, Lee B., and Mack, John E. "The Firesetter Syndrome." *Psychiatry* 1968, *31*, 277–288.

McKenzie, Roderick Duncan. *The Neighborhood: A Study of Local Life in the City of Columbus, Ohio.* Chicago: University of Chicago Press, 1923.

Miller, S. M. "The Participant Observer and Over-Rapport." *American Sociological Review* 1952, *17*, 97–99.

Molotch, Harvey. "Racial Integration in a Transition Community." *American Sociological Review* 1969, *34*, 878–893.

Schwartz, Morris S., and Schwartz, Charlotte G. "Problems in Participant Observation." *American Journal of Sociology* 1955, *60*, 350–351.

Suttles, Gerald D. *The Social Order of the Slum: Ethnicity and Territory in the Inner City.* Chicago: University of Chicago Press, 1968.

Valentine, Charles A. *Culture and Poverty: Critique and Counter-Proposals.* Chicago: University of Chicago Press, 1968, pp. 173–189.

Vandersall, Thornton A., and Wiener, Jerry M. "Children Who Set Fires." *Archives of General Psychiatry.* 1970, *22*, 63–71.

Vidich, Arthur J. et al., eds. *Reflections on Community Studies.* New York: Wiley, 1964.

Webb, Eugene J.; Campbell, Donald T.; Schwartz, Richard D.; and Sechrest, Lee. *Unobtrusive Measures: Nonreactive Research in the Social Sciences.* Chicago: Rand McNally, 1966.

Weick, Karl E. "Systematic Observational Methods." In *The Handbook of Social Psychology,* vol. 2, 2nd ed., edited by Gardner Lindzey and Elliot Aronson. Reading, Mass.: Addison-Wesley, 1968, pp. 357–451.

Whyte, William Foote. *Street Corner Society: The Social Structure of an Italian Slum.* 2d ed., Chicago: University of Chicago Press, 1955.

Whyte, William Foote. "On Street Corner Society." In *Contributions to Urban Sociology,* edited by Ernest W. Burgess and Donald J. Bogue. Chicago: University of Chicago Press, 1964, pp. 256–268.

Zorbaugh, Harvey Warren. *The Gold Coast and the Slum.* Chicago: University of Chicago Press, 1929.

11
Fire Alarms as Urban Social Indicators

Fire alarms normally include three kinds of events: (1) calls to the fire department because of the need to extinguish fires, (2) calls because of the need for emergency or ambulance (but nonfire-related) aid, and (3) false alarms. In the aggregate, the alarms are a record of physical and social deterioration in the central city; the highest incidence of alarms in any large city is nearly always found in the neighborhoods with the lowest-income population and with buildings in the poorest condition. Moreover, the incidence of alarms often varies directly with other forms of urban disorder. The U.S. Riot Commission (1968), for instance, noted that fires, along with rock throwing or sniping at control forces and along with the looting of stores, were the most common events that characterized the urban riots of the mid-1960s. Thus the record of fire alarms constitutes a potentially valuable resource as an urban social indicator. The purpose of this chapter is to explore this possibility in greater detail by examining three types of alarm patterns: cross-city trends, seasonal (temporal) patterns, and neighborhood differences.

CROSS-CITY COMPARISONS

The incidence of alarms in the largest United States central cities rose sharply for the decade from 1960 to 1970. However, the alarm incidence

---

This chapter is based on material excerpted from a previously unpublished paper, "The Development of Social Indicators" (delivered at the 21st Annual Meeting of the Eastern Sociological Society, Boston, April 1972).

FIRE ALARMS AS URBAN SOCIAL INDICATORS

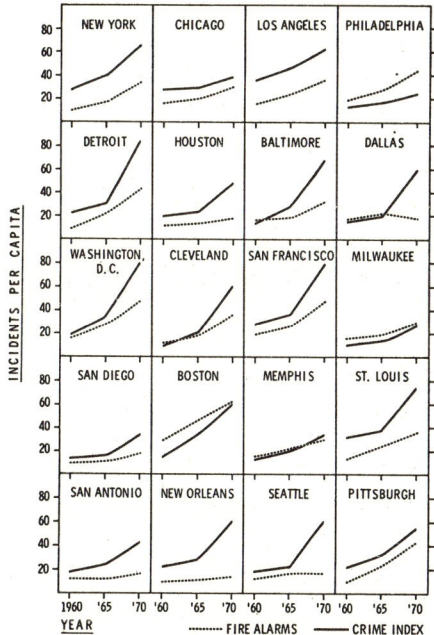

Figure 6. Per capita fire alarms and FBI Index crimes, twenty largest United States cities, 1960–1970. (Based on alarm and crime incidences for 1960, 1965, and 1970 [*Fire Journal* and *Uniform Crime Report*], and on census populations for 1960 and 1970.)

varied from city to city, and increased at varying rates in different cities, as shown graphically in Figure 6. The precise reasons for these variations, and for differences in the relationship between alarm incidence and the incidence of another commonly used indicator of urban disorder, the FBI Index crimes (shown for comparison purposes in Figure 6), are not yet known. The variations may be a result of different population characteristics in the cities, different types of police and fire protection services, or different reporting systems.

However, some interesting observations can be made just by ranking these cities according to the percentage of increase in their per capita alarm rates (Table 16, column 1). For purely numerical reasons, it might have been expected that those cities that began the decade with the lowest per capita rates would have shown the largest percentage increases; but that was not the case (column 2). Neither was a similar expectation that the percentage increase was merely an inverse function of city size; if anything, the more populated cities tended to have the large percentage increases (column 3). In contrast, the percentage increases in alarm rates seemed to be higher in

Table 16
Increase in per Capita Alarms for Twenty Largest Central Cities, 1960–1970

City	(1) Percent increase in per capita alarms, 1960–1970	(2) Per capita alarms 1960	(3) Rank by total population, 1960	(4) Percent increase in number of alarms, 1960–1970	(5) Percent change in total population, 1960–1970
Pittsburgh	331	9.7	16	272	−14
Detroit	282	10.9	5	244	−10
Cleveland	193	12.3	8	151	−14
Washington, D.C.	183	15.6	9	181	− 1
New York City	177	12.1	1	180	1
St. Louis	167	13.3	10	120	−17
San Francisco	145	19.2	11	137	− 3
Los Angeles	124	16.0	3	155	14
Philadelphia	118	20.3	4	111	− 3
Memphis	105	15.1	20	156	25
Boston	105	30.1	13	88	− 8
Baltimore	89	17.0	6	82	− 4
San Diego	80	9.9	18	118	22
Milwaukee	78	16.6	12	72	− 4
Chicago	76	16.9	2	67	− 5
Seattle	49	10.1	19	39	− 6
San Antonio	46	11.2	17	65	12
Houston	45	11.9	7	91	31
New Orleans	33	10.5	15	26	− 5
Dallas	0	17.1	14	24	24

those cities that, during the decade of the sixties, experienced *both*: (a) large percentage increases in the absolute number of alarms (column 4), and (b) a stable or declining population base (column 5). Moreover, the cities with more rapidly increasing alarms generally consisted of the older and eastern cities, where social and physical conditions are known to have declined more than in other cities.

These findings suggest a relationship between fire alarms and urban deterioration. The findings also highlight the general fiscal and social dilemma faced by the contemporary central city: As the population base and thus the municipal revenue resources have leveled off or declined, the needs for many municipal services, measured in absolute terms, have increased considerably.

FIRE ALARMS AS URBAN SOCIAL INDICATORS

A rising number of fire alarms requires, of course, increased service from fire protection forces, accomplished either through the realization of new efficiencies, or the addition of new resources, or both. How cities cope with this general dilemma is certainly a continuing challenge for municipal administrators.

The general rise in urban fire alarms over the last decade, however, should not obscure the fact that fire alarms also exhibit marked temporal and geographic regularities. For instance, there are well-known day-of-the-week patterns. In New York City, the pattern takes the form of a rise in alarms to a Friday-Saturday-Sunday peak and then a decline during the middle of the week. Alarms also follow a regular hourly pattern, in which the number of alarms rises as the late afternoon and early evening hours are reached, then declines after those hours. These and other consistent alarm patterns all appear to be independent of the recent historical rise in alarms, suggesting that fire alarms are an indicator of other urban phenomena in addition to the general pattern of physical and social deterioration. To illustrate this point, let us examine in greater detail two different alarm patterns: the seasonal variation in alarms and the neighborhood variation in alarms. Although both bases will draw on New York City alarm data, parallel situations evidently exist in other cities.

SEASONAL ALARM PATTERNS

In New York City, different types of alarms have different seasonal patterns. Both *false alarms* and alarms associated with *nonbuilding fires* (garbage, brush, rubbish, abandoned vehicle, and other outdoor fires) rise during the late spring and decline during the fall. Alarms associated with *building fires*, on the other hand, exhibit a double peak, one in the summer and another in the winter. Figure 7 shows the seasonal trends for one type of alarm, false alarms, by comparing the alarms to another seasonal indicator, the maximum daily temperature.

Note that the seasonal pattern persists in spite of the overall rise in false alarms during the 1964–1969 period; similar patterns persist for the other alarm types as well. In fact, Senator Daniel Patrick Moynihan, in his infamous "benign neglect" memo, suggested that because fire alarms increased in black low-income neighborhoods during July and August of every year, the alarms represented an endemic situation of which the 1964–1968 urban riots were epidemic conditions. Our own related research has shown that the seasonal pattern does indeed exist at the level of small geographic areas such as neighborhoods, but that it exists whether those areas are dominated by middle- or lower-income groups, or by white or nonwhite populations. Thus the

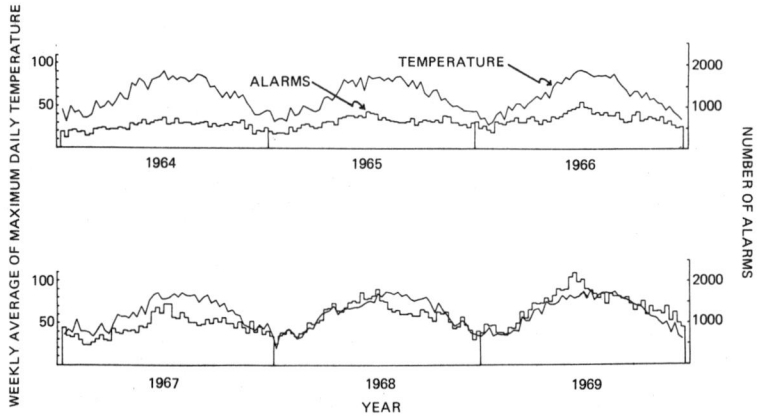

Figure 7. Weekly false alarms and temperature, New York City, 1964–1969.

seasonal pattern appears to reflect some general cycle of urban activity, and not one that is confined to low-income areas.

More detailed examination of the seasonal pattern has shown that the weekly variation of false but not other types of alarms is associated with the occurrence of a few holidays and with rises in temperature above seasonal norms. In other words, whenever there was a week with either: (a) one of several holidays—Easter, Independence Day, Labor Day, Halloween, Thanksgiving, and New Year's Day—or (b) a higher weekly average temperature than the preceding or following weeks, there tended to be more false alarms than in the preceding or following weeks (interestingly, the relationship to temperature changes was just as strong in the winter as in the summer). The observation of increases in false alarms during holiday periods led many people to suggest that the effect was attributable not so much to holidays as to the fact that more children, who are suspected to be the main perpetrators of false alarms, are out of school. This hypothesis was found to have little support, because the false alarms were not higher on weeks with school days off.[1]

Table 17 summarizes these findings. The method of analysis was to determine for the years 1964–1969 the overall number of *peak alarm weeks* for each of three types of alarms: false alarms, alarms associated with non-

---

[1] Fortunately for analytic purposes, school days off can be distinguished from holidays because there is no large overlap between national holidays and days off on the New York City public school calendar; several days off are associated with local events like Yom Kippur or Election Day, and when most national holidays fall on a weekend, they are not observed with a day off from school.

Table 17
Analysis of Weekly Fire Alarms, New York City, 1964–1969

Category of weeks	False alarms		Nonbuilding fire alarms		Building fire alarms	
	Peak	Nonpeak	Peak	Nonpeak	Peak	Nonpeak
1. All weeks, 1964–1969[a]	86	220	82	224	81	225
2. Weeks with any of five holidays[b]	25	5	14	16	14	16
3. Peak temperature weeks	48	41	35	54	26	63
(April–October)	(24	27)	(21	30)	(17	34)
(rest of year)	(24	14)	(14	24)	(9	29)
4. Weeks with either five special holidays or peak temperatures	62	45	40	67	33	74
5. Weeks with school days off	22	33	17	38	23	32

[a]Only the fifty-one whole weeks for each year were included. Thus fractional weeks at the beginning and end of the year, and hence New Year's Day, were excluded from the analysis.
[b]Easter, Independence Day, Labor Day, Halloween, and Thanksgiving.

building fires, and alarms associated with building fires. A peak alarm week was simply defined as a week that had more alarms than both the week preceding it and the week following it. Weeks with holidays, peak temperatures (again, an average temperature higher than that of the preceding or following week), and school days off were also separately identified, and analyzed according to whether they occurred during peak alarm weeks or not.[2] The analysis showed the disproportionate number of peak false alarm weeks (62 out of 86, or 72 percent) that fell on either holidays or high-temperature weeks (Table 17, row 4). The analysis also showed that the other types of alarms did not conform to the false alarm pattern.

---

[2]A word should be said about the use of weeks as a unit of analysis, since the incidents being studied, holidays and high temperatures, are daily events. There were three reasons for the use of weeks. First, prior analysis of hourly alarm patterns had shown that the holiday and temperature effects often spread to more than one day, for example, the following morning, a long weekend, and in the case of holidays only, the preceding night. Second, weeks form comparable units. Any analysis of daily alarm patterns would have been difficult because of the potential confusion created by the day-of-the-week pattern. Third, the weekly analysis, though less precise, gave emphasis to the magnitude of the increase in alarms, namely, that during holiday or high temeprature periods, false alarms increased to the extent that the false alarm total for the entire week had substantially increased.

164   **CHAPTER 11**

This analysis of seasonal alarm patterns has thus suggested that false alarms are a potential indicator of a general urban activity that is: (a) associated with several national holidays and with rises in temperature, but not with school days off, and (b) independent of either the general rise in urban fire alarms or neighborhood variations in alarms.

NEIGHBORHOOD ALARM PATTERNS

An examination of fire alarms according to their neighborhoods shows that some neighborhoods characteristically have more alarms per unit area than others. Once again, the neighborhood differences persist in spite of the general rise in citywide alarms. This fact is shown in Figure 8, in which the twelve community planning districts of Manhattan (New York City Planning Commission, 1969), "super" neighborhoods to be sure, have been ranked by their 1965 incidence of fire alarms. Virtually the same rankings persisted for 1970, even though all districts had experienced a sharp rise in alarms. (The exact location of the districts is shown on the map in Figure 9.)

These neighborhood alarm patterns are not a simple function of differences in total population or in the number of dwelling units in the districts. Figure 8, for instance, also shows the population per square mile for the twelve districts, and shows how the population does not relate closely to the alarm incidence. Instead, the neighborhood variations in alarms are related

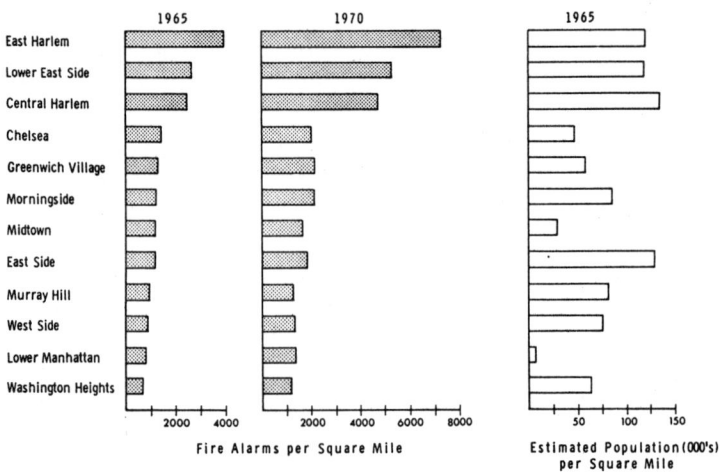

Figure 8. Fire alarms for Manhattan, by community planning district, 1965 and 1970.

FIRE ALARMS AS URBAN SOCIAL INDICATORS

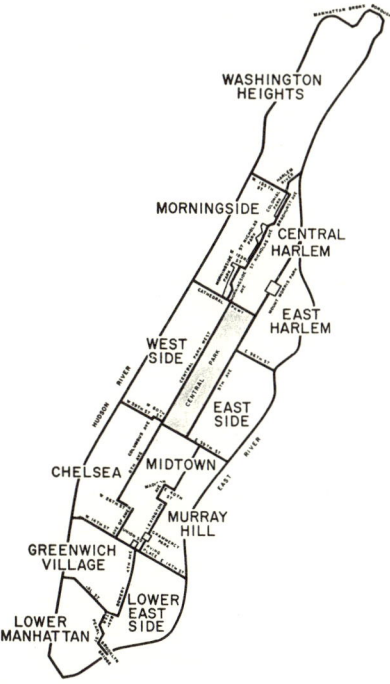

Figure 9. Community Planning Districts, Manhattan. (Adopted by the City Planning Commission, 1 March 1968.)

to the socioeconomic condition of the neighborhoods. Higher rates of alarms are nearly always found in low-income areas like Harlem, East Harlem, and the Lower East Side. That fire alarms should be higher in these areas should come as no surprise, for a high incidence of urban fires is a manifestation of such conditions as uncollected garbage in the streets, deteriorating buildings with poor electrical wiring and malfunctioning stoves, and poorly supervised children's play. Obviously, in this respect, fires act as both a cause and an effect in the vicious cycle of ghetto life; deteriorating buildings lead to more fires, but fires also lead to more building deterioration.

As neighborhood indicators, however, fire alarms potentially have a much greater value than merely serving to identify the poorer and deteriorating areas of the city. There are many other ways of making such identifications, and fire alarms would be redundant with those other ways. By far the greater importance of fire alarms as a neighborhood indicator lies in the possibility that alarms also reflect *general* types of neighborhoods and *general* processes of neighborhood change.

The possibility regarding a neighborhood typology arises from the fact that neighborhoods not only differ in gross alarm rates but also have characteristic differences for single types of alarms. To illustrate this point, Table 18 shows the rank order of the twelve community planning districts, first for building fire alarms, and second for false alarms. The rank orders for each type of alarm remain virtually the same for 1965 and 1970, even though the percentage of building fires increased in all cases for this period. Second, there is by no means an inverse or simple relationship between the percentage of building fire alarms and the percentage of false alarms.[3] Instead, the suggestion here is that the districts can be categorized along at least two dimensions—false alarms and building fires—and that areas high on both are likely to be different kinds of neighborhoods than areas high on one and low on the other, low on both, and so on. Thus, for example, Table 18 suggests that Central Harlem (high on building fires, medium on false alarms) might be a more aging neighborhood than East Harlem (low on building fires, high on false alarms), even though both are characteristically considered low-income neighborhoods.

As for neighborhood change, firemen have often noted that an initial rise in false alarms following years of stable alarm rates may be an early sign of a "tipping" neighborhood. Conversely, a decline in false alarms following years of high alarm rates may be an early sign of neighborhood renewal. The potential value of such use of fire alarms is that, although neighborhood change and evolution necessarily occur over long periods, the important shifts in that evolution may occur over much briefer periods, and fire alarms may be helpful in identifying those shifts in a timely and accurate manner.[4]

SUMMARY

Fire alarms are multiple indicators of urban conditions. There are many distinguishable alarm patterns, and three of them have been examined here: cross-city comparisons, seasonal variations, and neighborhood patterns. Each of these patterns reflects different aspects of urban social conditions, with the citywide rate relating to the overall physical and social deterioration of the central city, the seasonal variation relating to general cycles of urban activity,

---

[3] It should be remembered that these two types of alarms account for only about half of all alarms, with emergency calls and nonbuilding fire alarms accounting for the other half.
[4] There have been many hints about stage or other sequential theories of neighborhood change, but no definitive results have been produced. The literature begins with Park and Burgess's exposition of the zonal hypothesis in 1925; for two examples of more recent developments, see Hartshorn (1971) and Birch (1971).

Table 18
Twelve Community Planning Districts Ranked According to
Incidence of Different Types of Alarms, 1965

	1965	1970
Proportion of all alarms that were for building fires (%)		
Central Harlem	47	34
Midtown	41	31
West Side	40	32
Morningside	40	31
East Side	40	29
Murray Hill	36	27
Chelsea	35	29
Greenwich Village	32	22
East Harlem	30	20
Lower East Side	30	20
Lower Manhattan	28	21
Washington Heights	27	23
Proportion of all alarms that were for false alarms (%)		
East Harlem	26	32
Lower East Side	24	32
Morningside	18	25
Washington Heights	18	21
Central Harlem	16	19
Greenwich Village	15	23
Chelsea	14	20
West Side	13	18
Lower Manhattan	12	15
Murray Hill	11	18
East Side	10	15
Midtown	10	13

and the neighborhood variation relating to differences in neighborhood condition. Thus it is apparent that the interpretation of fire alarms as urban indicators depends, among other things, on the temporal and geographic levels on which the alarms are analyzed.

This brief review of fire alarm patterns also has implications for the general development of social indicators (see Bauer, 1966; Sheldon and Moore, 1968). Because alarms are reported in fine spatial and temporal detail, a richer and more diverse analysis of urban conditions is possible. However, the availability of such rich sources of information for social indicators poses a new challenge for researchers and policy makers alike, bringing the development of real, operational social indicators one step closer to reality. In the future, it will be increasingly difficult to justify only general discussion of indicators or to ignore particular issues because of the lack of adequate social statistics; people will have to concern themselves much more with the ultimate purposes of specific social indicators, and with how these indicators are to be interpreted and used.

REFERENCES

Bauer, Raymond A., Ed. *Social Indicators.* Cambridge, Mass.: MIT Press, 1966.
Birch, David L. "Toward a Stage Theory of Urban Growth." *Journal of the American Institute of Planners* 1971, *37,* 78–87.
Hartshorn, Truman A. "Inner City Residential Structure and Decline." *Annals of the Association of American Geographers* 1971, *61,* 72–96.
New York City Planning Commission. *Plan for New York City.* Vol. 4. *Manhattan.* Cambridge, Mass.: MIT Press, 1969.
Park, Robert E., and Burgess, Ernest W. *The City.* Chicago: University of Chicago Press, 1925.
Sheldon, Eleanor Bernert, and Moore, Wilbert W., eds. *Indicators of Social Change: Concepts and Measurements.* New York: Russell Sage Foundation, 1968.
U.S. Riot Commission. *Report of the National Advisory Commission on Civil Disorders.* New York: E. P. Dutton, 1968.

12

Improving the Evaluation of Neighborhood Intervention Programs

THE NEED FOR PRACTICAL METHODOLOGICAL RESEARCH

Federal agencies have initiated a whole host of neighborhood intervention programs. The Community Development Block Grant (CDBG) program, the Urban Reinvestment Task Force (and Neighborhood Housing Services), the Neighborhood Strategy Areas, the Neighborhood Self-Help program, and neighborhood anticrime efforts are but the latter-day counterparts of earlier Model Cities, urban renewal, public housing, and economic development programs. In each case, the program is aimed at improving a *neighborhood site*.[1] This focus on a collective unit of analysis distinguishes these intervention programs from others that are aimed solely at improving individual persons or households. In these latter types of programs—for example, employment,

---

This chapter is a revised version of a previously unpublished paper, which was first written in 1979. The research was partially supported by the U.S. Department of Housing and Urban Development, though none of the comments should be construed as representing the official views of that agency.

[1]That does not necessarily imply a "physical" definition of neighborhoods; even if a neighborhood is defined in terms of its residents, the goal of the intervention is to improve the *collective* lot of those residents, which is presumed to be more than the sum of the specific improvements for each individual resident. Thus the unit of analysis is the collectivity.

169

welfare, or educational programs—the individual person can be the unit of analysis in the design of any program evaluation.[2]

The evaluation of neighborhood interventions ("neighborhood evaluations") poses peculiar difficulties *because of the collective nature of the unit of analysis.* For one thing, any intervention will only work unevenly across the whole unit of analysis; presumed changes in resident behavior or housing conditions cannot be translated into an overall "neighborhood" effect. For another, the sample of sites will probably be small, relative to the number of variables of interest. Finally, the sites are heterogeneous enough that they cannot be easily matched for any comparison purposes, and it is politically infeasible to "randomly" assign sites to different treatment conditions. For all these reasons, the designer of neighborhood evaluations may have to discard many of the traditional notions of research design (Yin, 1978).

Participants in the evaluation process, who include both *researchers* who conduct evaluations and *sponsors* of evaluation studies, have been aware of the practical difficulties of conducting neighborhood evaluations for some time (e.g., Horst et al., 1976). In fact, those currently involved in neighborhood evaluations have come to realize that a myth may have been perpetrated. This myth is that neighborhood evaluations should be designed to follow the traditional research designs—a myth fueled by the production of such handbooks as the EDA's *Evaluating Economic Development Programs* (Milkman, Toborg, Perez, and Boyd, 1978) or HUD's *Program Evaluation and Analysis* (Public Technology, Inc., 1978).[3] The myth leads to the continually frustrating position whereby some external observers, such as the GAO, apply incorrect and unreasonable criteria in assessing the worthiness of evaluation efforts (see Comptroller General, 1978a, 1978b); similarly, other participants, such as topflight researchers, may no longer desire to get involved in this type of evaluation research in the first place.

In contrast, if neighborhood evaluations are to be successfully conducted in the future, both researchers and sponsors need some practical advice on how to conduct evaluations, given reality-based circumstances—that is, within the contemporary political and administrative framework. The purpose of this final chapter is to suggest that HUD and other federal agencies supporting neighborhood interventions should initiate a series of *practical methodological research* studies. The goal of these studies would be to identify specific meth-

---

[2]Housing programs, as distinct from neighborhood programs, present a mixed situation. On the one hand, because the housing programs intervene with specific parcels, such parcels can serve as individual units of analysis; on the other hand, the broader aim of a housing program is often to improve the surrounding neighborhood, and here the unit of analysis would be a collective one.

[3]Along the same lines, another paper written by two HUD officials (Sumka and Gardner, 1980) claims that the use of traditional research designs can be a feasible goal.

IMPROVING THE EVALUATION OF NEIGHBORHOOD PROGRAMS

odological solutions to existing problems in the conduct of neighborhood evaluations. This chapter attempts to outline some of the problems and potential solutions that these studies should cover.

TYPICAL PROBLEMS FACED BY THE DESIGNERS OF NEIGHBORHOOD EVALUATIONS

At present, the typical neighborhood evaluation begins with the goal of determining the "impact" of a neighborhood intervention. A neighborhood intervention, as previously suggested, can consist of

- The provision of funds to improve municipal services and neighborhood facilities (e.g., the CDBG program—see Dommel, 1978; Office of Evaluation, 1978)
- The initiation of a crime prevention program for a residential area or a public housing project (e.g., LEAA or HUD anticrime programs)
- The encouragement of private sector activities, such as economic or community development, through the provision of seed money or low-interest loans (e.g., HUD or EDA urban development funds—see Office of Evaluation, 1979; Office of Policy Development and Research, 1975)

Whatever the program, a fair question at the outset is whether, after a reasonable period the program has improved the condition of the neighborhood. This basic informational need usually underlies the design of a program evaluation (Bernstein, 1976; Freeman, 1977; Nachmias, 1978).

In spite of the apparent reasonableness of this primary objective, most neighborhood evaluations encounter a series of problems that prevent the basic question from being answered if the traditional research design approach[4] is used. Four classes of problems may be identified: (1) those that are related to the basic nature of the intervention, (2) those that arise from the difficulties of establishing adequate measures (3) those that prevent the traditional research design approach from being implemented, and (4) those that involve the management of the evaluation study. Each of these classes of problems will be discussed in turn; the main recommendation is that these problems should help set the agenda for the proposed, practical methodological research studies.

---

[4]The traditional research design approach is considered any approach stemming from the experimental or quasi-experimental designs enumerated by Campbell and Stanley (1966); see also Caporaso and Roos (1973) and Cook and Campbell (1979).

Problems Related to the Nature of the Intervention

For the practical, problems related to the nature of the intervention will probably be considered unavoidable. This first class of problems emanates from the political and administrative reality of federally initiated programs, a reality that is unlikely to change and that will therefore continue to play havoc with any evaluation study. For the purposes of discussion, several of these problems will be described illustratively; one goal of the proposed practical methodological research studies would be to uncover other, related problems. However, these problems may have to be seen as the constraints under which evaluations must be conducted, rather than as problems about which anything can be done.

Staggered Initiation of Site Activities

Most neighborhood interventions involve a group of sites, generally spread across the country in some regionally representative fashion. Even if one makes the naïve assumption that the initiation of site activities is marked by the initial awarding of federal funds, the complex nature of the contemporary award process means that different sites will begin at different times. That is so even in a *formula* program, such as the CDBG program, where different cities are known to have initiated their spending in staggered fashion in spite of the fact that the funds were made available at the same time. In an *award* program the situation is blatantly worse; some sites simply do not receive their awards until many months after other sites.

This staggered initiation of site activities means that any data collection plans on the part of the evaluation study will be contaminated. If a "wave" of surveys is conducted, for instance, the interpretation of the data must, at a minimum, take the varied initiation periods into account. However, such variation introduces yet another variable in a situation that, as previously suggested, already has too many variables for the likely sample of sites.

Differences in the Intervention from Site to Site

A second common problem, also usually inherent in the nature of the intervention, is that a federal intervention is actually not a single "experiment," in which the treatment is the same from site to site. Instead and especially because of the political emphasis on local initiatives, the actual intervention is likely to differ considerably from site to site. In the extreme, the result of this variation is the creation of a federal program in which there are multiple local experiments, not a single national one.[5] However, documentation of this variation—for example, local criteria for selecting target neighborhoods—is scarce or nonexistent in most evaluation reports.

The Changing Nature of the Intervention over Time

A third problem is that the intervention activities themselves will change over time. The potential sources of such change are varied. New national political priorities may emerge, such as HUD's 1978 emphasis in the CDBG program on targeting low- and moderate-income groups, on encouraging increased citizen participation, or on increasing federal paperwork requirements to exercise more control over local CDBG programs. Local political turnover or shifts in decision-making power are another source of change that may be anticipated; for instance, the Brookings study of the CDBG program found notable shifts in the composition and relative influence of participants in CDBG decision making over a two-year period, with a greater role later being played by citizens (Dommel, 1978). Finally, the nature of the intervention can change, in desirable directions, as a result of early experiences and feedback about initial activities. If some activities appear more successful than others, then a site should adjust to this reality and shift the emphasis in its activities in future years.

All of these changes have created what has become popularly regarded as "moving target" research. In essence, an evaluation of a program is occurring that is not unitary over time. In some situations, the intervention program may so markedly shift its priorities and goals that the initial evaluation design may become irrelevant. Even if the shift is slight, however, a full-fledged national evaluation design might be so distorted as to be rendered useless.

The Role of Technical Assistance Groups

Many contemporary neighborhood intervention programs involve assistance from a technical consulting group, whose role is to promote the intervention and ease its implementation at any given site. Such has especially been the case with anticrime programs, where technical assistance contractors have been funded, by federal agencies, to provide consultation to local groups and agencies.

---

[5]It is also true that the intervention may vary *within* site, as is the case when CDBG funds are divided and then administered by differect city agencies. In this situation there would have to be multiple evaluation designs within sites, and not just across sites.

The presence of a technical assistance contractor at each site also serves to increase the variability in the nature of the intervention. Now, not only are there the differences attributable to staggered starting times, local initiatives, and changes in the intervention over time, but there is also the difference in the "treatment" provided by the technical assistance group. Nevertheless, the technical assistance group plays a potentially vital role in the intervention: Without technical assistance, many sites would not be able to implement the intervention in the first place. For the evaluation team, the presence and role of the technical assistance group must be accepted as another fact of life; variations in technical assistance may be measured—with difficulty—but cannot by any means be controlled.

Summary

These are but four of the potential problems created by the nature of the intervention itself; others could have been identified. The overall conclusion, however, is that these problems are inherent in the administrative process and therefore represent constraints in the design and conduct of any neighborhood evaluation. Although it is important to recognize these types of problems, little can be done about them, and future evaluations should be designed to assume these constraints.

Problems Related to Measurement

A second class of problems arises from the difficulties of establishing adequate measures of what is occurring at an intervention site. In some cases the costs of adequate measurement are too high; in other cases the existing state of the art provides little guidance for determining the relevant measures. Whichever the situation, measurement problems are a topic that should be directly addressed by practical methodological research in the future.

Measuring Ultimate Objectives

A common expectation is that a program can be evaluated in terms of its impact on ultimate objectives. These objectives usually involve the quality of neighborhood life or improvements in the local economy. However, such goals are usually defined broadly; specific objectives providing standards for local or national achievement are not explicitly stated. As a result, in a recent GAO assessment of HUD's evaluation system (Comptroller General, 1978a), the reviewers found that most program evaluations did an adequate job of describing program activity; however, because program objectives and performance standards were lacking or poorly established, "progress toward program goals" could not be adequately addressed. During the period covered by the GAO review, HUD's Office of Policy Development and Research completed 38 evaluation studies, of which only 12 used performance standards (e.g., legislative or departmentally written goals) to measure program achievement. The existence of this problem suggests that the search for performance measures of ultimate objectives may have to be enhanced by alternative approaches.

Conflicts among Ultimate Objectives

Second, not only may ultimate objectives be broadly and unclearly specified, but the objectives themselves may cover conflicting courses of action or effects. For instance, among the major goals of the CDBG legislation are: neighborhood stabilization and revitalization, spatial decentralization of low- and moderate-income groups, and geographic and income targeting. Yet these objectives cannot in reality be achieved simultaneously; funds used to improve the physical environment and the social services for low- and moderate-income persons in target areas may hinder the spatial decentralization goal by encouraging those persons to remain in a predominantly low-income area.

These and other conflicting goals may nevertheless have to be covered by an evaluation study. One obvious approach is to use a multiplicity of outcome measures, rather than to focus on a single measure. Whether this is the best or only approach should be addressed in further methodological research.

Measuring Private Behaviors

A private behavior is one that is generally inaccessible to direct observation or measurement by the researcher (whether the researcher is personally present or represented by some mechanical recorder). Because a researcher cannot make any direct observations of such behaviors, he must rely on indirect sources (e.g., verbal recall), which produce measurement error and bias. The criminal act is the classic private behavior, with only the victim and the offender actually present.[6] For neighborhood policy, important private behaviors are the amount and quality of home or property maintenance activity, as well as the frequency of intrafamily loans to cover housing costs.

These and other types of private behaviors may be critical determinants of the outcomes of a neighborhood intervention program, but are difficult to

---

[6]The main exception is the filming of bank robberies. Otherwise researchers have had very little direct access to the criminal act.

measure. Property maintenance or intrafamily loan behavior can, for instance, significantly affect a neighborhood housing market. The main goal is for the researcher to recognize that direct observation is impossible and that only indirect measures are being used. However, a challenge for the future might be the development of direct measures of these private behaviors.

Problems Related to Traditional Research Designs

A third set of problems arises from the inability to implement a traditional experimental (or quasiexperimental) research design in conducting a neighborhood evaluation. The research design problems mean that, even if the seriously identified problems can be alleviated, causal inferences from the traditional standpoint would be difficult if not impossible to make, in attributing certain impacts to the neighborhood intervention program in question.

The research design problems are numerous; it has already been noted that, where neighborhood sites are the units of analysis, there is likely to be an inability to "match" sites and thereby to establish any sort of comparison or control groups. It has also been suggested, again with sites as the units of analysis, that the number of sites is unlikely to be large enough to permit inferences about the large number of relevant variables. Typically, as in HUD's anticrime program, a number on the order of thirty to fifty sites may be involved in a single intervention; such a number is clearly insufficient to test any interactive hypotheses among variables. In addition to these previously noted problems, two others are worthy of attention.

The Likely Existence of Multiple Interventions

A common design problem is that the program under evaluation is not likely to be the only program that has been operating at each site in question. Other programs, both federally and locally sponsored (as well as private activities), are likely to have been in operation—especially for the typical urban, low-income neighborhood. For instance, the Urban Homesteading program at first appears to be a singular intervention in that it deliberately transfers HUD-owned property to neighborhood residents in participating cities; homesteaders willing to rehabilitate the housing are selected and aided in obtaining funds and contracts for the rehabilitation (Office of Policy Development and Research, 1977). However, from the inception of the program, homesteading alone was deemed insufficient to stabilize and preserve neighborhoods. Therefore a package of mutually reinforcing interventions—for example, CDBG funds for housing rehabilitation, technical assistance, and program administration; 312 loan authority for rehabilitation financing; and city guarantees of service improvements in target neighborhoods—was strongly encouraged by HUD. In practice, this package mandate was significantly realized, and an early evaluation of the Homesteading program pointed to the considerable overlap of programs.[7] The evaluation thus noted the likely difficulty of distinguishing the unique contribution of homesteading per se.

If it is a needy neighborhood, the existence of multiple interventions makes eminent political and administrative sense. However, as the above example suggests, evaluation studies will have a difficult time attributing any single effect (even if measurable) to any single program. To this extent the basic goals of the evaluation will be difficult to fulfill.

Prior, Intervention-Related Activities

A variety of new neighborhood programs have taken advantage of or have extended previous neighborhood efforts. This continuity in local operational activity causes another problem for the evaluation study: It is difficult to determine when the intervention actually began. With the Urban Reinvestment Task Force, most Neighborhood Housing Services (NHS) began with informal neighborhood coalitions of residents, city government officials, and private lenders, which had to be formed *before* the Urban Reinvestment Task Force could be approached for assistance in establishing an NHS. Is the formation of such centrally important coalitions part of the intervention? Furthermore, certain NHS's were in operation prior to the initiation of federal funds; similarly, urban homesteading was in operation in at least two cities (Philadelphia and Wilmington, Delaware) before it became a federal demonstration program. Are the earlier nonfederal efforts part of the intervention? Finally, categorical programs were operational across the country before the CDBG consolidation of these programs occurred, and the anticrime demonstrations under the Public Housing Urban Initiatives program openly permitted extensions of previous public housing activities to qualify for the new funding for crime prevention efforts.

All of these examples suggest that few neighborhood interventions began from a zero base. In fact, given the history of federal interventions over the past thirty years (Yin, 1980), any urban neighborhood is likely to have carried out relevant activities prior to the initiation of funds from a new neighborhood

---

[7]For example, each of the 40 target neighborhoods was also a designated CDBG area; 5 coincided with NHS target areas; 10 had code enforcement programs; 17 had other loan and grant programs for rehabilitation; and 13 of the 23 demonstration cities relied wholly or in part on the 312 loan program as a source of rehabilitation finance. In some cities, the 312 funds were also used to rehabilitate nonhomestead property, making it even more difficult to attribute neighborhood revitalization effects to the homesteading program alone (Office of Policy Development and Research, 1977).

intervention. This fact of life, in which specific sites do not begin from a zero baseline activity, is yet another example of a problem posed for the traditional research designs. Numerous other problems might have been mentioned. In the aggregate, the problems probably challenge the notion that any traditional experimental or quasiexperimental design can be feasibly executed in a neighborhood evaluation.

Problems Related to the Management of the Evaluation Study

As if these three classes of problems were not enough, there is a fourth class that has become increasingly prominent over the last few years. This class involves the management of the evaluation study, in which research investigators as well as research sponsors must cope with a variety of constraining conditions. We shall discuss three such problems.

Adequate Level of Funding

The first problem is that sponsoring agencies usually commit themselves to an overall dollar amount to support an evaluation, and *then* design the needed evaluation within the perceived limits of this dollar amount. However, in some cases the dollar amount may be so low that few, if any, important research questions can be answered. Under such circumstances, a neighborhood evaluation may be doomed from the outset. If a certain level of resources is required to conduct the "bare-bones" evaluation, this amount must simply be set aside by the sponsoring agency. The only way such a problem can be alleviated is for the sponsoring agency to have first articulated (even to itself) a crude design for the evaluation and then to determine the necessary level of funding. One suspects, however, that this sequence of decision making rarely takes place.

Forms Clearance

For studies in which public opinion is to be surveyed, special clearance must be obtained for the survey instrument and design. The purpose is to assure that the public is not overwhelmed by federally funded data collection activities or by an unnecessary invasion of privacy. Both these objectives are eminently justifiable, but the way in which the clearance process has been implemented creates delay and timing problems for the evaluation study.

The delay has been in the nature of ninety days, the minimum period that has been required from the time of submission to the time of approval. Although this delay creates difficulties, these are controllable as long as the costs of the delay have been anticipated.

A more significant effect that the clearance process has had on the management of evaluation studies is in the timing of study activities. In the past, and in studies in which clearance has not been needed, researchers have typically allowed a long period for developing their survey instruments, including adequate conceptualization and pilot testing. The instrument-development process, in fact, can fill a major part of the overall time allotted to a study, with data collection a relatively quick step (even for a large survey, where one may be "into" and "out of" the field in a matter of weeks). The need for clearance, however, has sharply curtailed this instrument-development activity. Thus researchers have been forced to develop their instruments and sampling plans prematurely (or to rely on old instruments and sampling plans). The problem has not been adequately solved and continues to cause dilemmas in the basic sequencing of evaluation activities. The most unfortunate situation is where the scheduling of an evaluation study's entire activities is designed around the need for forms clearance.

Research for Formative Purposes

A third prevalent problem in the management of evaluation studies is that research sponsors (or those operating the neighborhood intervention program) often desire to have formative results from the evaluation. The traditional experimental or quasiexperimental design, which is aimed at producing summative findings, is not necessarily flexible enough to yield early results. Because of this limitation of the summative design, the requirements for formative reporting are usually poorly integrated into the overall evaluation study plan.

Other Related Problems

These problems that have been enumerated are only the more prominent of those facing neighborhood evaluations. Additional problems could have been described, including

- The problem that most of the important impacts will only occur over a period that is usually longer than that allotted for the evaluation[8]
- The problem that the rules for reviewing the final report are rarely specified in enough detail to avoid excessive and costly redrafting—

---

[8]A good example here is the urban renewal program, whose effects have changed considerably over a period of decades.

in many cases, the evaluation contract only allows for one cycle of comments even though reviewers may wish two or three cycles

The important thing to note is that the problems do appear to fall into four classes. Of the four, the nature of the intervention itself is not one over which much control can be exerted. Thus, in initiating further research on *practical methodologies,* a research sponsor such as HUD should focus on the elaboration of the three remaining classes of problems: research measurement, research design, and research management.

ILLUSTRATIVE SOLUTIONS THAT DESERVE FURTHER INVESTIGATION

The preceding section has suggested that the identification of evaluation problems should form one portion of the research agenda for practical methodological studies in the future. A second portion of the research agenda, however, should be directed at the potential solutions that can be implemented.

Many potential solutions have already been identified in an ad-hoc fashion by those who must write research solicitations (i.e., research sponsors) of those who must conduct neighborhood evaluations. What is lacking is a systematic effort to create an inventory for future reference. The examples below are intended to illustrate a few approaches that are worthy of further exploration. Again, the intention is to suggest topics for further research on practical methodology, rather than to defend or support any particular approach. These examples have been organized according to the three topics of research measurement, research design, and research management, but no attempt has been made to find a solution to every problem that has previously been enumerated.

Potential Approaches to Measurement

There is a long history of attempts to develop neighborhood indicators and proxy measures for key neighborhood phenomena.[9] Such attempts have not been overly successful, and more research of this sort is therefore not being recommended here under the guise of practical methodological studies (research on indicators, however, might be continued as part of a longer-term research effort). Instead, more practical approaches might cover three possibilities.

[9]See Chapter II for an example.

Developing Measures of Dysfunction or Ineffectiveness

To overcome the typical difficulty of measuring program performance, in which ultimate objectives are hard to define in measurable terms, an alternative approach might be one in which the burden of evidence is placed on those who would like to show that the activities are dysfunctional or ineffective. Note that such measures are not merely the observation of null effects of effectiveness measures. Moreover, there are numerous potential candidates for dysfunction measures. For housing rehabilitation activities, as used in the evaluation of the Urban Homesteading program, dysfunction measures might include such items as

- Evictions of renters for renovation or conversion
- Increases in rent or property taxes
- Nonhomesteader dissatisfaction with the kinds of residents the program brings into the neighborhood
- Defection of private lending institutions from neighborhood coalitions
- Defaults on rehabilitation loans

For a neighborhood crime prevention activity, dysfunction measures might include

- Errors (e.g., false arrests, unnecessary injuries)
- Complaints by participants
- Complaints by residents
- Failure to gain cooperation from the police

Some of these measures are more easily quantified and monitored than the typical effectiveness measures that evaluation studies attempt to use. It is not clear why programs cannot be compared in terms of these dysfunctional or ineffectiveness measures, which do provide a realistic comparative framework for evaluation. Naturally, supporters of a program will still want to assess its performance in positive terms, so that the notable accomplishments can be publicized. This assessment can still be done by collecting anecdotal and less systematic evidence (ironically, as is presently done for ineffectiveness measures), but the main burden of systematic evaluation measurement would be placed on the use of the dysfunction measures.

Developing Substitute Measures

The term "substitute" measure is used to imply a much looser relationship—between the phenomenon that one wants to measure and the available measures—than is the case with the "indicators" or "proxy" measures. A prime example of a substitute measure would be the number of candidate sites that wish to participate in an intervention program, probably normalized for the amount of dollars involved. If a neighborhood intervention has attracted a large number of candidates, either at the outset or during the period of the intervention, this substitute measure of enrollment or reenrollment would suggest that the intervention program has been satisfying some client group. Although enrollment or reenrollment data do not tell us *how* a program is functioning, such measures can be a substitute for determining *how well* the program is functioning in terms of client receptiveness. Where a program such as the Urban Reinvestment Task Force attracts a large waiting list of sites in spite of the low dollar amounts involved, the substitute measure indicates that the program must be moving in the right direction.

There may be other opportunities in which substitute measures may be more easily obtained than direct measures of program effectiveness. All other things being equal, for instance, high turnover rates among program managers (or even among program monitors in the supporting agency) are a potential substitute for assessing the quality of the implementation process. Thus the notion of substitute measures deserves consideration in further methodological research.

Developing Better Input Measures

A third approach to measurement is to place more emphasis on what have traditionally been regarded as "input" measures—for example, the number of loans made in a rehabilitation program, the number of patrol hours in a citizen crime prevention effort, or the number of residents contacted in the outreach phase of a neighborhood campaign. Most of these measures have been ignored, especially in neighborhood crime prevention programs (Yin, 1979), as a result of the undue attention given to the achievement of ultimate objectives. Furthermore, in those few cases where such data have been collected, as in the CDBG program, little analysis of the data has been conducted.

The use of input measures serves a potentially dual purpose in conducting a neighborhood evaluation. First, as will be further described below, the input measure is the basic unit by which program *accountability* may be established. Typically, the failure to collect or analyze input measures means that it is impossible to determine what the intervention program produced in the narrowest sense. Second, the input measures may be the only fair measure by which to judge program performance. If it can be shown, for instance, that an investment of a certain level of funds resulted in the production of a certain amount of loan or patrol activities, that may be sufficient for evaluation purposes. To further determine the relationship between the amount of loan activity and neighborhood revitalization, or the amount of patrol activity and any reduction in crime may require the development of a fuller theory of neighborhood change than is currently available.

Potential Approaches to Research Design

Much of the problem with contemporary evaluations may ultimately be related to the fact that they are tailored after the traditional research design approach. What may be needed is the development of alternative approaches to research designs. Such an expectation is reasonable, if only because it should be remembered that the traditional research designs all emanate from a behavioral science model. This model is based on individuals as the units of analysis; yet the major point of this chapter is that neighborhood interventions involve a collective unit of analysis. Thus other social sciences, such as economics, history, or political science, may involve highly empirical efforts that are more relevant to neighborhood evaluations. Unfortunately, the research designs used in these other fields have not been documented as well as those of the behavioral sciences.

The development of alternative approaches should not be seen as an attempt to identify the single best research design. Instead it should be understood that several approaches are possible, and may even be used within the same evaluation study. Two such approaches are discussed below.

An Accountability Approach

Although program sponsors are often concerned with judging program performance by ultimate outcomes, there is actually a prior step that deserves more attention. This step is simply the one whereby program accountability can be assessed, that is: Were the immediate products of the site activity a worthy outcome for the public funds that were invested?

The methodologies for assessing program accountability have not been fully discussed or developed by previous research. Yet the payoffs have potential bearing both on the narrower question of accountability itself as well as on the broader issue of program evaluation. The broader purpose might be served, for instance, if it were found that programs were having difficulty spending their allocations and developing sufficient immediate products. At sites where such was the case, there would be no need to attempt any further broader evaluation.

Unfortunately, for some neighborhood interventions, as in most crime prevention activities, the necessary data are not usually available, and efficient approaches to accountability need to be developed. In other neighborhood interventions, the basic accountability methodology can be tested with existing data. For instance, the Grantee Performance Report data requested of CDBG recipients (though criticized for being incomplete, vague, and invalidly reported) are in principle useful for accounting for program spending and the immediate outcomes of specific activities. Collected at regular intervals and according to informative and useful categories, such data could provide local program directors and policy makers as well as HUD officials with timely reports on the incremental progress being made by local programs.

Within-Site Designs

The traditional research designs generally attempt to accommodate cross-site statements and comparisons. Because the traditional designs have been tuned mainly to the behavior of individuals, in which within-individual behavior is relatively straightforward or irrelevant, little attention has been given to within-site processes and activities, other than as points of measurement for the cross-site comparisons. However, in most neighborhood interventions, the site processes and activities are a highly complex mixture of implementation plans, ongoing neighborhood turnover, and other market and political forces. As a result it is usually difficult to explain what has happened, even within a single site, if the traditional research design is followed.

More work needs to be done to develop within-site research designs (e.g., see Yin, 1981). Such designs might begin, for instance, with the construction of a basic site chronology or history. Additional data could then be used to try to explain what happened at the site and why, and thereby to derive insight into the neighborhood intervention and its outcomes. Note that cross-site comparisons could still be made, because both the various site histories and the various site explanations could be compared across sites to develop a model picture and possibly an overall explanation for the outcome of the intervention program. At present, however, there has been little methodological investigation of within-site research designs. For instance, questions concerning the relevant sources of information, the appropriate time span and intervals, or even the level of detail in searching for an explanation are not covered well by existing methodological studies. Yet, if one cannot explain the events at any given site, even the adequate measurement of programmatic outcomes will not produce more than a summative, go-no-go evaluation; and without an understanding of the intervention process, few policy recommendations can be made regarding modifications in the intervention design.

Potential Approaches to Research Management

Within the context of managing an evaluation study, several steps can be considered as potential ways of alleviating some of the problems mentioned earlier. For illustrative purposes, three different tactics are discussed below.

Using Split Samples to Reduce Costs

Because of the complexity of activities at any given site, the evaluation study is often caught between the necessity for making intensive observations at each site and the necessity for covering a large number of sites. Within the typically available level of funding for evaluation studies, it is difficult to increase depth without sacrificing scope, and vice versa. One potential approach to this problem is to use split samples within the research design. Basically, different sites can be covered to differing extents in order to accommodate managerial realities. Some of the possible splits might be as follows.

Site Visitors versus Telephone Sites. Data can be collected either through field visits or through telephone interviews. Some sites can be selected for intensive field visitation; other sites can be selected for telephone interviewing only. Recent methodological research has shown that telephone interviews can yield a large amount of accurate information; the split sample would allow the work done at the field-visited sites to be enhanced by the interview information from the larger number of (telephone) sites. This type of split sample has been used in recent studies of municipal innovations.

Process versus Outcome Sites. A second way of using a split sample would be to have some sites in which outcome data alone are collected (whether that includes "input" measures only or also covers ultimate objectives), and a small subset of sites in which both outcome and process data are collected. Thus the small subset would have to be the source of any conclusions regarding causal explanations of outcomes; however, the larger sample, in which data collection costs might be considerably lower, would provide summative information so that the intervention could be judged on the basis of a larger number of sites.

Use of Site Monitors. A third way of dividing the sample of sites is related to the use of site monitors, as in the Brookings study of the CDBG program. The Brookings study made use of a national network of "resident observers,"[10] who were experienced researchers living near and familiar with the local community (Dommel, 1978). The monitors used a uniform analytic framework to study the social and political processes of local CDBG programs, and the success of the Brookings experience with resident observers should be assessed. To the extent that such monitors are found valuable, and because of the additional expense of maintaining site monitors, such persons could be identified at a handful of potential sites, and engaged in more intensive data collection than at the larger number of sites, which would have no site

---

[10]However, the Brookings study has been limited to the situation in which the site monitors are academically-based individuals. The site-monitoring functions can also be fulfilled by municipal officials who may be working as part of the intervention program.

monitor. Again, the larger number of sites would allow an evaluation study to develop a fuller picture of the overall impact of an intervention program and, if properly designed, to add to the external validity of the study.

There are several other ways in which the sample of sites can be divided in an evaluation study. The main point is that these possibilities should be considered not only from the standpoint of research design but also from that of research management. The reason is that the selection and division of sites has great bearing on the ultimate costs of the evaluation study.

Using Expert Panels for Formative Feedback

The need for formative information from an evaluation study is related to the desire to improve an intervention program while it is in progress. For multiple-year interventions, such formative feedback can be necessary because of funding decisions regarding the intervention program. However, the need for such information often interferes with the overall design of the evaluation study, which is typically based on summative considerations (again, the traditional research designs tend to be summative designs). The result is the often-voiced complaint that the researcher must continually interrupt the study and jeopardize the summative design, much as a novice might constantly want to uproot a plant in order to see whether it was growing properly.

An alternative approach to the satisfaction of formative needs is to consider the formative design separately from the summative design. Such a separation can be made in the initial solicitation for research. Thus the formative aspects of an evaluation study—its costs, scheduling, design, and payoffs—can be considered independently of the summative design, rather than as by-products of the latter. Given such an approach, some steps can be taken that may not markedly enhance the costs of the study.

For instance, it is commonly the case that research sponsors (or policy makers who have been operating the intervention program) desire to have some early indication of how each site is progressing. This early indication can be obtained through the use of a visiting panel of experts, who might travel to several sites (for a large number of sites, several panels could be used). These experts, through field observations, on-the-spot inquiries of local officials and residents, and examination of data already collected by the evaluation team can provide a qualitative analysis of the progress, problems, and accomplishments of a site's activities. Such informed judgments could even be made, if desired, at regular intervals and could serve as a ready source of information on program status. Furthermore, site visit reports would be a quick and relatively low-cost way of tracking program activities at a number of sites. Common problems or solutions could be identified and shared with all the operating sites.

IMPROVING THE EVALUATION OF NEIGHBORHOOD PROGRAMS

The use of a panel of experts is but one example of an evaluation activity that is geared specifically to formative needs, but that need not interfere, managerially,[11] with the other evaluation activities. There may very well be several other ways of fulfilling formative needs. The main goal, whatever the approach, would be to use a procedure that is flexible and not overly expensive, so that information can be gathered at key intervals during the life of the intervention program.

Using Oral Briefings for Formative Feedback

Another way of improving formative information is the more frequent use of oral briefings. Currently, there is usually a disproportionate emphasis in favor of *written* rather than oral reports, with many evaluation contracts containing long lists of "deliverables." The written reports may be necessary for certain types of administrative accountability, but these reports, especially if they are of the interim variety, require an inordinate effort for preparation and do not usually convey all the information that is needed by the research sponsor (or the sponsor of the intervention program). The reports are difficult to read, lengthy, and fail to contain many relevant (though sometimes speculative) materials because of the evaluation team's natural reluctance to divulge results prematurely.

In contrast, oral briefings may be arranged at any reasonable time during the life of an evaluation study, and may provide program or research sponsors with more relevant information in communicable form. That is so because researchers can be confronted verbally and will often be willing to give their best judgments, as of the moment, if such judgments do not have to be committed to writing. Of course, abuses of oral briefings are always possible, but the general idea is that a greater use of such briefings may produce better formative information than is normally contained in written, interim reports.

SUMMARY

The preceding sections have aimed at describing a set of illustrative problems and solutions in the current conduct of neighborhood evaluations. Most of these problems and solutions are not addressed by contemporary guides to evaluations, yet these issues dominate both the work of the evaluation team as well as the work of the research sponsor. In effect, there

---

[11]The visits, as well as any other formative activities, of course, would have an effect on the overall program outcomes and therefore would have to be accounted for, in a technical sense, in the summative effort.

appears to be a gap between practice (the conduct of evaluation studies) and scientific knowledge (guides for conducting evaluation studies).

To improve this situation, this chaper has advocated further methodological research, but of the sort that focuses directly on *practical* methodologies for conducting evaluations. The data for such research would consist of the neighborhood evaluations that have recently been completed or are still under way; in each case, information about the practical problems and their tentative solutions—from both the evaluator's and the sponsor's point of view—could be sought. To give the reader an idea of the types of topics that could be covered, this chapter has described a range of different problems as well as a range of potential solutions.

REFERENCES

Bernstein, Ilene N., ed. *Validity Issues in Evaluation Research*. Beverly Hills, Calif.: Sage Publications, 1976.

Campbell, Donald T., and Stanley, Julian C. *Experimental Designs for Research*. Chicago: Rand McNally, 1966.

Caporaso, James A., and Roos, Leslie L., Jr. *Quasi-Experimental Approaches*. Evanston, Ill.: Northwestern University Press, 1973.

Comptroller General of the United States. "HUD's Evaluation System Assessment." Washington, D.C., 20 July, 1978a.

Comptroller General of the United States. "Management and Evaluation of the Community Development Block Grant Program Need to Be Strengthened." Washington, D.C., 30 August, 1978b.

Cook, Thomas D., and Campbell, Donald T. *Quasi-Experimentation: Design and Analysis Issues for Field Settings*. Chicago: Rand McNally, 1979.

Dommel, Paul R. *Decentralizing Community Development*. Washington, D.C. Brookings Institution, 1978.

Freeman, Howard. "The Present Status of Evaluation Research." In *Evaluation Studies: Vol. 2, Annual Review* Edited by Marcia Guttentag, Beverly Hills, Calif.: Sage Publications, 1977.

Horst, *Pamela et. al.* "Program Management and the Federal Evaluator." *Public Administration Review* 1976, *36*, 220–235.

Milkman, Raymond H., Toborg, Mary A., Perez, Una M., Boyd, Brian. *Evaluating Economic Development Programs: A Methodology Handbook*. Washington, D.C.: Lazar Management Group, July, 1978.

Nachmias, David. *Public Policy Evaluation*. New York: St. Martin's Press, 1978.

Office of Evaluation. "Community Development Block Grant Program: Third Annual Report." Washington, D.C.: U.S. Department of Housing and Urban Development, 1978.

Office of Evaluation. "Preliminary Review of the Urban Development Action Grant Program (UDAG)." Washington, D.C.: U.S. Department of Housing and Urban Development, 1979.

Office of Policy Development and Research. "The Neighborhood Housing Services Model." Washington, D.C.: U.S. Department of Housing and Urban Development, 1975.

Office of Policy Development and Research. "Evaluation of the Urban Homesteading Demonstration Program: Second Annual Report." Washington,D.C.: U.S. Department of Housing and Urban Development, 1977.

Public Technology, Inc. *Program Evaluation and Analysis: A Technical Guide for State and Local Governments.* Washington, D.C; Public Technology, Inc., 1978.

Sumka, Howard J., and Gardner, John L. "Evaluation of Programs for Neighborhood Reinvestment and Preservation in the United States." Paper presented at the Fourth Conference on Urban and Regional Research, Economic Commission for Europe, 1980.

Yin, Robert K., "Are Traditional Research Designs Responsive?" In *Accountability in Urban Society,* edited by Scott Greer, R. D. Hedlund, and J. L. Gibson, Beverly Hills, Calif.: Sage Publications, 1978, pp. 293–299.

Yin, Robert K. "What Is Citizen Crime Prevention?" In *How Well Does It Work?* Washington, D.C.: National Institute of Law Enforcement and Criminal Justice, 1979, pp. 107–134.

Yin, Robert K., "Creeping Federalism: The Federal Impact on the Structure and Function of Local Government." In *The Urban Impacts of Federal Policies.* edited by Norman Glickman, Baltimore: Johns Hopkins University, 1980, pp. 595–618.

Yin, Robert K. "The Case Study Crisis: Some Answers." *Administrative Science Quarterly,* 1981, *26,* 58–65.

Index

Accountability, program, assessment of, 182, 183–184
Active-user information delivery system, 85–87
Architectural design in housing projects, 96–97

Banfield, Edward, 68, 71, 110
Blacks
 community protection patrols, 48
 in housing projects, 98
Boards, citizen organization, 5, 6, 13–14
Branch libraries. *See* Libraries
Brookings Institution study of CDBG program, 185
Budget control and organizational success, 6–7, 8
Building fires
 correlates, 153
 neighborhood patterns, 152, 166, 167
Building patrols, 30, 32, 34–37

Cable television, 85–87
Centralization
 information systems, 90
 service delivery, 72–74, 77
Citizen participation, 1–15, 51–61
 benefits, 53
 case studies, list of, 59–61
 federal policy toward groups, 54–55, 59
  revenue sharing, proposal for, 55–58
 structure of groups, 11–13
 success of groups, correlates of, 3–4

Citizen participation (*Cont.*)
 organizational characteristics, 5–15, 23
 See also Crime patrols and guards; Feedback mechanisms
Citizens' Advice Bureau (CAB), 112
City halls, little, 21, 23, 104–106
Community Development Block Grant (CDBG) program
 Brookings study, 185
 changes, 173
Community planning districts, Manhattan, N.Y.
 fire alarm patterns, 164–166, 167
 map, 165
Community protection patrols, 30, 47–48
Comparative neighborhood studies, need for, 129
 participant-observation, 135
Crime
 FBI Index, 159
 rates in public housing, 94
 reduction by patrols and guards, 34–35, 38–40, 44
Crime patrols and guards, 26–50
 building, 30, 32, 34–37
 community protection, 30, 47–48
 definitional criteria, 27–28
 expenditures, 48
 implementation factors, 49–50
 neighborhood, 30–31, 37–43
 outcomes, 32
  building patrols, 34–37

Crime patrols and guards (*Cont.*)
  outcomes (*Cont.*)
    citizen participation, 36, 42, 46–47
    crime reduction, 34–35, 38–40, 44, 49
    neighborhood patrols, 38–43
    police-related, 35–36, 40–41, 45–46
    sense of security, 35, 40, 44–45
    social service patrols, 44–47
    vigilantism, 36, 41–42, 46, 49
  social service, 31, 43–47
  typology, 28–31
Decentralization
  information systems, 90
  urban programs, 66, 77–78
Dohrenwend, Barbara, 143 n
Dysfunction (ineffectiveness) measures, concept of, 122, 181

Education. *See* Information delivery systems
Elections for citizen organizations, 14
Evaluation studies, 122, 169–188
  problems, 170, 171, 179–180
    in management of study, 178–179
    in measurement, 174–176
    from nature of intervention, 172–174
    with traditional research designs, 170, 176–178
  solutions to problems, potential, 180
    of management, 184–187
    of measurement, 180–183
    of research design, 183–184

False alarms
  neighborhood patterns, 152, 166, 167
  participant-observation study, 149–150, 152, 153, 154
  seasonal patterns, 19, 161, 162, 163–164
  solutions, potential, 76–77, 149
Family characteristics in housing projects, 98
FBI Index crimes, 159
Feedback, police, to neighborhood patrols 39
Feedback mechanisms, citizen, 17–24
  outside executive branch, 18–19
  grievance procedures, 20–21, 24
    ombudsman distribution, 22
  neighborhood facilities, 21, 23

Feedback mechanisms (*Cont.*)
  neighborhood meetings, 20
  neighborhood organizations, 23–24
  success, factors in, 24
  urban indicators, 19
Fire alarms, 158–167
  cross-city comparisons, 158–160
  false
    neighborhood patterns, 152, 166, 167
    participant-observation study, 149–150, 152, 153, 154
    seasonal patterns, 19, 161, 162, 163–164
    solutions, potential, 76–77, 149
  neighborhood patterns, 152, 164–166, 167
  streetcorner observations, 148–149, 150, 151–154
  temporal patterns, 19, 161–164
Fire hydrants, use and misuse of, 144–148
Firefighting, nineteenth-century, 67
Formative needs of evaluation study, 186–187

Games, hydrant use for, 146
Garbage survey in field study, 139, 141, 151, 155
  statistics, 152, 153
Geocoding routines, 127
Government, federal, *See* Neighborhoods: federal government, role of
Government initiatives, local. *See* Service delivery
Grievance procedures
  citywide, 20–21, 24
    ombudsman distribution, 22
  investigations by citizen groups, 8, 9
Guards and patrols. *See* Crime patrols and guards

Harness program for hydrants, 145
Health centers, study of, 5–6, 10
High-rise housing projects, 97
Holidays and fire alarms, 162, 163
Homesteading, urban, 176–177
Housing
  building patrols for, 30, 32, 34–37
  in neighborhood typology, 126
  See also Public housing
Hydrant use and abuse, 144–148

INDEX

Immigrant city, service delivery in, 67–70
Indicators, urban social, 19, 135, 155, 167–168, 180. *See also* Fire alarms
Ineffectiveness measures, concept of, 122, 181
Information and referral centers
  libraries as, 106, 111–114
  outside library system, 112
Information delivery systems, 80–91
  centralization and effectiveness, 90
  definition, 80
  equity problems, 81, 83, 85, 87–89, 90
  research agenda on, 90–91
  types, 81–82
    active-user, 85–87
    mixed-user, 83–85
    passive-user, 82–83
Information networks in neighborhoods, 102–103
  institutions compensating for, 103–105
Input measures, 182

Jacobs, Jane, 2, 117, 129

Keller, Suzanne, 102–103

Libraries
  declines in utilization, 107–108, 109
  dissemination improvements, 110–111
  numbers of, in largest cities, 107
  roles, possible, 23
    information and referral centers, 106, 111–114
  user base, options concerning, 108, 110
Little city halls, 21, 23, 104–106

Maintenance costs for public housing, 97
Meetings, neighborhood, 20
Membership base, organizational, and funding, 57–58
Mixed-user information delivery system, 83–85
Monitors, site, use of, 185–186
Moynihan, Daniel Patrick, 161
Multiservice centers, 105

National Commission on Urban Problems, 105
National Institute of Education (NIE)
  goal, 80, 90

National Institute of Education (*Cont.*)
  R&D Utilization (RDU) program, 83–85
Neighborhood Action Task Force, 104
Neighborhood Housing Services, (NHS), 177
Neighborhood Information Center project, 113
Neighborhood patrols, 30–31, 37–43
Neighborhood Pilot Centers program, 104
Neighborhoods
  defining, problem of, 121–122
  external events affecting, 128
  federal government, role of, xiv, xvii, 54–55, 59, 63, 74
  programs, evaluating. *See* Evaluation studies
  revenue sharing, proposal for, 55–58
  functions and dysfunctions, xiii
  improved prospects, xv–xvi
  indicators, 19, 135, 155, 167–168, 180
    See also Fire alarms
  information network, informal, 102–103
    institutions compensating for, 103–105
  typologies, 124–125, 126
  See also Citizen participation; Research on neighborhoods; Service delivery
New York, N.Y.
  field study. *See* Participant-observation: New York City field study
  fire alarms
    neighborhood patterns, 152, 164–166, 167
    and participant-observation, 148–150, 151–154
    seasonal patterns, 161–163

Ombudsmen, 21
  distribution, 22
Oral briefings in evaluation studies, 187

Participant-observation
  advantages, 134, 154–155
  history, 133
  modification of traditional approach, 134–136
  New York City field study, 136–155
    conclusions about method, 142–143, 154–155

New York City field study (*Cont.*)
  conclusions about method (*Cont.*)
    fire alarms and streetcorners, 148–154
    fire hydrant use and misuse, 144–148
    initial phase, 138–139, 148–149
    neighborhoods in, 136, 137
    role changes, 141
    rotation, 139–140
    uses, 143
    problems, 133–134, 142–143
  public housing studies, 93–94, 97
Passive-user information delivery system, 82–83
Patrols and guards. *See* Crime patrols and guards
Play activities, hydrant use for, 146
Police
  crime patrols and, 30, 47–48
    building, 35–36
    neighborhood, 39, 40–41
    social service, 45–46
  fire hydrants, closing of, 145
  loss of social symmetry, 75–76
  supervision over, problem of, 68–69
Policy makers, participant-observation modifications for, 134, 135
Political centralization, 72, 73–74
Population changes in central cities, 109
Private behaviors, measurement of, 175–176
Professionalization in service delivery, 72
Protocols, standardized, 125
Proximity-based dynamics, 120
Public housing, 92–99
  attitudes toward, 92–93
  building patrols, 35–36, 37
  managerial intitiatives
    architectural design, 96–97
    site selection, 95–96
    tenant selection, 97–99
  research biases, 93–94
  social impact, 94–95

R&D utilization (RDU) program, 83–85
Racial composition of housing projects, 95–96, 98
Reform movements, political, 73–74
Relocation patterns of families, 19
Research on neighborhoods, 117–130
  characteristics justifying, 120

Research on neighborhoods (*Cont.*)
  obstacles
    false, 121–122
    true, generally overlooked, 127–129
    true, generally recognized, 123–125, 127
  See also Evaluation studies; Participant-observation
Resident patrols and guards. *See* Crime patrols and guards
Residential turnover, 103, 123, 124, 128
Revenue sharing with community groups, proposal for, 55–58
Riot prevention, institutions for, 104
Rubinstein, Jonathan, quoted, 68
Rumor control centers, 104

Scatter-site housing, 96
Service delivery, neighborhood, 65–78
  bargaining nature of, 69–70
  changes, explanations for, 70–71
  centralization, 72–74
  citizen organizations overseeing, 3–15
  control, problems of, 68–69
  crisis, 1960s, 74–77
  decentralization trend, 66, 77–78
  in history, 67, 68, 70, 71, 72–73
  information about, 103–105
  participant-observation, uses of, 143
  social symmetry in, 70
    loss of, 75–76
  See also Information delivery systems; Libraries; Public housing
"Sesame Street" (television program), 82–83
Site selection for housing projects, 95–96
Social area analysis, 125
Social indicators, 19, 135, 155, 167–168, 180. *See also* Fire alarms
Social service patrols, 31, 43–47
Social symmetry in service delivery, 70
  loss of, 75–76
Split samples, use of, 185–186
Spray cap program for hydrants, 145
Staff resources
  in citizen groups, 8–9, 13, 23
  indigenous service staff, 10
Standardized protocols, 125
Streetcorner observations, 138–139, 148–149, 150–154
Substitute measures, 181–182

Task forces, neighborhood, 104
Technical assistance groups for interventions, 173–174
Technology and service centralization, 73
Television
  cable, 85–87
  "Sesame Street" program, 82–83
Temperatures and fire alarms, 162, 163
Tenant selection for public housing, 97–99
Transportation, development of, 73

Umbrella versus unitary organizations, 12–13
Urban cable television, 85–87

Urban Homesteading program, 176–177
Urban indicators, 19, 135, 155, 167–168, 180. *See also* Fire alarms
Urban Reinvestment Task Force, 177

Vigilantism in crime patrols, 36, 41–42, 46, 49

Welfare boards, 5
Whyte, William Foote, study by, 133, 134, 142
Wisconsin Information Service, 112

Youth patrols, social service, 43, 44, 46